BASEBALL AMERICA PRESENTS

BEFORE THEY WERE BRAVES

BASEBALL AMERICA INC. · DURHAM, N.C.

Baseball America

ESTABLISHED 1981
P.O. BOX 12877, DURHAM, NC 27709 · PHONE (919) 682-9635

EDITOR AND PUBLISHER B.J. Schecter *@bjschecter*
EXECUTIVE EDITORS J.J. Cooper *@jjcoop36*
Matt Eddy *@MattEddyBA*
CHIEF REVENUE OFFICER Don Hintze
DIRECTOR OF BUSINESS DEVELOPMENT Ben Leigh
DIRECTOR OF DIGITAL STRATEGY Mike Salerno

EDITORIAL
ASSOCIATE EDITORS Kegan Lowe *@KeganLowe*
Josh Norris *@jnorris427*
Justin Coleman *@ElJayColes*
SENIOR WRITER Ben Badler *@benbadler*
NATIONAL WRITERS Teddy Cahill *@tedcahill*
Carlos Collazo *@CarlosACollazo*
Kyle Glaser *@KyleAGlaser*
WEB EDITOR Mark Chiarelli *@Mark_Chiarelli*
SPECIAL CONTRIBUTOR Tim Newcomb *@tdnewcomb*

PRODUCTION
CREATIVE DIRECTOR James Alworth
GRAPHIC DESIGNER James Alworth

BUSINESS
TECHNOLOGY MANAGER Brent Lewis
ACCOUNT EXECUTIVE Kellen Coleman
OFFICE MANAGER & CUSTOMER SERVICE Angela Lewis
CUSTOMER SERVICE Melissa Sunderman

STATISTICAL SERVICE
MAJOR LEAGUE BASEBALL ADVANCED MEDIA

Alliance
⟩⟩⟩⟩ BASEBALL ⟨⟨⟨⟨

BASEBALL AMERICA ENTERPRISES

CHAIRMAN & CEO Gary Green
PRESIDENT Larry Botel
GENERAL COUNSEL Matthew Pace
DIRECTOR OF MARKETING Amy Heart
INVESTOR RELATIONS Michele Balfour
DIRECTOR OF OPERATIONS Joan Disalvo
PARTNERS Jon Ashley
Stephen Alepa
Martie Cordaro
Brian Rothschild
Andrew Fox
Ian Ritchie
Dan Waldman
Sonny Kalsi
Glenn Isaacson
Robert Hernreich
Craig Amazeen
Peter Ruprecht
Beryl Snyder
Tom Steiglehner

3 S T Ξ P

MANAGING PARTNER David Geaslen
CHIEF CONTENT OFFICER Jonathan Segal
CHIEF FINANCIAL OFFICER Sue Murphy

BASEBALL AMERICA (ISSN 0745-5372/USPS 591-210) August 6, 2019, Vol. 39, No. 8 is published monthly, 12 issues per year, by Baseball America Enterprises, LLC, 4319 South Alston Ave, Suite 103, Durham, NC 27713. Subscription rate is $92.95 for one year; Canada $118.95 (U.S. funds); all other foreign $144.95 per year (U.S. funds). Periodicals postage paid at Durham, NC, & additional mailing offices. Occasionally our subscriber list is made available to reputable firms offering goods and services we believe would be of interest to our readers. If you prefer to be excluded, please send your current address label and a note requesting to be excluded from these promotions to Baseball America Enterprises, LLC, 4319 South Alston Ave, Suite 103, Durham, NC 27713, Attn: Privacy Coordinator. POSTMASTER: Send all UAA to CFS (See DMM 707.4.12.5); NON-POSTAL & MILITARY FACILITIES: send address corrections to Baseball America, P.O. Box 420235, Palm Coast, FL 32142-0235. CANADA POST: Return undeliverable Canadian addresses to IMEX Global Solutions, P.O. Box 25542, London, ON N6C 6B2. Please contact 1-800-381-1288 to start carrying Baseball America in your store.
©2019 by Baseball America Enterprises, LLC. All Rights Reserved. Printed in the USA.

BASEBALL AMERICA PRESENTS
BEFORE THEY WERE BRAVES

Compiled by
J.J. Cooper

Editors
Matt Eddy, Kegan Lowe and Carlos Collazo

Contributing Editors
Chris Hilburn-Trenkle, M'Lynn Dease, Jared McMasters,
Tyler Henninger and Michael Magnuson

Database and Application Development
Brent Lewis

Design & Production
James Alworth

Programming & Technical Development
Brent Lewis

Cover Photos
MAIN PHOTOS: Chipper Jones.
Photo by Scott Cunningham/Getty Images

Greg Maddux
Photo by Scott Cunningham/WireImage/Getty Images

Tom Glavine
Photo by Harry How/Getty Images

For additional copies, visit our Website at
BaseballAmerica.com or call 1-800-845-2726 to order.
US $19.95 / CAN $27.00, plus shipping
and handling per order. Expedited shipping available.
Distributed by Simon & Schuster.
ISBN-13: 978-1932391909
Statistics provided by Major League Baseball Advanced
Media and Compiled by Baseball America.

ABOUT THE BOOK

In the back corner of the Baseball America's offices there is a tiny treasure chest. It may look like an ordinary closet stacked with shelves, but inside there are back issues stretching back to Baseball America's first days in 1981. Nearly four decades of baseball history sits in those binders, and there are insights on many of yesterday's and today's stars from the time before they were household names.

It's an easy place to lose a few hours, jumping from one surprising discovery to another. On one page, there's draft preview notes from when Ken Griffey Jr. was still a high school star. Over here, there's a reminder of the time when Oddibe McDowell was a bigger star than Arizona State teammate Barry Bonds.

As valuable as the perspective of time can be, there's also a lot of value in seeing what how everything was viewed contemporaneously. And Baseball America's archives do just that, providing story after story that was telling the story of high school, college, minor league and major league baseball as it happened.

Unfortunately, we cannot let everyone just rumage through our archives in person–it's not a very big closet and we need to hold on to all of those magazines. But we also know that there are many fans out there just like us—fans who enjoy going back and remembering when Hall of Famers of today were just kids with dreams of future stardom.

So with that in mind, we created the "Before They Were Stars" book, providing contemporaneous scouting reports on more than 100 of the best players of the past 40 years. The logical follow-up was to produce a book that focused on the homegrown stars of one team. And if we were going to pick one team to first spotlight, the Atlanta Braves were the logical choice. Over the span of Baseball America's nearly four decades, no organization has had a more consistently talented farm system, producing a number of Hall of Famers as well as numerous all-stars.

So here is our attempt to tell the story of the Braves of the Baseball America era. The Braves were generally woeful in the 1980s at the big league level, but they did start developing the stars of their 1990s teams in the late-1980s, so the book divides up relatively easily into decade-by-decade chapters looking at the best stars of each era. The stories included are unchanged from how they ran at the time, but we have included notes to provide insights we have now with the benefit of hindsight.

Personally, this book was a labor of love. I grew up in Middle Georgia in the late-1970s and 1980s. Fulton County Stadium was the first place I saw a major league game (and the only MLB stadium I had visited until after I graduated college). Watching Braves games on TBS was an experience I shared with my parents, brother and grandparents.

While my fandom was put aside as I became a professional journalist, I was fortunate enough to continue covering the Braves through the 1990s before coming to Baseball America in 2002. While Chipper Jones, Tom Glavine and Andruw Jones may have become household names, this book also attempts to shine spotlights on some of the behind-the-scenes coaches, scouts and other officials who were also key to developing young prospects into big leaguers. ∎

JJ COOPER
EXECUTIVE EDITOR, BASEBALL AMERICA

In 1991 and 1992, Steve Avery, John Smoltz and Tom Glavine gave the Braves a trio of front-of-the-rotation arms.

A HISTORY OF BASEBALL AMERICA PROSPECT RANKINGS

A few hundred minor league prospects have matured into major league stars in the 38 years that Baseball America has been ranking prospects as comprehensively as only BA can.

Prospect rankings have been an integral part of BA from its beginnings in 1981. The October issue from that year ranks the Top 10 Prospects for all the full-season minor leagues.

The first scouting report to appear in that issue belongs to 20-year-old Phillies shortstop Julio Franco, whose age has since been revised upward by two years. Franco ranked No. 1 in the Eastern League in 1981 and was considered a "can't-miss player who someday soon will replace Larry Bowa in Philadelphia."

Among the other prospects we highlighted in that 1981 issue are current major league managers Terry Francona and Don Mattingly and current broadcasters Ron Darling and Harold Reynolds.

BA began ranking the Top 10 Prospects for each organization beginning with the 1983 season. The National League West was the first division to be featured, and future big leaguers such as Eric Davis, Ozzie Guillen, Kevin McReynolds and Mitch Williams all received reports in that issue.

Best Tools balloting was the next major prospect enhancement. It first appeared on the minor league side in 1986, when minor league managers singled out David Cone, Randy Johnson and Larry Walker as having loud tools that would impact the game.

The final prospect ranking breakthrough came in the form of the Top 100 Prospects, which was introduced in 1990 and was headlined that year by Steve Avery, Ben McDonald and John Olerud in the top three spots. ■

TABLE OF CONTENTS

Outfielder Albert Hall
hit for the cycle in 1986.
Considering how dire
some of the Braves late-
'80s season were, there
were few moments like
this to remember.

A decade of futility sets stage for future success

Baseball America has ranked the talent level in all major league farm systems for 35 years. And what we have found is that talent ebbs and flows. One team's farm system is on the rise. Another is entering a fallow period. Over the course of a few decades, It's almost impossible for a team to consistently have excellent talent growing on the farm.

Almost.

For 28 of the 30 major league teams, their average minor league talent ranking sits between 10th and 20th. Every great stretch of producing prospects is eventually equalled by a span where the team lacks significant impact talent in the minors. Often that is because of a team picking late in the draft, or has used parts of the farm system as trade chips to acquire big leaguers.

Twenty of the 30 big league clubs' average org talent rank is between 14 and 16—smack dab in the middle. The Blue Jays (powered by an outstanding run in the late 1980s and early '90s) and Rays have an average rank of 10th, a clear step above the average team. The Tigers (average rank of 22nd) are the only team whose average rank is worse than 20th.

Standing alone are the Braves. The Braves have averaged ranking eighth in baseball over those 35 years. Since 1989, Baseball America has declared the Braves have had the best farm system in baseball six different times. Over that same time frame, the Braves have ranked outside of the top 10 just five times.

It has been an eye-popping run. During the 1990s and 2000s, the Braves made 14 consecutive playoff appearances—interrupted only by the players' strike and cancelled playoffs in 1995. Atlanta made five more playoff appearances in the 2010s. And while the club has managed to land some successful free agent and pulled off several astute trades, the core of the team's success year after year has been a reliance on scouting and player development.

It wasn't always that way. For the first 20 years of their time in Atlanta, the Braves believed that the club's best path to success was to bludgeon its opponents. Years before the Colorado Rockies joined the National League, Fulton County Stadium was known as the "Launching Pad."

From Hank Aaron and Orlando Cepeda to Bob Horner and Dale Murphy, the Braves believed that they could outscore and overwhelm. Come draft time, the Braves regularly focused on big, strong hitters. Often, they didn't have a lot of defensive value.

There was another aspect of Braves baseball, one that was much more ruinous than the focus on

11

In the 1980s, all too often the Braves traded away promising young players like outfielder Brett Butler in the quest to find a short-term fix. It very rarely worked out.

bats. Owner Ted Turner was willing to spend, which would seem to be a very good thing, but that spending was focused on helping the big league team immediately. The Braves were one of the teams willing to spend as free agency became more and more pervasive, but they lost draft picks because of the free agent signings. It was a short-term approach, but one that generated notice and was intended to help boost TV ratings.

The Braves were a vital part of the programming lineup for Turner's TBS Superstation. All summer throughout the South (and around the country), fans could watch and listen to Skip Caray, Pete Van Wieren and Ernie Johnson Sr. call Braves wins and losses.

There were a lot more losses than wins—which sometimes made Caray's acerbic wit even more enjoyable. The Braves did win the National League West in 1969 and again in 1982, but in both cases they failed to win a playoff game. More often, the Braves were far out of the pennant race by August. Caray was often excusing fans to feel free to walk their dogs in the late innings of blowout losses—as long as they promised to patronize the sponsors.

Turner's Braves kept looking for quick fixes. Gaylord Perry, Claudell Washington, Terry Forster and Bruce Sutter were brought in as free agents.

And sometimes the Braves traded away young talent for older veterans. The acquisition of righthander Len Barker was the worst example. He was supposed to help the Braves' playoff push in 1983. The Braves were a half game up in the NL West when they acquired Barker. They lost their next six games, which included a poor start by Barker, fell out of first place and ended up finishing three games behind the Dodgers.

Barker ended up going 10-20 with a 4.64 ERA in two and half seasons with the Braves before he was released (with three years left on his contract). Outfielder Brett Butler and third baseman Brooks Jacoby, two of the young players the Braves traded away to acquire Barker, both went on to have long, successful careers. The Braves also traded away their two best first-round picks (Duane Ward and Ken Daley) from 1980-85 early in their careers for veterans.

The Braves were happy to spend money on flashy free agents, but when it came to the draft, Atlanta was much more likely to close its wallet. The Braves drafted future Hall of Famer Randy Johnson out of high school in the fourth round in 1982 but failed to sign him. A year later, they drafted and failed to sign Jay Buhner, a two-time all-star, in the ninth round. In 1986, the Braves drafted Steve Finley (11th round), Tim Salmon (18th) and future No. 1 overall pick Ben McDonald (27) but whiffed on inking all three.

By the middle of the decade, there was a realization that a change was needed. And a familiar name was brought in to make the fixes. Bobby Cox had been the manager of the Braves from 1978-81 before being fired. He then managed the Blue Jays from 1982-85, making the playoffs in his final year in Toronto.

The Braves were a bad team at the time seemingly headed in the wrong direction, so there was some surprise when Cox left a talented Blue Jays team to take over as the Braves general manager. It took a while to turn around the club, but Cox quickly decided to focus on developing young pitchers rather than big sluggers.

"Nothing changes until it gets better there," catcher Bruce Benedict told Baseball America in 1989 while pointing to the pitcher's mound. "They tried to do it here for so long with big guys who could hit it out of the park, and that didn't work. They're trying it the other way now."

The Braves drafted Kent Mercker, Derek Lilliquist and Steve Avery with their first three first-round picks of the Cox era. Lefthander Tom Glavine was already in the organization. He was the club's second-round pick in 1984.

"Get all the lefties you can get," Cox said then. "From my own experience, they can be very valuable. A good lefthander is always better than a good righthander in my book. I don't know why it works that way, but it just somehow happens."

Cox didn't focus only on lefties, but he did keep a laser focus on acquiring quality pitchers. Righthander John Smoltz was acquired in an August 1987 trade where the Braves reversed their previous approach. In this case, Atlanta traded away veteran Doyle Alexander and reaped the rewards of acquiring a top young talent.

"It doesn't matter where you're playing," Cox said to Baseball America in 1989. "You have to have pitching. There aren't too many places where you can get by with bad pitching. You have to have good pitching to win here."

Not everyone was on board with the changes. The Braves went 54-106 in 1988 as Cox put a halt to the free agent spending. The big league club finished last three times and second-to-last twice in Cox's first five years with the Braves.

There was dissent in the meetings of the Braves' board of directors, but president Stan Kasten helped back Cox.

"Everyone believes in what Bobby is doing," Kasten told Baseball America at the time. "We all feel this is the best way to go. A couple of years ago, what we had was a last-place team with the highest average salary in the majors. A big part of that was caused by free agency. The only way you can do it is to build a solid minor league system.

"It's the old Branch Rickey theory of the more players you have playing, the better chance you have of finding someone. We're all behind Bobby in this."

Cox pushed the Braves to become the first team in baseball to expand to eight minor league affiliates. That granted extra roster spots to help try to develop more pitchers.

And just as importantly, he bolstered the support staff. Bobby Dews became the club's field coordinator in charge of the coaching of the club's minor leaguers. That meant Paul Snyder could focus on being the club's scouting director in charge of the draft. Soon the Braves were proud to say they had more scouts, more coaches and more minor league teams than anyone else in baseball.

In the 1980s, that rebuilding effort didn't have a big league payoff—though watching young players like Glavine, Smoltz and Ron Gant figuring out the major leagues was more exciting than watching veterans on the tail end of their careers.

But Braves fans would have to wait for the 1990s to arrive to see major league success. ∎

The Braves didn't develop many pitchers in the 1980s before the Tom Glavine-John Smoltz-Pete Smith group arrived. Zane Smith was one of the few who emerged.

BA Braves Top 10 Prospects year by year

1983

Player, Pos.	WAR	What happened
1. Brad Komminsk, OF	2.2	Highly-touted prospect never hit for average or power expected in up-and-down eight-year MLB career.
2. Brian Fisher, RHP	0.8	Braves' 1980 second-round pick was traded to Yankees in 1984 for Rick Cerone. Threw 640 MLB innings.
3. Duane Ward, RHP	10.1	Braves' 1982 first-round pick was traded for Doyle Alexander. Went on to become dominant closer for Blue Jays.
4. Miguel Sosa, INF	—	Shortstop didn't hit in upper minors and was out of baseball at age 27.
5. Gerald Perry, 1B	-0.1	Perry made one all-star appearance, but his lack of power didn't fit at first base.
6. Brook Jacoby, 3B	15	Two-time all-star was traded in ill-fated Len Barker trade and played nine years for the Indians.
7. Zane Smith, LHP	20.2	Smith spent 13 years in the majors, going 100-115, 3.74 in a solid, lengthy career.
8. Albert Hall, OF	-0.7	Hall hit for the cycle in 1987, but lack of power limited him to part-time role in nine-year MLB career.
9. Kenny Clark, SS	—	Braves' 1981 seventh-round pick was a career .207 minor league hitter who never reached Double-A.
10. Matt West, RHP	—	West reached Triple-A, but proved to be more of a organizational arm than a significant prospect.

1984

Player, Pos.	WAR	What happened
1. Brad Komminsk, OF	2.2	Highly-touted prospect never hit for average or power expected in up-and-down eight-year MLB career.
2. Jeff Dedmon, RHP	1.4	Dedmon was a three-time first-round pick. He worked in the Braves' bullpen from 1983-87.
3. Duane Ward, RHP	10.1	Braves' 1982 first-round pick was traded for Doyle Alexander. Went on to be closer for Blue Jays.
4. Miguel Sosa, 2B	—	Shortstop didn't hit in upper minors and was out of baseball at age 27.
5. Gerald Perry, 1B	-0.1	Perry made one all-star appearance, but lack of power didn't fit at first base.
6. Brian Fisher, RHP	0.8	Braves' 1980 second-round pick was traded to Yankees in 1984 for Rick Cerone. Threw 640 MLB innings.
7. Zane Smith, LHP	20.2	Smith spent 13 years in the majors, going 100-115, 3.74 in a solid, lengthy career.
8. Albert Hall, OF	-0.7	Hall did hit for the cycle in 1987, but lack of power limited him to part-time role in nine-year MLB career.
9. Craig Jones, RHP	—	A rare draftee from Army, Jones spent three seasons at Triple-A Richmond.
10. Andres Thomas, SS	-5.7	Thomas was the Braves' everyday shortstop in the late 1980s despite a very light bat.

1985

Player, Pos.	WAR	What happened
1. Duane Ward, RHP	10.1	Braves' 1982 first-round pick was traded for Doyle Alexander. Went on to be closer for Blue Jays.
2. Drew Denson, OF	-0.1	Denson fit the Braves' desire for big (6-foot-5) sluggers, but power didn't show up until he was a minor league vet.
3. Tom Glavine, LHP	80.7	Glavine was the cornerstone of Braves' rebuilding effort. Top-of-scale changeup led him to the Hall of Fame.
4. Milt Thompson, OF	18.6	Braves' continual quest for catching cost them Thompson and Steve Bedrosian in the 1985 Ozzie Virgil trade.
5. Marty Clary, RHP	-0.3	A fill-in starter in 1989-90, Clary went 1-10, 5.67 in his last stint in the majors.
6. Paul Zuvella, SS	-2.3	Zuvella served as an emergency callup middle infielder for most of the 1980s, hitting .222/.275/.277 in 209 games.
7. Miguel Sosa, 2B	—	Shortstop didn't hit in upper minors and was out of baseball at age 27.
8. Jeff Blauser, SS	20.9	Seen as a good-glove, light bat, Blauser proved to be the opposite on his way to two all-star appearances.
9. Zane Smith, LHP	20.2	Smith spent 13 years in the majors, going 100-115, 3.74 in a solid, lengthy career.
10. Andres Thomas, SS	-5.7	Thomas was the Braves' everyday shortstop in the late 1980s despite a very light bat.

1986

Player, Pos.	WAR	What happened
1. Duane Ward, RHP	10.1	Braves' 1982 first-round pick was traded for Doyle Alexander. Went on to be closer for Blue Jays.
2. Tom Glavine, LHP	80.7	Glavine was the cornerstone of Braves' rebuilding effort. Top-of-scale changeup led him to the Hall of Fame.
3. Drew Denson, OF	-0.1	Denson fit the Braves' desire for big (6-foot-5) sluggers, but power didn't show up until he was a minor league vet.
4. Andres Thomas, SS	-5.7	Thomas was the Braves' everyday shortstop in the late 1980s despite a very light bat.
5. Jeff Blauser, SS	20.9	Seen as a good-glove, light bat, Blauser proved to be the opposite on his way to two All-Star appearances.
6. Paul Assenmacher, LHP	13.0	Traded for very modest returns in 1989, Assenmacher was a reliable lefty reliever from 1986-1999.
7. Matt West, RHP	—	West reached Triple-A, but proved to be more of a organizational arm than a significant prospect.
8. John Kilner, LHP	—	Kilner eventually struggled in Richmond and quickly was sent back to Double-A for good.
9. Tommy Greene, RHP	7.2	Traded with franchise icon Dale Murphy in 1990, Greene had two solid seasons in Phillies' rotation.
10. Greg Tubbs, OF	-0.1	Tubbs always got on base and stole bases, but his only MLB time was 59 at-bats with Reds in 1993.

1987

Player, Pos.	WAR	What happened
1. Jeff Blauser, SS	20.9	Seen as a good-glove, light bat, Blauser proved to be the opposite on his way to two All-Star appearances.
2. Tom Glavine, LHP	80.7	Glavine was the cornerstone of Braves' rebuilding effort. Top-of-scale changeup led him to the Hall of Fame.
3. Tommy Greene, RHP	7.2	Traded with franchise icon Dale Murphy in 1990, Greene had two solid seasons in Phillies' rotation.
4. Dave Justice, OF	40.6	A three-time all-star and Rookie of the Year; he homered in deciding game of Atlanta's lone World Series title.
5. Sean Ross, OF	—	Outfielder spent eight years in minors, but career .310 minor league on-base percentage kept him from an MLB role.
6. Brian Deak, C	—	Deak's high-OBP, high-power, low average package would have been more valued a decade later.
7. Ron Gant, 2B	34.1	Gant needed to move to the outfield, but his power and speed stood out for late '80s, early '90s Braves.
8. Drew Denson, OF	-0.1	Denson fit the Braves' desire for big (6-foot-5) sluggers, but power didn't show up until he was a minor league vet.
9. Kent Mercker, LHP	12	Mercker bounced between rotation and pen, but versatile lefty had two no-hitters and pitched until he was 40.
10. John Kilner, LHP	—	Kilner struggled in Richmond and quickly was sent back to Double-A for good.

1988

Player, Pos.	WAR	What happened
1. Derek Lilliquist, LHP	4.7	Lilliquist made it to Atlanta in just two years, but he was traded away a year later and became a reliever.
2. Tommy Greene, RHP	7.2	Traded with franchise icon Dale Murphy in 1990, Greene had two solid seasons in Phillies rotation.
3. Kevin Coffman, RHP	-1.9	After struggling in Braves' rotation, Coffman was traded to Cubs to bring yet another catcher—Jody Davis.
4. Ron Gant, 2B	4.1	Gant needed to move to the outfield, but his power and speed stood out for late '80s, early '90s Braves.
5. Andy Nezelek, RHP	—	Nezelek seemed on a fast track until 1990, then injuries kept cropping up.
6. John Smoltz, rhp	69.0	Braves' best big-game playoff pitcher had one of the best sliders in baseball, which led to eight all-star appearances.
7. Ed Whited, 3B	-0.8	Acquired from the Astros for Rafael Ramirez in 1987, Whited didn't hit in his lone big league stint in 1989.
8. Dave Justice, OF	40.6	A three-time all-star and Rookie of the Year; he homered in deciding game of Atlanta's lone World Series title.
9. Dave Nied, RHP	2.7	Nied was the No. 1 pick in the 1992 expansion draft, but struggled with injuries with the Rockies.
10. Tom Redington, 3B	—	Redington cracked the first BA Top 100 Prospects after an excellent '89 season, but he never reached Triple-A.

1989

Player, Pos.	WAR	What happened
1. Steve Avery, LHP	13.8	At one point, Avery seemed destined for stardom. He was great for a brief stretch in the early 1990s.
2. Kent Mercker, LHP	12.0	Mercker bounced between rotation and pen, but versatile lefty had two no-hitters and pitched until he was 40.
3. Derek Lilliquist, LHP	4.7	Lilliquist made it to Atlanta in just two years, but he was traded away a year later and became a reliever.
4. John Smoltz, RHP	69.0	Braves' best big-game playoff pitcher had one of the best sliders in baseball, which led to eight all-star appearances.
5. Tommy Greene, RHP	7.2	Traded with franchise icon Dale Murphy in 1990, Greene had two solid seasons in Phillies' rotation.
6. Barry Jones, OF	—	Lefty first baseman/corner outfielder had a lengthy minor league career but never reached the majors.
7. Dennis Burlingame, RHP	—	Righthander was supposed to be part of next wave of Braves pitching prospects, but he peaked at Triple-A in 1993.
8. Dennis Hood, OF	—	An athletic outfielder, Hood's struggles to make contact doomed him to a long minor league career.
9. Mark Lemke, 2B	6.1	Lemke spent eight years as Braves' second baseman and had some significant postseason moments.
10. Jimmy Kremers, C	-0.1	Biggest contribution was as one of the players dealt to the Expos for center fielder Otis Nixon.

Of all the Braves' stars of the 1990s, Glavine was the one with the deepest ties to the bad teams of the late 1980s. He made his Braves debut in 1987.

TOM GLAVINE, LHP

BIOGRAPHY

PROPER NAME: Thomas Michael Glavine. **BORN:** March 25, 1966 in Concord, Mass.
HT.: 6-0. **WT.:** 205. **BATS:** L. **THROWS:** L. **SCHOOL:** Billerica (Mass.) HS.
FIRST PRO CONTRACT: Selected by Braves in second round of June 1984 draft; signed June 22, 1984.

Predicting which pitching prospects will turn into big league stars is a maddening pursuit. A pitcher's career path can change dramatically because of one injury or a newly discovered pitch. In Glavine's case, the pitch he will forever be remembered for was not one that he threw as a minor league prospect. Glavine did not discover his circle-changeup grip until 1989, after he had already spent a year and a half in the majors.

That pitch made Glavine a 300-game winner and one of the best lefthanders of all time. And it couldn't be predicted by any scout or coach watching him pitch in the minors in the mid-1980s. But Glavine was already a top pitching prospect before he found his changeup, and if you read the scouting reports, it focuses on other things that were apparent—an outstanding, focused mentality and a drive and determination that hinted at greatness to come.

CAREER STATISTICS

Year	Club (League)	Class	W	L	ERA	G	GS	CG	SV	IP	H	R	ER	HR	BB	SO	AVG
1984	Braves (GCL)	R	2	3	3.34	8	7	0	0	32	29	17	12	0	13	34	.236
1985	Sumter (SAL)	A	9	6	2.35	26	26	2	0	169	114	58	44	6	73	174	.193
1986	Greenville (SL)	AA	11	6	3.41	22	22	2	0	145	129	62	55	14	70	114	.237
	Richmond (IL)	AAA	1	5	5.63	7	7	1	0	40	40	29	25	4	27	12	.260
1987	Richmond (IL)	AAA	6	12	3.35	22	22	4	0	150	142	70	56	15	56	91	.248
	Atlanta (NL)	MAJ	2	4	5.54	9	9	0	0	50	55	34	31	5	33	20	.279
1988	Atlanta (NL)	MAJ	7	17	4.56	34	34	1	0	195	201	111	99	12	63	84	.270
1989	Atlanta (NL)	MAJ	14	8	3.68	29	29	6	0	186	172	88	76	20	40	90	.243
1990	Atlanta (NL)	MAJ	10	12	4.28	33	33	1	0	214	232	111	102	18	78	129	.281
1991	Atlanta (NL)	MAJ	20	11	2.55	34	34	9	0	247	201	83	70	17	69	192	.222
1992	Atlanta (NL)	MAJ	20	8	2.76	33	33	7	0	225	197	81	69	6	70	129	.235
1993	Atlanta (NL)	MAJ	22	6	3.20	36	36	4	0	239	236	91	85	16	90	120	.259
1994	Atlanta (NL)	MAJ	13	9	3.97	25	25	2	0	165	173	76	73	10	70	140	.268
1995	Atlanta (NL)	MAJ	16	7	3.08	29	29	3	0	199	182	76	68	9	66	127	.246
1996	Atlanta (NL)	MAJ	15	10	2.98	36	36	1	0	235	222	91	78	14	85	181	.249
1997	Atlanta (NL)	MAJ	14	7	2.96	33	33	5	0	240	197	86	79	20	79	152	.226
1998	Atlanta (NL)	MAJ	20	6	2.47	33	33	4	0	229	202	67	63	13	74	157	.238
1999	Atlanta (NL)	MAJ	14	11	4.12	35	35	2	0	234	259	115	107	18	83	138	.287
2000	Atlanta (NL)	MAJ	21	9	3.40	35	35	4	0	241	222	101	91	24	65	152	.244
2001	Atlanta (NL)	MAJ	16	7	3.57	35	35	1	0	219	213	92	87	24	97	116	.261
2002	Atlanta (NL)	MAJ	18	11	2.96	36	36	2	0	225	210	85	74	21	78	127	.252
2003	New York (NL)	MAJ	9	14	4.52	32	32	0	0	183	205	94	92	21	66	82	.288
2004	New York (NL)	MAJ	11	14	3.60	33	33	1	0	212	204	94	85	20	70	109	.252
2005	New York (NL)	MAJ	13	13	3.53	33	33	2	0	211	227	88	83	12	61	105	.279
2006	New York (NL)	MAJ	15	7	3.82	32	32	0	0	198	202	94	84	22	62	131	.267
2007	New York (NL)	MAJ	13	8	4.45	34	34	1	0	200	219	102	99	23	64	89	.281
2008	Myrtle Beach (CAR)	HiA	0	0	2.25	1	1	0	0	4	3	1	1	0	1	4	.214
	Mississippi (SL)	AA	0	1	3.60	1	1	0	0	5	4	3	2	0	1	1	.222
	Atlanta (NL)	MAJ	2	4	5.54	13	13	0	0	63	67	40	39	11	37	37	.288
2009	Mississippi (SL)	AA	0	0	4.50	1	1	0	0	2	3	1	1	1	1	0	.300
	Gwinnett (IL)	AAA	1	0	3.38	2	2	0	0	8	11	3	3	1	2	3	.333
	Rome (SAL)	LoA	1	0	0.00	1	1	0	0	6	3	0	0	0	0	2	.143
Major League Totals			**305**	**203**	**3.54**	**682**	**682**	**56**	**0**	**4413**	**4298**	**1900**	**1734**	**356**	**1500**	**2607**	**.257**
Minor League Totals			**31**	**33**	**3.19**	**91**	**90**	**9**	**0**	**562**	**478**	**244**	**199**	**41**	**244**	**435**	**.250**

The master of the outside corner

JULY 1985

SUMTER LEFTHANDER MADE RIGHT DECISION SIGNING WITH BRAVES

by **RICHARD CHESLEY**

Sumter's Tom Glavine is probably one of the few people in South Carolina who was following the National Hockey League playoffs this spring.

Glavine, from North Billerica, Mass., is considered one of the top pitching prospects in the Atlanta Braves' organization. The Braves expended their second selection in the June 1984 draft on him—even though there were serious questions whether they could sign him.

A Massachusetts high school hockey star, Glavine was a top prospect for a career in the NHL when the Braves drafted him. He was a fourth-round pick of the Los Angeles Kings within a matter of days of being selected by Atlanta.

That set up a bidding war, of sorts, which the Braves won—although they paid a price to get Glavine.

"They must have thought highly of him," said Sumter general manager Dean Brannon. "They had to outbid the LA Kings. I understand they went way over what they planned on for signing him.

"He's a quality kid. A smart kid with a lot on the ball and a lot of talent," Brannon said. "And it doesn't hurt that he is lefthander. That just improves the chances of making it."

Glavine appreciates all the positive talk, but he knows his career is up to him, not what somebody says.

"It is nice to hear. It's flattering," Glavine said. "But I have to ignore it. I have to do what I can, work hard, learn and improve."

It will be hard to improve on his start this season in the South Atlantic League.

Through May 23, Glavine was 4-0 and among the Sally League leaders with a 1.88 ERA. He had allowed just 42 hits and struck out 65 in 58 innings.

With statistics like that in his first full professional season, it would seem that Glavine might not have had a difficult decision on what career to choose.

But he did. The 6-foot, 175-pound lefty was a four-time league all-star and all-conference player in baseball, and a three-time all-star and all-conference selection in hockey.

The *Boston Globe* named him its player of the year in both baseball and hockey and named him its scholar-athlete two years running—something no other Boston-area prep star had ever done before.

"It was a really difficult decision as far as what was really best," admitted Glavine. "But I looked at the longevity of what a career would be, and baseball was the way to go.

"It would have been baseball anyway. I've dreamed of playing professionally for a long time." ∎

EDITOR'S NOTE: Glavine was right in his assessment. He ended up spending 22 years in the major leagues, winning 305 games on his way to being inducted into the Hall of Fame in 2014.

MARCH 1996

ATLANTA'S OVERLOOKED ACE

by NICK CAFARDO

The questions are so much different now. The spring after the Braves won the World Series championship, Tom Glavine can't help but notice.

"It used to be, 'Do you think you'll ever win a world championship?' " Glavine says. "Now it's, 'Do you think you will be able to repeat?' or 'Do you think you have enough drive to win another one?' "

"I had the answers to the other question down pat. I'm glad I don't have to answer it anymore. Now I've got to come up with new answers for this one. I suspect by the end of spring training, I'll have it down pretty good."

Everyone expects Glavine, part of the Fab Four pitching staff, will have another stellar season. He's the winningest pitcher of the last five years, with one more victory than teammate and four-time Cy Young Award winner Greg Maddux. And he's motivated to perform at a high level for many years to come.

Glavine, 30, has been a Brave longer than any of his teammates. He's the major link between the current team and the poor teams of the late 1980s. Having experienced winning, he says his drive comes from never wanting to lapse back into those 100-loss seasons, when years were over by Memorial Day.

"After having been through the process every year since 1991, we understand what needs to be done to get back there," Glavine says. "We've been on every side of this and the side we despised the most was the losing side and all the frustration and sadness that came along with it. I think that's motivation enough to win. And to keep winning."

Glavine's story is of a hard-working kid from the blue-collar town of Billerica,

In his World Series clinching Game Six win in 1995, Glavine did not allow a hit through five innings.

Mass., torn between hockey and baseball, who rose to become a Cy Young Award recipient, 20-game winner three-straight years, goat of the strike and finally hero of the World Series.

The run culminated with a celebration at Atlanta Fulton County Stadium when the tomahawking Braves fans finally showed emotion that David Justice complained was lacking right before Game Six. Glavine held the Indians to one hit over eight innings, Justice homered in the sixth and Mark Wohlers held the Indians in the ninth to win the clinching game 1-0.

Glavine's was as masterful a performance as you could get in a game of that magnitude. It wasn't perhaps as gutsy as Jack Morris' 10-inning affair against the Braves in Game Seven of the 1991 Series, but for pure pitching, this was more artistic.

From retiring the Indians in order in the first to striking out Albert Belle in the eighth, Glavine lived on the plate's outside corner, neutralizing the Indians' righthanded hitters.

"After the first inning I really started to relax and settle in," Glavine says. "I wanted to leave the mound feeling confident that I had good stuff, and that I felt that from the outset. It wasn't that the rest of the game was going to be a breeze, but I knew I had the stuff to beat them that night.

"All I needed to do was keep my concentration level where it was. And if I did that, I was confident I was going to have a good night."

He actually had a no-hitter through five innings. There's enough pressure to pitch well, but a no-hitter in a World Series game?

It was, of all people, light-hitting Tony Pena who broke that spell, looping a leadoff single to right-center on a pitch low and away.

"It was actually a pitch I would throw him again in that situation," Glavine says. "At least the no-hitter possibility was over and done with, and now it was up to me to not fall apart."

While Glavine knew he had great stuff, the Braves' offense didn't. They had squandered opportunities against Dennis Martinez early, and everyone wondered whether the Braves would ever score themselves. In the bottom of the sixth, Justice put an end to that notion with his home run.

Glavine had hoped to be out on the mound when the final out was secured safely in Marquis Grissom's mitt, but he tired and stiffened. He decided the best course of action was to turn the game over to Wohlers.

"It was good to see the fans celebrating like that," Glavine says. "They deserved it. They'd been through a lot over the years and the frustration of not winning was just as bad for them as it was for us. That's why when people ask me about motivation, I say I'd like to win three or four world championships just to make up for ones we let slip past us."

Glavine's offseason was hectic but pleasurable. Billerica threw him a parade in December and his No. 15 was retired at Billerica Memorial High a week before Christmas. Many of his high school and youth coaches attended. A few days later Governor William Weld declared Tom Glavine Day in Massachusetts.

"You can win all the awards you want," Glavine says, "but it's being honored by the community you grew up in and in the state you grew up in that means the most and that I'll always remember."

He soon found it difficult to walk around Atlanta and its suburbs without being noticed as a World Series hero. A year before, his reputation was much different because of his vocal stance on baseball's labor dispute. How quickly things had changed.

"I felt like I was the one everyone was targeting because I was the guy who was always on TV," Glavine says. "I think after a while I was considered the problem.

"I think if I had to do it over again, I wouldn't make myself available for so many interviews. I'd just attend the negotiating sessions and then go back to my room and make calls to my players I think our message was too complicated. We couldn't get it out to fans clearly and concisely."

One of the highlights of the talks was getting to visit with President Clinton at the White House. Glavine and other players were able to speak to Clinton about sports and college basketball as the President attempted to get the sides together, which of course never happened.

Despite his frank answers to tough questions, Glavine said he hoped he didn't burn bridges with the owners--or the fans who root for him, the Braves or baseball in general. For the fans, at least, it seems all is forgiven.

"It makes me feel good," Glavine says. "The fans deserve my time and my attention and I'm more than willing to sign an autograph or just say hello.

"After what happened in the strike, the fans deserved our undivided attention, and it's a tribute to them that they got into baseball again. That was pretty neat. I remember the days in Atlanta when you could walk down the street in anonymity. This sure beats those days.

Glavine played both hockey and baseball from a young age. But he loved hockey long before he ever took up baseball. The center led the Merrimack Valley in scoring with 84 points as a senior in high school. His early heros were Bobby Orr and Phil Esposito.

He was drafted in the fourth round by the NHL's Los Angeles KIngs in June 1984. By that time, Glavine had already committed to the University of Massachusetts-Lowell, where he would have played both hockey and baseball.

Some scouts had him projected as the top lefty in the country, but a fear he would jump to hockey caused him to drop to the second round and the Braves. Until Glavine signed, scouting director Paul Snyder sweated out the possibility he would go to the Kings. He didn't and began his baseball career.

A 19-year-old Tom Glavine pitched for low Class A Sumter in 1985 and led the South Atlantic League with a 2.35 ERA over 26 starts.

Sports Illustrated reprinted a scouting report by an unnamed NHL scout three years ago that described Glavine this way: "Good skating ability . . . long stride with good balance . . . good acceleration . . . excellent scorer, smart around the net . . . has several moves and can finish off . . . excellent slap and wrist shots with a quick release . . . tough and durable, will not be intimidated . . . excellent competitor."

Wayne Gretsky later was traded to the Kings and could have been a linemate of Glavine's. To this day, Glavine wonders how good a hockey player he could have been.

"When I look back at all the players who are currently in the NHL that I played with or against--Kevin Stevens and Tom Barrasso are two--I wonder if I could have made it," he said. "I would have had to get a lot stronger. But I had the skills."

Glavine received a $90,000 bonus to sign with the Braves. At his first professional camp he worked with legendary pitching coach Johnny Sain and was first exposed to the throwing program that Braves pitching coach Leo Mazzone has become noted for.

Throwing every day strengthened Glavine's arm and enabled him to successfully make the jump from high school to the pros.

"People thought Johnny was crazy for making pitchers throw every day," Glavine says. "Maybe Johnny was just a little ahead of his time and now Leo has perfected it."

"If you look at our pitching staff today, we don't have many people with arm problems because Leo makes us throw every single day. Not all-out, but at a pace where you gradually build up strength toward your next start. It's hard to believe people still question it."

Glavine developed his signature two-seam changeup in 1989, discovering it almost by accident. He was retrieving an errant ball when shagging during spring training when his ring finger and middle finger settled on the ball, creating an odd grip.

"The key to the pitch was I didn't have to slow down my arm speed or change anything in my delivery," says Glavine, who went 14-8 that season, his breakthrough year.

In 1991, after new general manager John Schuerholz improved the Braves' defense by adding third baseman Terry Pendleton, first baseman Sid Bream and center fielder Otis Nixon, Glavine vowed to live up to the potential Braves brass thought he had. The rest is history. Glavine went on to go 20-11, 2.55, win the Cy Young and establish himself as the best lefty in the game.

Mazzone compared Glavine to Hall of Famer Whitey Ford. During spring training in 1993, in fact, Braves manager Bobby Cox introduced Mazzone to his idol, Ford, and Mazzone turned to Ford and said as he pointed to Glavine, "This is the Whitey Ford of the '90s."

Glavine, who got to the 20-win level again in '92 and '93 but has 29 since, wants to get back to that elite level. He says his 1995 performance, in which he went 16-7, 3.08, was the best of his career because he has matured and understands pitching more.

"What's made me a better pitcher over the last five years is that I can win a game where I don't have my best stuff," he said, "and if I don't have my best stuff I can go to Plan B and win the game."

What about the next five years? Both Glavine and Maddux are under contract this year and have option years in 1997. Scherholz could take it a year at a time before deciding what to do. But the conventional wisdom is that Schuerholz will sign both to three-year extensions after this season.

"It's not something that's gnawing at me every day," Glavine says. "I've signed a contract and I'll honor it. I think one of the things my role in the labor dispute taught me is about the business of baseball. If the Braves want to renegotiate, fine. If they don't, I'm here for two more years and we'll take it from here.

"I love playing in Atlanta and this is where I'd like to finish my career, but I'm not naive. I know that there comes a time when a team has to go in a different direction. If I'm a part of that decision, I'll understand. It would be great, though, to keep this pitching staff together. We could do a lot of damage the next few years." ∎

EDITOR'S NOTE: The Braves and Glavine stayed together for another seven seasons after his heroic World Series win in 1995. He eventually left to pitch for the Mets from 2003-2007, but he did return to Atlanta in 2008 for his final season. His 244 wins with the Braves are fourth-most in team history.

A 19-year-old Tom Glavine pitched for low Class A Sumter in 1985 and led the South Atlantic League with a 2.35 ERA over 26 starts.

Tom Glavine scouting reports

ATLANTA BRAVES
NO. 3 PROSPECT AFTER 1984

With Andrew Denson in the first round and Glavine in the second round, the 1984 draft could go down as a big one in Braves history.

Glavine's win-loss record was ordinary (3-3 with a 3.34 ERA in the Gulf Coast League) but check out the other numbers: 32 innings, 29 hits, 13 walks and 34 strikeouts. Then consider that he's from New England, where he was an outstanding hockey player (fourth-round pick of the Los Angeles Kings in NHL draft last June) and didn't have the amateur background in baseball that a lot of other players have had.

Glavine has good movement with a sinking fastball, which he runs in on hitters. As far as makeup—he was a hockey player. In other words, he is a battler. But that's not all. As a junior he became the first Boston-area prep to be selected both the outstanding high school athlete and academic athlete by the *Boston Globe*—a pair of awards he won again as a senior.

1985 SOUTH ATLANTIC LEAGUE
NO. 6 PROSPECT

If baseball loses its appeal, Glavine can always hit the ice.

The Atlanta Braves' second-round pick in the June 1984 draft, Glavine was also a fourth-round pick of the Los Angeles Kings of the NHL. A bidding war ensued, and the Braves couldn't be happier they won it.

Glavine, 6-foot, 175 pounds, went 9-6 with a league leading 2.35 ERA while striking out 174 and allowing only 114 hits and 73 walks in 168 innings.

Beyond statistics, Glavine received praise as a class individual and he has everybody pulling for him to make the major leagues because of his attitude.

ATLANTA BRAVES
NO. 2 PROSPECT AFTER 1985

Glavine defies logic. He really is 20; he really has concentrated on baseball as his No. 1 sport for only a year and a half; he really is a lefthander.

Just the same, he already is a pretty polished young pitcher who has outstanding composure, command of four pitches, and the ability to throw as hard as he needs to against certain hitters in certain situations. It is a sinking fastball that Glavine already realizes he has to run in on hitters—lefthanded or righthanded—to succeed.

Check out the ratios from his first full pro season at Sumter: 169 innings, 114 hits, 73 walks and 174 strikeouts.

The Braves' second pick in June 1984, Glavine turned down a college scholarship to play hockey and a pro hockey offer from the Los Angeles Kings, who drafted him in the fourth round of the NHL draft. The hockey background is obvious in the tenacity with which Glavine approaches pitching. He doesn't give in or get down when things go bad. He has that confidence that he can get out of the mess.

He combines his athletic ability and attitude along with the intelligence to learn quickly from instruction and mistakes. He was selected the Boston-area prep athlete and academic athlete of the year as a junior and senior — the only athlete to receive both honors in the same year.

ATLANTA BRAVES
NO. 2 PROSPECT AFTER 1986

Growing up in the Boston area, Glavine's baseball experience was limited. He spent more time on the ice than the baseball field—and was a fourth-round pick of the Los Angeles Kings in addition to being the Braves' second-round selection in the 1984 draft.

Glavine has, however, developed quickly since devoting his attention to baseball. He spent the bulk of last year at Double-A Greenville, where his 3.41 ERA ranked fourth in the Southern League.

Despite being young, a lefthander and not from an area with an emphasis on baseball, Glavine has command of all four pitches, including a sinking fastball that runs. His biggest asset, however, is his knowledge of pitching. He's the type of pitcher who can win games on days when he doesn't have good stuff because he will think his way through the game and remain in command of his emotions—regardless of the situation.

John Smoltz spent two decades with the Braves, proving he could be an elite starter, then an elite closer and then an elite starter again.

JOHN SMOLTZ, RHP

BIOGRAPHY

PROPER NAME: John Andrew Smoltz. **BORN:** May 15, 1967 in Warren, Mich.
HT.: 6-3. **WT.:** 220. **BATS:** R. **THROWS:** R. **SCHOOL:** Waverly HS, Lansing, Mich.
FIRST PRO CONTRACT: Selected by Tigers in 22nd round of June 1985 draft; signed Sept. 22, 1985.

When the Tigers considered trading John Smoltz to land Doyle Alexander in their push toward the 1987 playoffs, they were trading away a hard-throwing pitcher who could potentially be written off as a future reliever because of his delivery. In some ways, the Tigers were right. Smoltz was a great reliever. But was also a great starting pitcher and Hall of Famer.

CAREER STATISTICS

Year	Club (League)	Class	W	L	ERA	G	GS	CG	SV	IP	H	R	ER	HR	BB	SO	AVG
1986	Lakeland (FSL)	A	7	8	3.56	17	14	2	0	96	86	44	38	7	31	47	.242
1987	Glen Falls (EL)	AA	4	10	5.68	21	21	0	0	130	131	89	82	17	81	86	.268
	Richmond (IL)	AAA	0	1	6.19	3	3	0	0	16	17	11	11	2	11	5	.266
1988	Richmond (IL)	AAA	10	5	2.79	20	20	3	0	135	118	49	42	5	37	115	.233
	Atlanta (NL)	MAJ	2	7	5.48	12	12	0	0	64	74	40	39	10	33	37	.285
1989	Atlanta (NL)	MAJ	12	11	2.94	29	29	5	0	208	160	79	68	15	72	168	.212
1990	Atlanta (NL)	MAJ	14	11	3.85	34	34	6	0	231	206	109	99	20	90	170	.240
1991	Atlanta (NL)	MAJ	14	13	3.80	36	36	5	0	230	206	101	97	16	77	148	.243
1992	Atlanta (NL)	MAJ	15	12	2.85	35	35	9	0	247	206	90	78	17	80	215	.224
1993	Atlanta (NL)	MAJ	15	11	3.62	35	35	3	0	244	208	104	98	23	100	208	.230
1994	Atlanta (NL)	MAJ	6	10	4.14	21	21	1	0	135	120	69	62	15	48	113	.239
1995	Atlanta (NL)	MAJ	12	7	3.18	29	29	2	0	193	166	76	68	15	72	193	.232
1996	Atlanta (NL)	MAJ	24	8	2.94	35	35	6	0	254	199	93	83	19	55	276	.216
1997	Atlanta (NL)	MAJ	15	12	3.02	35	35	7	0	256	234	97	86	21	63	241	.242
1998	Greenville (SL)	AA	0	1	2.57	3	3	0	0	14	11	4	4	2	3	16	.216
	Macon (SAL)	LoA	0	0	3.60	2	2	0	0	10	7	4	4	1	1	14	.179
	Atlanta (NL)	MAJ	17	3	2.90	26	26	2	0	168	145	58	54	10	44	173	.231
1999	Greenville (SL)	AA	0	0	4.50	2	1	0	0	4	5	2	2	0	1	7	.294
	Atlanta (NL)	MAJ	11	8	3.19	29	29	1	0	186	168	70	66	14	40	156	.245
2000	Did not play--Injured																
2001	Macon (SAL)	LoA	0	0	1.80	1	1	0	0	5	4	1	1	0	0	5	.235
	Greenville (SL)	AA	0	0	0.00	3	1	0	0	6	3	0	0	0	0	6	.150
	Atlanta (NL)	MAJ	3	3	3.36	36	5	0	10	59	53	24	22	7	10	57	.238
2002	Atlanta (NL)	MAJ	3	2	3.25	75	0	0	55	80	59	30	29	4	24	85	.206
2003	Atlanta (NL)	MAJ	0	2	1.12	62	0	0	45	64	48	9	8	2	8	73	.204
2004	Atlanta (NL)	MAJ	0	1	2.76	73	0	0	44	82	75	25	25	8	13	85	.245
2005	Atlanta (NL)	MAJ	14	7	3.06	33	33	3	0	230	210	83	78	18	53	169	.243
2006	Atlanta (NL)	MAJ	16	9	3.49	35	35	3	0	232	221	93	90	23	55	211	.251
2007	Atlanta (NL)	MAJ	14	8	3.11	32	32	0	0	206	196	78	71	18	47	197	.249
2008	Mississippi (SL)	AA	0	0	0.00	1	0	0	0	1	1	0	0	0	0	0	.250
	Rome (SAL)	LoA	0	0	0.00	2	1	0	0	3	1	0	0	0	0	4	.091
	Atlanta (NL)	MAJ	3	2	2.57	6	5	0	0	28	25	8	8	2	8	36	.229
2009	Portland (EL)	AA	0	0	2.70	1	1	0	0	3	3	1	1	0	0	2	.231
	Greenville (SAL)	LoA	0	0	1.13	2	2	0	0	8	5	1	1	0	0	8	.172
	Pawtucket (IL)	AAA	1	1	3.38	3	3	1	0	16	10	6	6	2	4	11	.179
	Boston (AL)	MAJ	2	5	8.33	8	8	0	0	40	59	37	37	8	9	33	.343
	St. Louis (NL)	MAJ	1	3	4.26	7	7	0	0	38	36	18	18	3	9	40	.248
Major League Totals			213	155	3.33	723	481	53	154	3473	3074	1391	1284	288	1010	3084	.237
Minor League Totals			22	26	3.86	81	73	6	0	448	402	212	192	36	169	326	.220

The Braves' big-game hunter

MAY 1988

HOLY SMOLTZ! A YOUNG RYAN?

by JOHN PACKETT

When the Triple-A Richmond Braves broke camp in late March and headed north for the International League season, they were expected to have excellent pitching, thanks to young prospects Derek Lilliquist and Tommy Greene.

Lilliquist, 22, Atlanta's top pick in the draft last year, and Greene, a former No. 1 selection who turned 21 the day before the season opened, were considered the most likely to succeed in 1988. A summons by the parent club was not out of the question.

It hasn't worked out that way. Greene and Lilliquist have struggled the early part of the 1988 season, while righthander John Smoltz has turned in the best numbers of the spring on the R-Braves pitching staff.

John who? For those with short memories, Smoltz was traded from Detroit to Atlanta last August for Doyle Alexander, who went 9-0 and helped the Tigers win the American League East title. Smoltz was sent to Richmond, where he was 0-1 in three starts with an ERA of 6.19. Detroit clearly gained all the short-term benefits from the deal.

"I was really shocked," said Smoltz, who will be 21 on May 15. "I just didn't think I would be traded. Not at that time, late in the season. I was upset at the time, because I really wanted to play for Detroit. But they had to do what they needed to do to win the pennant, and it worked out.

"I'm not bitter. It's not to the point where I don't watch them or anything," said Smoltz, a native of Detroit who grew up as a Tigers fan.

Smoltz is concentrating on making it in the Atlanta organization, and the 6-foot-3, 185-pound righthander has gotten off to a blazing beginning. In three starts for the R-Braves, Smoltz was 2-0 with an ERA of 1.42. In 19 innings, he's struck out 19 and walked seven, giving up nine hits.

"The only surprise, as far as I'm concerned," Richmond pitching coach Leo Mazzone said, "is the command of his pitches. We knew he had a strong arm, but no matter how hard you throw the fastball, if you don't have a good curve, you're not going to get anybody out."

Smoltz began to change his curve and regain confidence in himself by working with Mazzone in instructional league last fall.

"We didn't work on any mechanics or lack of concentration," said Smoltz. "Just one pitch. My curveball. We tried to tighten it up. That's going to make or break me. If I can get the curveball over, I'll be much more effective."

In two of his three outings, Smoltz's curve consistently fooled batters looking for the heater.

"He had a breaking ball that broke real big," Mazzone said. "Now he's tightened it up. He's going to more of a throw–and–turn breaking pitch. He's been real successful with it and feels real comfortable. He's getting a nasty break on it."

Atlanta, with its struggling pitching staff, is already casting greedy glances toward Smoltz, and general manager Bobby Cox is comparing his farmhand to a "young Nolan Ryan."

Even though Smoltz has impressive statistics so far, Mazzone hopes his protege stays down on the farm for the foreseeable future.

"I think he should be right here for 180 innings," Mazzone said. "Then, when he does go to the big leagues, it won't be a shuttle run. He'll stay up there." ∎

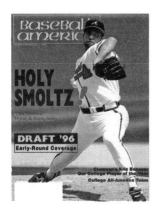

JUNE 1996

SMOLTZ FINALLY PLEASES HIS CRITICS

by BILL BALLEW

About six hours before the start of Game 7 of the 1991 National League Championship Series, Braves pitcher John Smoltz and media relations manager Glen Serra hailed a cab at the Vista International Hotel in Pittsburgh, their identities unknown to the driver.

"So you guys are going to the game, eh?" said the cabbie, donning a Pirates cap. "We'll take 'em, easy. We got (John) Smiley going for us. Who do they got?"

"Smoltz," Serra said.

"Oh yeah. He ain't got nothing. It's in the bag."

For the remaining 10 minutes of the drive, Serra applied his best wrestling submission hold on the pitcher in the back seat. Upon arriving at Three Rivers Stadium, Smoltz had more pent-up energy than a groom on his wedding day.

"Man, I really wanted to get after that guy," Smoltz said, "but I'll show him what I got."

Before the clock struck midnight Smoltz was true to his word. The righthander gave up six hits and one walk and fanned eight Pirates in a 4-0 shutout, his second victory of the playoffs.

In many ways, that day serves as a microcosm of Smoltz's career since jumping to the majors in 1988. He has tasted nearly as much success as any pitcher in the game, but his accomplishments rarely seem to be enough to gain the respect of the masses. As a result, Smoltz has found himself battling others' expectations as aggressively as he does opposing hitters.

John Smoltz threw an additional 209 innings in the post-season, going 15-4, 2.67 with four saves. He pitched in four World Series and nine NL Championship Series.

Until now.

No pitcher was more dominant than Smoltz during the first two months of this 1996 season. After dropping his first start in the third game of the year, the right-hander proceeded to win his next 11 outings, the last coming May 29. How rare is this? The Elias Sports Bureau revealed that the Giants' Joe McGinty, who went on to post a 35-8 mark in 1904, is the only pitcher in the National League to have won 10 games more quickly at the start of the season, reaching the mark on May 21 some 92 years ago.

Smoltz, naturally, has received some help during the streak. The Braves averaged 6.3 runs every time the righthander took the mound. The only close call occurred in Pittsburgh for his 10th win on May 24. Smoltz had been pulled for a pinch-hitter but remained the pitcher of record when Atlanta pushed across three runs in the top of the seventh of a 5-3 win, giving him his 100th career victory.

"Realistically, I couldn't have gotten off to a better start," Smoltz says. "But the way I approached it, I felt that I could do this. The team has definitely helped me out in many situations, but at the same time I haven't really allowed them to get in a hole. I've stayed ahead and kept things quiet. The runs the other teams have been scoring have come late, when we had a 7-1 or 9-0 lead."

With impeccable command and a vast array of nasty pitches, Smoltz limited opposing hitters to a .173 average during his blazing start. He also led the National League in strikeouts with 97, placed second with a 2.24 ERA and had allowed less than a baserunner an inning.

"He's had his best stuff," Atlanta manager Bobby Cox said. "He's about as good as they come right now. John's on one of those rolls where he's almost unstoppable."

The scenario creates an endless stream of reporters scurrying to Smoltz's locker to ask one short, monotonous question: What's causing all this success?

"Health is the biggest reason," says Smoltz, 29. "For the first time in a long time, I'm free of pain and can go out there and do what I feel I'm capable of doing.

"The command is where it is because of my health. I can throw the ball to a spot. Because I've been inhibited at certain times in my career, it's affected my control and, quite honestly, I feel that's a big part of my game."

Smoltz's health began to deteriorate in late 1991, when he was finishing his 14-13 season with the Braves' division-clinching win against Houston on Oct. 5. Dr. Joe Chandler, Atlanta's orthopedic surgeon, diagnosed the ailment as bone chips in Smoltz's right elbow, which started to affect him regularly a year later. Chandler recommended surgery at the end of the 1992 season and again the following winter after Smoltz had decided against it.

"The bone chips had been causing havoc for quite some time," Smoltz says. "It was periodic—the pain would come and go. I'd have two bad weeks, then two good weeks. During that time, I couldn't throw anything slow. When I'd throw the ball hard, I was fine. But when I had to put any touch on a pitch, that's where it was very difficult.

"Still, there were enough good times to make me feel like I could bear the pain. I was getting through it. I was successful, and I was winning a lot of games. Maybe not as many as some thought I could win, but through it all I had some pretty darn good games. I just bit the bullet and pitched as much as I could."

The pain finally became too much to ignore during the 1994 season. With a disappointing 6-10 record and a career-high 4.14 ERA, Smoltz realized during a July 31 start against Philadelphia that he no longer could ignore his problem. He had the surgery six weeks later, with Chandler removing a large bone spur and some chips from the back of Smoltz's right elbow.

"I cost myself some games," Smoltz said. "But if I didn't pitch all the times I didn't feel good, it would have been less than 50 percent. That's not a good ratio. And they pay me a lot of money to pitch a lot of games. So I don't look back and say I regret pitching those games."

Smoltz's competitive spirit was obvious to Braves scouting director Paul Snyder more than a decade ago. Snyder scouted the Lansing, Mich., prep product in the spring of 1985 and was interested in the youngster's services before the home-state Tigers drafted Smoltz in the 22nd round and signed him just before he was to attend classes at Michigan State.

Two years later, Detroit was battling Toronto in the American League East and needed a veteran pitcher down the stretch. The Tigers set their sights on Doyle Alexander, a malcontent who acted like a prisoner in Atlanta's rebuilding clubhouse. The Braves gave Detroit its hired gun in exchange for a 20-year-old Double-A pitcher with an 11-18 record in 38 minor league starts.

The Tigers traded the future for the present and, behind Alexander's 9-0 record, outlasted the Blue Jays for the AL East title. The Braves got what they wanted as well: a key component of their rotation for years to come

"I hadn't seen John since he was in high school, but I knew what kind of pitcher we were dealing with," Snyder said. "He was an outstanding athlete who had arm strength. He was just having trouble with locating the breaking ball and getting to the same release point every time, just like a lot of young pitchers do.

"I was there the night he joined us in (Triple-A) Richmond. He was trying to throw too many pitches at that time. We eliminated some of the breaking balls and got John into a routine. Pretty soon he started to do what we thought he could."

After a 10-5 start at Triple-A in 1988, which led to his being named the top prospect in the International League, Smoltz joined Atlanta's rotation July 23 and hasn't missed more than a half-dozen starts since. During that time his achievements easily created a full resume:

■ In 1989, his first full season in the majors, Smoltz became the youngest all-star pitcher in Braves history after reaching the break with an 11-6, 2.10 record.

■ Building on his 1991 postseason success, including 7.1 innings of shutout pitching against Minnesota in Game 7 of the World Series, Smoltz won two more games in the 1992

John Smoltz made his first all-star appearance in 1989 as a 22-year-old. He made his final all-star appearance in 2007 as a 40-year-old.

NLCS and posted a 2.66 ERA in three starts to earn series MVP honors.

■ He led the league with 215 strikeouts in 1992, then placed second a year later with 208.

■ Through June 1 of this year, his 73 wins since the beginning of 1990 ranks third among active NL pitchers, behind only teammates Tom Glavine (96) and Greg Maddux (95).

"He's been one of the best pitchers in the game for six years," Atlanta pitching coach Leo Mazzone said. "He don't give a – – – – if it's 1991 or 1996. He has been, not just right now. Someone asked me what made him turn a corner. I said there wasn't a corner for him to turn."

As true as Mazzone's comments may be, Smoltz has never received much acclaim. One reason centers on his standing in the shadows of Maddux and Glavine. Another involves how Smoltz has never won 15 games in a season despite the fact that many observers rate his fastball, curveball and slider among the best in the game.

A third reason focuses on Smoltz's perceived makeup. Much was made about his tremendous turnaround in 1991, the season he staggered through a 2-11, 5.16 first half before going on a 12-2, 2.62 tear in the final three months.

Smoltz began seeing psychologist Jack Llewellyn, who worked with him on concentrating only on those aspects of his life he can control.

The therapy took nearly four years for Smoltz to fully accept and embrace. He now considers all aspects of his life—family, religion and baseball—to be in proper perspective, which has created an even better and more dominating pitcher.

"The kid has everything so in control now it's amazing," Llewellyn says. "Nothing bothers him like it used to. He's as tough as they come."

"I'm a totally different pitcher as far as my mindset goes," said Smoltz, who adds that he never reads the paper and refuses to allow comments, from either Pittsburgh cabbies or sportswriters, affect him.

Some observers point out that Smoltz's timing couldn't be better. He'll be a free agent at the end of the season, and Atlanta general manager John Schuerholz already has started designing how, despite the cost that rises with each start, to keep a tomahawk across the righthander's chest.

Smoltz, meanwhile, has little to say about his next contract or any other aspect of the future. He's too busy following advice from "Wayne's World," which is to "live in the now," regardless of whether it involves answering the same endless questions, putting up with his sarcastic teammates (Could you sign this ball and put 11-1 under it? Maddux asked) or dealing with lingering questions about whether he finally has become the pitcher everyone expected.

"Pitching is hard. Greg makes it look easy. Certain other guys make it look easy," Smoltz said. "But it can be hard if you have a lot of other things on your mind. Right now, I'm just pitching and not worrying about anything other than getting the ball to the plate. And as a pitcher, especially for me, that makes this game a heck of a lot easier." ■

EDITOR'S NOTE: The 1996 season did prove to be special for Smoltz. He finished the season with a 24-8, 2.94 mark as he led the league in wins and innings pitched (253.2) to win his only Cy Young award..

John Smoltz showed control and command issues in the minors, but those problems rarely arose in the majors.

John Smoltz scouting reports

DETROIT TIGERS
NO. 9 PROSPECT AFTER 1985 SEASON

Smoltz is one of the Tigers' true products. A high school phenom out of Lansing, Mich., the Tigers gambled that they could talk Smoltz out of attending school at Michigan State by drafting him in the 22nd round last June—and won.

Smoltz, however, signed too late to make his pro debut, choosing instead to pitch in the World Junior Championships. He did, however, show up at instructional league, where major league pitching coach Billy Muffett began what will be a long-term project of refining Smoltz's crude pitching mechanics.

1985 FLORIDA STATE LEAGUE
NO. 5 PROSPECT

Smoltz brought his blazing fastball with him and jumped out to a 4-0 record and 1.57 ERA before injuring his elbow and sitting out most of the midseason. After the long layoff, Smoltz slumped and finished with a 7-8 mark and 3.45 ERA. He struck out 51 in 99 innings, while walking 31.

Lakeland manager Tom Burgess blamed himself for part of Smoltz's slump. "I didn't let him pitch out of some of the jams he got into, because I didn't want to risk re-injuring his arm," Burgess said.

Smoltz was a 22nd-round draft pick out of high school in Lansing, Mich. The Tigers had to talk him out of attending Michigan State before signing him to a contract in late summer 1985.

DETROIT TIGERS
NO. 2 PROSPECT AFTER 1986 SEASON

The Tigers took a shot in the dark by drafting Smoltz in the 22nd round of the 1985 draft, then came up with what it took at the 11th hour to convince him to sign instead of playing baseball at Michigan State.

Signing late cost him his 1985 season, and an elbow injury put a damper on 1986. He was 4-0 with a 1.57 ERA at Class A Lakeland before being hurt. Initially, he came back and was tentative in throwing the ball, but by the end of the season was going strong again.

He needs to smooth out his mechanics, but has a legitimate fastball, good straight change-up and both a hard and soft curveball.

1986 EASTERN LEAGUE
NO. 9 PROSPECT

Whenever you hear Smoltz's name, you hear "great arm" mentioned quickly afterward. The Tigers traded Smoltz to Atlanta late in the season for Doyle Alexander.

Smoltz has a blazing fastball but didn't have the control of it to get Double-A hitters out consistently and had a relatively high ERA.

Reading manager George Culver, for one, thinks Smoltz will end up as a reliever in the mold of Goose Gossage.

"He'll blow you away for an inning or two and show way above-average stuff," Culver said. "But then he will lose it and show nothing special. That's why I think you'll see him as a reliever."

1988 INTERNATIONAL LEAGUE
NO. 1 PROSPECT

From the way he conducted himself on the mound to his repertoire of pitches, IL managers thought Smoltz was a major league pitcher even before his promotion to Atlanta.

"He has the best combination of fastball and breaking ball for a guy his age I've seen in a long time," Maine manager George Culver said. Even teams that defeated Smoltz wondered how. "He got stronger, threw harder, as the game went along," one manager said.

Add in Smoltz's maturity and Culver sees a winner. "He's growing by leaps and bounds," he said. "It's just fun to watch someone pitch with that kind of stuff."

ATLANTA BRAVES
NO. 6 PROSPECT AFTER 1987 SEASON

Don't let his numbers last summer deceive. This is a young man with an armful of potential. His command has been a major problem—123 walks and 133 strikeouts in 244 innings—but the Braves seemed to get that worked out in instructional league.

Smoltz was a victim of too much advice with the Tigers. Trying to please his instructors, he was trying to throw a variety of breaking balls and changeups, and had not mastered any of them. The Braves finally had him settle down on one breaking ball and one changeup to complement an overpowering fastball. Suddenly, the strike zone does not appear to be the twilight zone.

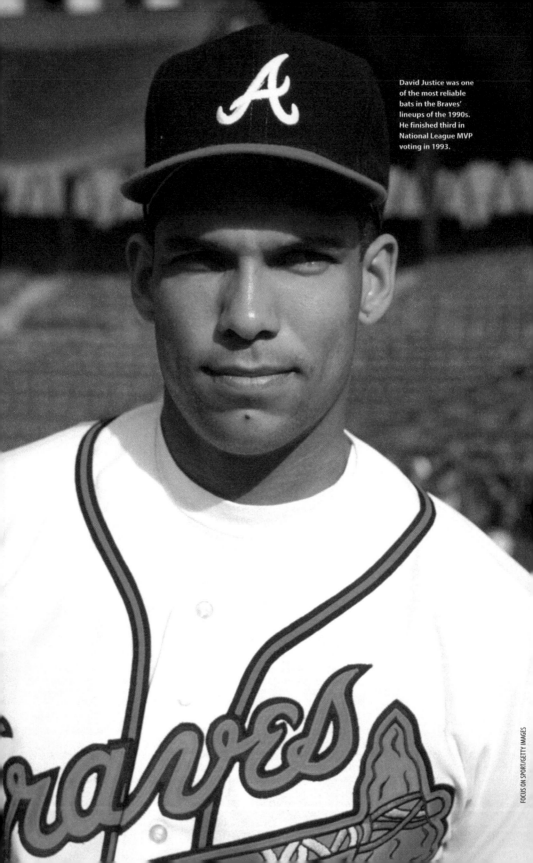

David Justice was one of the most reliable bats in the Braves' lineups of the 1990s. He finished third in National League MVP voting in 1993.

DAVID JUSTICE, OF

BIOGRAPHY

PROPER NAME: David Christopher Justice. **BORN:** April 14, 1966 in Cincinnati, Ohio.
HT.: 6-3. **WT.:** 200. **BATS:** L. **THROWS:** L. **SCHOOL:** Thomas More (Ky.).
FIRST PRO CONTRACT: Selected by Braves in fourth round of 1985 draft.

David Justice never shied from the spotlight. The biggest moment in Braves history is his sixth-inning home run in Game 6 of the 1995 World Series. That one swing was the only run in the clinching game of the franchise's lone World Series title in Atlanta. Braves fans woke up that morning to read comments from Justice decrying their lack of energy compared to the crowds of previous Braves' World Series appearances. They were going crazy that night after Justice's home run provided the only run Tom Glavine and Mark Wohlers needed in a one-hit shutout of Cleveland. Justice had proven throughout the early 1990s to be the Braves' player most comfortable in the spotlight and had a knack for rising to the occasion.

CAREER STATISTICS

Year	Tm	Lev	AVG	G	AB	R	H	2B	3B	HR	RBI	BB	SO	SB	OBP	SLG
1985	Pulaski (APP)	Rk	.245	66	204	39	50	8	0	10	46	40	30	0	.361	.431
1986	Sumter (SAL)	A	.300	61	220	48	66	16	0	10	61	48	28	10	.425	.509
1986	Durham (CAR)	A	.279	67	229	47	64	9	1	12	44	46	24	2	.413	.485
1987	Greenville (SL)	AA	.227	93	348	38	79	12	4	6	40	53	48	3	.327	.336
1988	Greenville (SL)	AA	.278	58	198	34	55	13	1	9	37	36	43	6	.392	.490
1988	Richmond (A-A)	AAA	.203	70	227	27	46	9	1	8	28	39	55	4	.311	.357
1989	Atlanta (NL)	MLB	.235	16	51	7	12	3	0	1	3	3	9	2	.291	.353
1989	Richmond (A-A)	AAA	.261	115	391	47	102	24	3	12	58	59	66	12	.360	.430
1990	Atlanta (NL)	MLB	.282	127	439	76	124	23	2	28	78	64	92	11	.373	.535
1990	Richmond (A-A)	AAA	.356	12	45	7	16	5	1	2	7	7	6	0	.442	.644
1991	Atlanta (NL)	MLB	.275	109	396	67	109	25	1	21	87	65	81	8	.377	.503
1991	Macon (SAL)	A	.200	3	10	2	2	0	0	2	5	2	1	0	.308	.800
1992	Atlanta (NL)	MLB	.256	144	484	78	124	19	5	21	72	79	85	2	.359	.446
1993	Atlanta (NL)	MLB	.270	157	585	90	158	15	4	40	120	78	90	3	.357	.515
1994	Atlanta (NL)	MLB	.313	104	352	61	110	16	2	19	59	69	45	2	.427	.531
1995	Atlanta (NL)	MLB	.253	120	411	73	104	17	2	24	78	73	68	4	.365	.479
1996	Atlanta (NL)	MLB	.321	40	140	23	45	9	0	6	25	21	22	1	.409	.514
1997	Cleveland (AL)	MLB	.329	139	495	84	163	31	1	33	101	80	79	3	.418	.596
1998	Cleveland (AL)	MLB	.280	146	540	94	151	39	2	21	88	76	98	9	.363	.476
1999	Cleveland (AL)	MLB	.287	133	429	75	123	18	0	21	88	94	90	1	.413	.476
2000	Cleveland (AL)	MLB	.265	68	249	46	66	14	1	21	58	38	49	1	.361	.582
2000	New York (AL)	MLB	.305	78	275	43	84	17	0	20	60	39	42	1	.391	.585
2001	New York (AL)	MLB	.241	111	381	58	92	16	1	18	51	54	83	1	.333	.430
2001	Norwich (EL)	AA	.000	2	8	0	0	0	0	0	0	0	1	0	.000	.000
2002	Oakland (AL)	MLB	.266	118	398	54	106	18	3	11	49	70	66	4	.376	.410
Major League Totals			**.279**	**1610**	**5625**	**929**	**1571**	**280**	**24**	**305**	**1017**	**903**	**999**	**53**	**.378**	**.500**
Minor League Totals			**.255**	**547**	**1880**	**289**	**480**	**96**	**11**	**71**	**326**	**330**	**302**	**37**	**.367**	**.431**

David Justice did not play high school baseball, but he quickly took to the sport in college.

David Justice scouting reports

ATLANTA BRAVES
NO. 4 PROSPECT AFTER 1986 SEASON

Justice is another late developer. He did not even play baseball in high school, opting to concentrate on academics and basketball. Basketball was also his main emphasis at Kentucky's Thomas More College, but the Braves saw enough to make Justice their fourth-round selection in 1985.

He hasn't disappointed. An outstanding natural athlete, Justice has a smooth swing and a good knowledge of the strike zone (94 walks, 52 strikeouts in 449 at-bats at Sumter and Durham last season), especially for an inexperienced player. He does not sacrifice power—22 home runs, 25 doubles and 105 RBIs.

ATLANTA BRAVES
NO. 8 PROSPECT AFTER 1987 SEASON

A basketball player in high school who concentrated on that sport during his days at Kentucky's Thomas More University, Justice has turned raw ability into reality since signing with the Braves.

He can play all three outfield positions well and has as smooth a swing as anybody in the Braves' system. After getting his feet on the ground in 1986, Justice appeared ready to explode in 1987, but a broken wrist suffered while trying to make a diving catch at the end of spring training knocked him out of action for the first 12 weeks of the 1987 season.

ATLANTA BRAVES
NO. 6 PROSPECT AFTER 1989 SEASON

Justice has a lovely swing, and is considered the premier athlete in the organization. But he is plagued by his own potential. He graduated high school at 16, was selected in the fourth round of the 1985 draft and amassed 22 home runs and 105 RBIs in his first full season. But he faltered at Richmond in 1988, and went a timid 1-for-20 last May in his major league debut. He went 11-for-31 in Atlanta in September.

The Braves knew Ron Gant could give them a middle-of-the-lineup bat. It just took a little while longer to figure out where he fit defensively.

RON GANT, OF/2B

BIOGRAPHY

PROPER NAME: Ronald Edwin Gant. **BORN:** March 2, 1965 in Victoria, Texas.
HT.: 6-0. **WT.:** 192. **BATS:** R. **THROWS:** R. **SCHOOL:** Bolles HS, Jacksonville.
FIRST PRO CONTRACT: Selected by Braves in fourth round of 1983 draft; signed June 14, 1983.

In 1988, Gant looked like a budding star for the Braves. He had 19 home runs and 19 stolen bases and finished fourth in Rookie of the Year balloting. He looked like a perennial power-speed threat with 30-30 potential at the major league level. A year later, a 24-year-old Gant found himself back playing for low Class A Sumter, because in addition to having 30-home run and 30-steal potential, he also had the chance to lead the league in errors at second base. The Braves tried him at third base, then decided to move him to the outfield instead. Gant accepted that he had to start over. After a short stint with Sumter, he returned to Triple-A Richmond as an outfielder. Gant's willingness to start over ended up making his career. In 1990, he logged a 30-30 season for Atlanta, and he ended up topping 30 home runs in three different seasons for the Braves, serving alongside David Justice as the best power hitters of the Braves' early-1990s clubs.

CAREER STATISTICS

Year	Tm	Lev	AVG	G	AB	R	H	2B	3B	HR	RBI	BB	SO	SB	OBP	SLG
1983	Braves (GCL)	Rk	.233	56	193	32	45	2	2	1	14	41	34	4	.366	.280
1984	Anderson (SAL)	A	.237	105	359	44	85	14	6	3	38	29	65	13	.291	.334
1985	Sumter (SAL)	A	.256	102	305	46	78	14	4	7	37	33	59	19	.332	.397
1986	Durham (CAR)	A	.277	137	512	108	142	31	10	26	102	78	85	35	.372	.529
1987	Greenville	AA	.247	140	527	78	130	27	3	14	82	59	92	24	.321	.389
1987	Atlanta (NL)	MLB	.265	21	83	9	22	4	0	2	9	1	11	4	.271	.386
1988	Richmond	AAA	.311	12	45	3	14	2	2	0	4	2	10	1	.333	.444
1988	Atlanta (NL)	MLB	.259	146	563	85	146	28	8	19	60	46	118	19	.317	.439
1989	Atlanta (NL)	MLB	.177	75	260	26	46	8	3	9	25	20	63	9	.237	.335
1989	Sumter	A	.385	12	39	13	15	4	1	1	5	11	3	4	.520	.615
1989	Richmond	AAA	.262	63	225	42	59	13	2	11	27	29	42	7	.345	.484
1990	Atlanta (NL)	MLB	.303	152	575	107	174	34	3	32	84	50	86	33	.357	.539
1991	Atlanta (NL)	MLB	.251	154	561	101	141	35	3	32	105	71	104	34	.338	.496
1992	Atlanta (NL)	MLB	.259	153	544	74	141	22	6	17	80	45	101	32	.321	.415
1993	Atlanta (NL)	MLB	.274	157	606	113	166	27	4	36	117	67	117	26	.345	.510
1995	Cincinnati (NL)	MLB	.276	119	410	79	113	19	4	29	88	74	108	23	.386	.554
1996	St. Louis (NL)	MLB	.246	122	419	74	103	14	2	30	82	73	98	13	.359	.504
1997	St. Louis (NL)	MLB	.229	139	502	68	115	21	4	17	62	58	162	14	.310	.388
1998	St. Louis (NL)	MLB	.240	121	383	60	92	17	1	26	67	51	92	8	.331	.493
1999	Philadelphia (NL)	MLB	.260	138	516	107	134	27	5	17	77	85	112	13	.364	.430
2000	Philadelphia (NL)	MLB	.254	89	343	54	87	16	2	20	38	36	73	5	.324	.487
2000	Anaheim (AL)	MLB	.232	34	82	15	19	3	1	6	16	20	18	1	.379	.512
2001	Colorado (NL)	MLB	.257	59	171	31	44	8	2	8	22	24	56	3	.345	.468
2001	Oakland (AL)	MLB	.259	34	81	15	21	5	1	2	13	11	24	2	.344	.420
2002	San Diego (NL)	MLB	.262	102	309	58	81	14	1	18	59	36	59	4	.338	.489
2003	Oakland (AL)	MLB	.146	17	41	4	6	0	0	1	4	2	9	0	.182	.220
Major League Totals			**.256**	**1832**	**6449**	**1080**	**1651**	**302**	**50**	**321**	**1008**	**770**	**1411**	**243**	**.336**	**.468**
Minor League Totals			**.258**	**627**	**2205**	**366**	**568**	**107**	**30**	**63**	**309**	**282**	**390**	**107**	**.341**	**.419**

In the early 1990s, Ron Gant (right) and David Justice (left) were fixtures in the middle of Atlanta's lineup.

Ron Gant
scouting reports

ATLANTA BRAVES
NO. 4 PROSPECT AFTER 1987 SEASON

A high school teammate of No. 3 prospect Kevin Coffman, Gant was the Braves' fourth-round selection in 1983. Like Coffman, Gant spun his wheels for a couple of years but started putting things together in 1986 at Durham, his third year at the full-season Class A level.

The biggest adjustment Gant has made has been mentally. He's learned to separate his offense from his defense—striking out doesn't mean he has to make errors.

He might not hit for a big average, but Gant will hit enough for a middle infielder, especially considering he is a definite run production threat (193 RBIs the last two years), who can steal a base (63 thefts the last two years).

ATLANTA BRAVES
NO. 7 PROSPECT AFTER 1986 SEASON

Gant's defensive ability is limited, but he is a hard-nosed player who gets the job done. If he can maintain average play in the field, his bat should make him an asset at second base, especially for a team who plays on natural grass. In spring training, the Braves had plans to move him to the outfield, but he improved enough at Class A Durham that they now want to keep him at second base.

Gant was one of just four players in the minor leagues this year who had double figures in doubles (31), triples (10), home runs (26) and stolen bases (35). And he was the only one of that group who also drove in 100 runs (102) and scored at least 100 (108).

JEFF BLAUSER, SS

The Braves' emphasis on up-the-middle defense during the early 1990s wasn't always a perfect fit for Blauser. Rafael Belliard was the no-hit, all-glove shortstop. Blauser was one of the best offensive shortstops in the National League, but his glove didn't compare with Belliard, so they shared time. But Blauser was sneakily productive. He was a two-time all-star who was generally good for 10-15 home runs a season at a time when few shortstops hit for power.

RANKED AS BRAVES NO. 8 PROSPECT AFTER 1984 SEASON

Don't be deceived by the fact that Blauser was selected in the secondary phase last June out of California's Sacramento City College. He only played at 18. And he does play.

He has a long way to go with the bat (.249 with 47 strikeouts in 62 games at Pulaski). But he already has come a long way in the field.

Start with the attitude—he plays hard—and he plays to win. Then check his range—well above-average. And his arm is better than that. And he has natural movements of a short-stop.

RANKED AS BRAVES NO. 5 PROSPECT AFTER 1985 SEASON

Blauser is another middle infielder with great defensive ability and offensive potential who just needs some time to develop with the bat.

Blauser has a plus arm that is not only strong but accurate, even when he throws off bal-ance. He has excellent range, and the natural movements of a shortstop.

His determination got a test early in the 1985 season when he went hitless in his first 33 at-bats at Sumter. Instead of giving up or complaining about being overmatched, Blauser made some adjustments and hit .254 the rest of the way. He is a patient hitter—some-times too patient—with 82 walks but 94 strikeouts in 422 at-bats.

RANKED AS BRAVES NO. 1 PROSPECT AFTER 1986 SEASON

Defensively he can handle the position at any level, and the Braves showed confidence by promoting him to Triple-A for the International League playoffs. He is fluid in the field with excellent range, and has an arm that is not only strong but accurate. He has soft hands and great instincts. Offensively Blauser will have to continue to adjust and improve at every level to live up to his defensive potential in the big leagues. There has been some talk Blauser will be moved to second base and eventually play alongside shortstop Andres Thomas in Atlanta. The Braves insist that they plan to leave him at shortstop next year.

STEVE AVERY, LHP

Avery was arguably too good, too soon. After he dominated the Appalachian League in his draft year, the Braves decided to push Avery to high Class A Durham, skipping him over low Class A. It wasn't enough. He posted a 1.45 ERA there and forced a promotion to Double-A at midseason 1989. He had barely turned 20 when he made his big league debut in 1990. A year later, he was the MVP of the NLCS, throwing 16.1 scoreless innings as he helped shut out the Pirates twice. Unfortunately for Avery and the Braves, his best days were done by the time he turned 24. His stuff slowly deteriorated in the second half of the 1990s, and a rotator cuff injury effectively ended his career by the time he was 29. But when he was young, he was exceptionally good.

RANKED AS BRAVES NO. 1 PROSPECT AFTER 1988 SEASON

The Braves, who considered economics heavily in the pre–Bobby Cox drafting days, gave the biggest bonus in their drafting history ($211,500) to sign Avery, the third pick overall in last year's draft. Considering this is the same team that gave Bob Horner $200,000 to weigh 215 pounds, the bonus is a huge bargain for the Braves.

In his first professional season. Avery showed incredible composure and poise. He also displayed remarkable control for a young lefthander. In 66 innings in the Appalachian League, Avery had 80 strikeouts and 19 walks.

Because of Avery's ability to throw his breaking pitch for strikes, the Braves think he could be at Double-A this year. The Braves brought him to major league camp this spring, and some in the organization believe he will return next spring to compete for a spot in the major league rotation.

RANKED AS BRAVES NO. 1 PROSPECT AFTER 1989 SEASON

The Braves struggle for reasons why Avery should be restrained. He has provided them none.

Age seems the best excuse. Not yet 20, Avery has dominated at every level, including a 6-3, 2.77 record at Double-A Greenville last season. Since being made the third overall selection in the 1988 draft, Avery has gone 19-8, 1.96.

He has a good fastball, and an overhand curve that really nosedives at the plate.

"I would not trade Steve Avery straight up for Wade Boggs," Bobby Cox said during December's Winter Meetings.

The club, which imposed a season-long pitch limit on its prize, refused to promote Avery to Triple-A Richmond at the end of last season. He should start this season at Richmond, and is expected to make his major league debut before season's end.

KENT MERCKER, LHP

Tom Glavine never threw a no-hitter. Neither did Greg Maddux. Nor did John Smoltz. Kent Mercker participated in two. In 1991, Mercker combined with Mark Wohlers and Alejandro Peña to no-hit the Padres. It was the Braves' first no-hitter since Phil Niekro also shut down the Padres in 1973. It was a serendipitous moment in Atlanta's amazing worst-to-first season. But Mercker wasn't done. Three years later, he did it again, throwing a complete-game no-hitter this time as he stymied the Dodgers. Mercker bounced between the Braves' rotation and bullpen throughout its World Series runs in the early 1990s. He became a starter for good in 1994, and handled that role for the rest of the decade before moving back to the bullpen for another six seasons.

RANKED AS BRAVES NO. 2 PROSPECT AFTER 1988 SEASON

The Braves started a three-year run of taking lefthanders in the first round of the draft by selecting Mercker in 1986. About a week later, Mecker injured an ankle while roughhousing at a high school party.

That was an omen for the Braves. Mercker's maturity lagged behind his pitching skills. His first season was marked by bouts with homesickness and childish activity. His second lasted only 12 innings because of an elbow injury.

Mercker, the person, caught up with Mercker, the pitcher, last year. His elbow healthy, Mercker was a combined 14–5, 2.91 ERA at Class A and Double-A. He allowed only seven home runs while getting 11.2 strikeouts per nine innings.

RANKED AS BRAVES NO. 4 PROSPECT AFTER 1989 SEASON

Mercker overpowered the International League with an explosive fastball (league high 144 strikeouts in 169 innings), but has yet to develop a consistent breaking pitch. Once untouchable, he has been offered in the Braves' search for a third baseman. Mercker is tentatively scheduled to return to Triple-A, where it's hoped he will become more aware of improving than of blowing away Triple-A hitters.

MARK LEMKE, 2B

Taken as a whole, Lemke's 10-year Braves career was a relatively modest one. He never hit .300, and he usually hit around .250. He never reached double digits in home runs. But with a dominant pitching staff and a solid lineup, the Braves were happy to have a reliable defender at second base. And Lemke did have his playoff highlights. He hit .417/.462/.708 during the 1991 World Series. He hit .333/.462/.381 during the NLCS against the Pirates the next season and he hit .444/.516/.630 during the 1996 NLCS against the Cardinals. So was Lemke a clutch hitter whose performance rose during the postseason? Well, he actually hit .272/.335/.353 overall in the postseason—not far above his normal production—but his highlights were spectacular.

RANKED AS BRAVES NO. 9 PROSPECT AFTER 1988 SEASON

He's Glenn Hubbard revisited. Like the Braves' long-time second baseman, Lemke is undersized but gritty and determined. He will not make the highlight-film play, but he will make the essential play.

That is enough for the Braves, who suffered as Ron Gant made 26 errors in 122 games and was a leading reason for the Braves' lowest double play total (138) for a full season since 1978. Lemke began spring camp as the starter at second base, but he must produce to keep the job. Jeff Blauser and Edwin Alicea, the Braves' ninth-round pick in the draft last June, lurk in the background.

RANKED AS BRAVES NO. 7 PROSPECT AFTER 1989 SEASON

The hard-nosed Lemke nearly made the Opening Day roster last spring before Bobby Cox purchased Jeff Treadway's contract from the Reds. Lemke returned to Richmond and collected himself for a .276 average, only 45 strikeouts in 518 at-bats and the MVP award at the Triple-A All-Star Game. Considered a more gifted version of Glenn Hubbard, Lemke should become at least a platoon partner with Treadway this spring.

David Justice's home run was the only run Atlanta needed in its 1995 World Series clinching Game Six win.

BRAVES 1990s

Homegrown pitching leads an amazing run

As general manager, Bobby Cox helped lay the groundwork for the Braves success of the 1990s, but the rebuild did not happen fast enough for him to remain as the GM.

When Braves president Stan Kasten told Cox that manager Russ Nixon had to be fired midway through the 1990 season, he also asked Cox to replace Nixon as manager.

Cox had a year and a half left on his five year, $2 million contract, so he didn't really have a whole lot of choice. It wasn't something Cox wanted to do. But he accepted it.

"Maybe I could have turned it down, but I also know that when a club asks you to do something, you should do it. It's like you have a choice, but you really don't, you know what I mean?" Cox said to Baseball America at the time.

"I didn't want to do this. It's upsetting when someone fails below you. It's the same as if you failed. Obviously, things haven't worked out here, and something had to be done."

After the season, Kasten didn't extend Cox's contract and also told him that he would be manager, but he wouldn't continue to be the GM.

"This just confirms my suspicions," Nixon told Baseball America at the time. "It's a (expletive) organization. This is just a soap opera for TBS is what it is. I think everyone knows who's in control down there. It's not Bobby. It's the other guy (Kasten). That's why it's so screwed up."

As bad as it may have looked at the time, Kasten's decision ended up helping put two men in the Hall of Fame. As a GM, Cox did some excellent work in the late 1980s, but as a manager, he ended up as one of the winningest managers of all time.

And to replace Cox as GM, the Braves hired Royals GM John Schuerholz. Schuerholz had led Kansas City to a World Series title in 1985 (his Royals knocked off Cox's Blue Jays team in the ALCS). Schuerholz had already been a successful executive, but the pairing of Schuerholz and Cox helped both of them to the Hall of Fame.

When Schuerholz was hired, the Braves appeared to be a disaster. Over the previous six seasons, the Braves had gone 389-577 (.402). But in reality there were signs of something impressive coming down the road. The Braves' farm system ranked second in

Bobby Cox's Braves teams made five World Series appearances in the 1990s.

baseball that year. Baseball America columnist Tracy Ringolsby actually predicted a surprise last to first run in 1990.

When Schuerholz arrived, he found a very young rotation (120 of the 162 starts in 1990 were made by pitchers who were 24 or younger) and a young nucleus of a lineup led by David Justice and Ron Gant. And in his last draft as GM, Cox along with scouting director Paul Snyder selected Chipper Jones with the No. 1 pick.

"I had preconceptions coming in. I think anybody would," Schuerholz said to Baseball America when he was hired. "My preconception was that this is an organization that has always been viewed with great potential. It's an organization that has been viewed as not having had the success that it could have."

Schuerholz promised that the team would be better in 1991 than they were in 1990. He ensured that would happen by adding some veterans to fill holes. Terry Pendleton proved to be an extremely astute free agent signing. Underappreciated in St. Louis, Pendleton won the National League MVP award in his first year in Atlanta (and was second in MVP voting in 1992). Sid Bream became the new first baseman and Juan Berenguer was signed as a free agent to bolster the bullpen.

The Braves seemed to have nothing but bad luck for much of the 1980s and 1990 – most famously free agent signee Nick Esasky played only nine games for the club in 1990 before succumbing to career-ending vertigo. All of a sudden, that luck turned in 1991.

The Braves won eight of their last nine games in 1991, rallying from two games back to edge the Dodgers by one game for the West Division title. The Braves wouldn't miss the playoffs again until 2006.

Ringolsby was right. He was just a year off in his prediction. The Braves ended up losing in the World Series in seven games to the Twins. But that worst to first run had turned the Southeast into manic Braves fans. It had also cemented the Schuerholz-Cox pairing – a year before, Cox was in the final year of his Braves contract. After the Braves' World Series appearance, it was unthinkable that he would be allowed to go anywhere else.

"Bobby's personality was such that it made this transition for me and for him much easier and much smoother than if somebody would have been worried about things other than getting the best job done for the Atlanta Braves," Schuerholz said to BA in 1991. "But that's all that Bobby cared about."

The Cox-Schuerholz pairing gave the Braves the foundation for lasting success. In addition to a World Series team, the club had Chipper Jones, Ryan Klesko, Javy Lopez and Mark Wohlers in the minors.

"You never know how it's going to turn out five or six years down the road, but we have confidence in the way things are going to go now," Cox told Baseball America after the 1991 season.

By 1992, the Braves had the enviable situation of being a World Series team that also had the top farm system in baseball. The 1992 Greenville Braves, who went a remarkable 100-43, are considered one of the best minor league teams of all time. That team had Chipper Jones, Lopez and 18 other future big leaguers on one roster.

Just as Chipper Jones was graduating, Andruw Jones was rising behind him. Andruw won back-to-back Baseball America Minor League Player of the Year awards before reaching the majors as a 19-year-old.

With a young core, the club had the financial freedom to sign Greg Maddux as a free agent before the 1993 season. He proved to be one of the best free agent signings of all time. He won three consecutive Cy Young awards in his first three seasons with the Braves and went 194-88, 2.63 in 11 years with the Braves.

The Braves were the best team in the National League throughout the decade. With the exception of 1994, when a strike forced a cancellation of the end of the season and the playoffs, the Braves won their division in every season from 1991 to 1999. The Braves made five World Series appearances in an eight-year stretch.

But the Braves only won one of those five World Series. Atlanta developed a reputation of failing to win the big one (interrupted only by the team's 1995 World Series win over Cleveland). It's a tag that still sticks to the Braves, but in hindsight, the Braves in the 1990s were one of the most successful teams baseball has seen in the free agency era, even if they are compared to a Yankees team that was even more successful in the 1990s. ■

Building with pitching prospects is a high-risk affair

The Braves had massive success developing Tom Glavine, John Smoltz, Steve Avery, Kent Mercker, Mark Wohlers and others in the early 1990s. In the late 1990s, it appeared that the Braves might manage to do it again.

Coming out of the 1998 season, the Braves had one of the best group of young pitchers in the minors. Five Braves pitchers ranked among the Top 100 Prospects in baseball. That does not include righthander Rob Bell, another Top 100 Prospect, was traded that offseason to the Reds in a deal to acquire Bret Boone and Denny Neagle.

"As always, we put an emphasis on pitching because you can never have enough," Braves scouting director Paul Snyder said to Baseball America in 1999. "We've won with pitching for the past seven years and we're trying to do everything we can to make certain that does not change."

At the time, it was logical to think that some combination of lefthanders Bruce Chen, Odalis Perez and Jimmy Osting and righthanders Jason Marquis, Kevin McGlinchy, Micah Bowie, Luis Rivera, Jason Shiell and Matt Belisle would replenish the Braves rotation as Tom Glavine, John Smoltz and Greg Maddux got older.

All 10 of those young pitchers ended up playing in the major leagues. But none would win 20 games for the Braves in their career. Marquis, Chen and Belisle all had very long MLB careers and Perez had some significant moments with the Dodgers, but none made an impact for the Braves as most of the prospects were traded.

"I don't think you can ever get enough pitching in an organization," Braves farm director Deric Ladnier said to BA in 1999. "There's so many factors and circumstances that can happen during the development of a pitcher. He might have injuries, he may not produce the way he's projected, he may turn out to be a reliever instead of a starter. With so many factors that affect these guys, I don't think you can ever have too many arms."

The Braves pitching prospects of the late 1990s are proof of that.

BA Braves Top 10 Prospects year by year

1990

Player, Pos.	WAR	What happened
1. Steve Avery, LHP	13.8	At one point, Avery seemed to be the future Hall of Famer in the Braves' rotation. He was great for a stretch.
2. Mike Stanton, LHP	14.3	Stanton was one of the most durable relievers in MLB history. His 1,178 appearances are second most all-time.
3. Tommy Greene, RHP	7.2	Traded with franchise icon Dale Murphy in 1990, Greene had two solid seasons in the Phillies' rotation.
4. Kent Mercker, LHP	12	A versatile power-armed lefty who had two no-hitters and pitched until he was 40.
5. Tyler Houston, C	1.4	A year before drafting Chipper Jones at 1-1, the Braves whiffed by taking Houston second overall.
6. Dave Justice, OF	40.6	A three-time all-star and rookie of the year, Justice homered in Game 6 of Atlanta's lone World Series title.
7. Mark Lemke, 2B	6.1	Lemke spent eight years as the Braves' second baseman, and he had some significant postseason highlights.
8. Dennis Burlingame, RHP	–	The righthander was supposed to be part of the Braves' next wave, but he peaked at Triple-A in 1993.
9. Tom Redington, 3B	–	Redington started strong but quickly flamed out. He never reached Triple-A.
10. Brian Hunter, OF	0.3	Hunter's power made him a useful part-time player over nine MLB seasons.

1991

Player, Pos.	WAR	What happened
1. Ryan Klesko, 1B	27	Few would have expected that Klesko would end up an outfielder, but his power was expected.
2. Chipper Jones, SS	85.2	One of the best switch-hitters to end up in Atlanta Braves history.
3. Tyler Houston, C	1.4	A year before drafting Chipper Jones at 1-1, the Braves whiffed by taking Houston second overall.
4. Javier Lopez, C	29.7	Lopez was one of the best-hitting catchers in the National League for a decade.
5. Mark Wohlers, RHP	3.9	Wohlers was a true fireballer, but wildness eventually cut short an impressive career as a reliever.
6. Melvin Nieves, 1B/OF	-2.3	Trading Nieves, Vince Moore and Keith Mitchell for Fred McGriff proved to be one of the Braves' best trades.
7. Ramon Caraballo, 2B	-0.4	With a little more luck and ability, Caraballo may have had a lengthy career as a backup infielder.
8. Paul Marak, RHP	0.7	Marak made seven starts for Atlanta in a magical 1990 season. The magic quickly departed.
9. Keith Mitchell, OF	0.2	Giants/Mets slugger Kevin Mitchell's brother, Keith quickly regressed after a solid 1991 MLB debut.
10. Ben Rivera, RHP	1.7	Accidentally unprotected, the Braves picked Rivera, their own player, with the No. 1 pick in the '88 Rule 5 draft.

1992

Player, Pos.	WAR	What happened
1. Chipper Jones, SS	85.2	One of the best switch-hitters of all-time, Jones is the best position player in Atlanta Braves history.
2. Ryan Klesko, 1B	27	Few would have expected that Klesko would end up an outfielder, but his power was expected.
3. Mark Wohlers, RHP	3.9	Wohlers was a true fireballer, but wildness eventually cut short an impressive career as a reliever.
4. Mike Kelly, OF	0.3	Kelly was one of the best players in Arizona State history, but his tools never translated to big league success.
5. David Nied, RHP	2.7	Nied was the No. 1 pick in the 1992 expansion draft, but he struggled with injuries with the Rockies.
6. Javier Lopez, C	29.7	Lopez was one of the best-hitting catchers in the National League for a decade.
7. Keith Mitchell, OF	0.2	Giants/Mets slugger Kevin Mitchell's brother, Keith quickly regressed after a solid 1991 MLB debut.
8. Melvin Nieves, OF	-2.3	Trading Nieves, Vince Moore and Keith Mitchell for Fred McGriff proved to be one of the Braves' best trades.
9. Napoleon Robinson, RHP	–	Robinson was effective in 1992 and 1993 in the minors, but he never made it to the majors.
10. Vince Moore, OF	–	The Braves loved speedy and athletic outfielders like Moore. He was dealt to the Padres for Fred McGriff.

1993

Player, Pos.	WAR	What happened
1. Chipper Jones, SS	85.2	One of the best switch-hitters of all-time, Jones is the best position player in Atlanta Braves history.
2. Javy Lopez, C	29.7	Lopez was one of the best-hitting catchers in the National League for a decade.
3. Ryan Klesko, 1B	27	Few would have expected that Klesko would end up an outfielder, but his power was expected.
4. Mike Kelly, OF	0.3	Kelly was one of the best players in Arizona State history, but his tools never translated to big league success.
5. Melvin Nieves, OF	-2.3	Trading Nieves, Vince Moore and Keith Mitchell for Fred McGriff proved to be one of the Braves' best trades.
6. Jamie Arnold, RHP	-1.4	The Braves' 1992 first-round pick, Arnold struggled but he did eventually reach the majors with the Dodgers.
7. Jose Oliva, 3B	-0.8	Acquired for Charlie Liebrandt, Oliva had both big power and big strikeout numbers with the Braves.
8. Chris Seelbach, RHP	-0.3	Seelbach was rarely dominant, but he eventually reached the majors in a return stint with the Braves in 2000-01.
9. Donnie Elliott, RHP	1.1	Elliott was yet another part of the franchise-altering Fred McGriff trade.
10. Jason Schmidt, RHP	29.5	Schmidt is an exception to the Braves' knack for wise trades. He had a lengthy career and won an ERA title.

1994

Player, Pos.	WAR	What happened
1. Chipper Jones, SS	85.2	One of the best switch-hitters of all-time, Jones is the best position player in Atlanta Braves history.
2. Ryan Klesko, 1B	27	Few would have expected that Klesko would end up an outfielder, but his power was expected.
3. Terrell Wade, LHP	0.9	Wade was a solid member of the Braves' bullpen in 1996. He was lost to the Rays in the 1997 expansion draft.
4. Javy Lopez, C	29.7	Lopez was one of the best-hitting catchers in the National League for a decade.
5. Glenn Williams, SS	0.1	Williams wowed Braves scouts with his power/athleticism, but the Aussie never hit for average in the minors.
6. Mike Kelly, OF	0.3	Kelly was one of the best players in Arizona State history, but his tools never translated to big league success.
7. Jamie Arnold, RHP	-1.4	The Braves' 1992 first-round pick, Arnold struggled but he did eventually reach the majors with the Dodgers.
8. Damon Hollins, OF	0.2	Another athletic Braves outfield prospect, Hollins had a brief stint as a fourth outfielder in the majors.
9. Andre King, OF	—	King ended up playing four years in the NFL after going to back to school to play football.
10. Jamie Howard, RHP	—	The Braves let Howard play football at LSU while he pitched. He was generally ineffective in both sports.

1995

Player, Pos.	WAR	What happened
1. Chipper Jones, SS	85.2	One of the best switch-hitters of all-time, Jones is the best position player in Atlanta Braves history.
2. Andruw Jones, OF	62.8	Considered one of the best defensive center fielders of all time, Jones also hit 434 MLB home runs.
3. Jason Schmidt, RHP	29.5	Schmidt is an exception to the Braves' knack for wise trades. He had a lengthy career and won an ERA title.
4. Glenn Williams, SS	0.1	Williams wowed Braves scouts with his power/athleticism, but the Aussie never hit for average in the minors.
5. Terrell Wade, LHP	0.9	Wade was a solid member of the Braves bullpen in 1996. He was lost to the Rays in the 1997 expansion draft.
6. Jermaine Dye, OF	20.3	Traded to the Royals, the strong-armed outfielder had a 14-year MLB career and made two all-star teams.
7. Damon Hollins, OF	0.2	Another athletic Braves outfield prospect, Hollins had a brief stint as a fourth outfielder in the majors.
8. Fernando Lunar, C	-0.2	An excellent defender, Lunar made it to the majors despite a career .220/.270/.304 minor league slash line.
9. Damian Moss, LHP	1.7	The Braves made a big push into Australia in the 1990s, and Moss was among the best of those signings.
10. Jose Oliva, 3B	-0.8	Acquired for Charlie Liebrandt, Oliva had both big power and big strikeout numbers with the Braves.

1996

Player, Pos.	WAR	What happened
1. Andruw Jones, OF	62.8	Considered one of the best defensive center fielders of all time, Jones also hit 434 MLB home runs.
2. Jason Schmidt, RHP	29.5	Schmidt is an exception to the Braves' knack for wise trades. He had a lengthy career and won an ERA title.
3. Jermaine Dye, OF	20.3	Traded to the Royals, the strong-armed outfielder had a 14-year MLB career and made two all-star teams.
4. Robert Smith, 3B	0	Lost to the Rays in the 1997 expansion draft, Smith showed an excellent glove but also a weak bat.
5. Terrell Wade, LHP	0.9	Wade was a solid member of the Braves' bullpen in 1996. He was lost to the Rays in the 1997 expansion draft.
6. Damon Hollins, OF	0.2	Another athletic Braves outfield prospect, Hollins had a brief stint as a fourth outfielder in the majors.
7. George Lombard, OF	-0.9	One of the top running back recruits in 1994, Lombard turned down Georgia for the Braves.
8. Ron Wright, 1B	-0.1	Wright eventually reached the majors for one game with Seattle—he went 0-for-3 and hit into a triple play.
9. Glenn Williams, SS	0.1	Williams wowed Braves scouts with his power/athleticism, but the Aussie never hit for average in the minors.
10. Damian Moss, LHP	1.7	The Braves made a big push into Australia in the 1990s, and Moss was among the best of those signings.

1997

Player, Pos.	WAR	What happened
1. Andruw Jones, OF	62.8	Considered one of the best defensive center fielders of all time, Jones also hit 434 MLB home runs.
2. Kevin McGlinchy, RHP	1.5	McGlinchy had an excellent rookie season, but shoulder issues torpedoed his chances of a long career.
3. Bruce Chen, LHP	10.3	Chen had a lengthy, 17-year MLB career. The hard-throwing lefty morphed into a crafty soft-tosser.
4. Jason Marquis, RHP	6.8	Marquis was a durable, back-of-the-rotation starter. He finished with nearly 2,000 MLB innings.
5. George Lombard, OF	-0.9	One of the top running back recruits in 1994, Lombard turned down Georgia for the Braves.
6. Damian Moss, LHP	1.7	The Braves made a big push into Australia in the 1990s, and Moss was among the best of those signings.
7. John LeRoy, RHP	0.2	LeRoy made one appearance with Atlanta in 1997. A Rays expansion draft pick, he never reached the majors again.
8. Robbie Bell, RHP	-0.6	Bell was a top prospect when he was dealt to the Reds in the Bret Boone trade.
9. Wes Helms, 3B	-1.7	Helms had a long career as a platoon corner infielder. He had 10 seasons of playing 80-plus MLB games.
10. Jimmy Osting, LHP	-0.3	Osting was a crafty lefty who saw his career slowed by Tommy John surgery.

1998

Player, Pos.	WAR	What happened
1. Bruce Chen, LHP	10.3	Chen had a lengthy, 17-year MLB career. The hard-throwing lefty morphed into a crafty soft-tosser
2. Robbie Bell, RHP	-0.6	Bell was a top prospect when he was dealt to the Reds in the Bret Boone trade.
3. Luis Rivera, RHP	0.4	Rivera was a massive talent, but shoulder injuries meant his career was finished as a 22-year-old.
4. Odalis Perez, LHP	8.9	Perez is the rare pitcher who slid from the bullpen in the minors to the rotation in the majors.
5. George Lombard, OF	-0.9	One of the top running back recruits in 1994, Lombard turned down Georgia for the Braves.
6. A.J. Zapp, 1B	—	Zapp's bat proved just a tick too light to get him to the major leagues in any role.
7. Troy Cameron, SS	—	Cameron had plenty of power, but his struggles to hit for average derailed his career.
8. Jason Marquis, RHP	6.8	Marquis was a durable, back-of-the-rotation starter. He finished with nearly 2,000 MLB innings.
9. Wes Helms, 3B	-1.7	Helms had a long career as a platoon corner infielder. He had 10 seasons of playing 80-plus MLB games.
10. Glenn Williams, 2B	0.1	Williams wowed Braves scouts with his power/athleticism, but the Aussie never hit for average in the minors.

1999

Player, Pos.	WAR	What happened
1. Bruce Chen, LHP	10.3	Chen had a lengthy, 17-year MLB career. The hard-throwing lefty morphed into a crafty soft-tosser.
2. George Lombard, OF	-0.9	One of the top running back recruits in 1994, Lombard turned down Georgia for the Braves.
3. Odalis Perez, LHP	8.9	Perez is the rare pitcher who slid from the bullpen in the minors to the rotation in the majors.
4. Luis Rivera, RHP	0.4	Rivera was a massive talent, but shoulder injuries meant his career was finished as a 22-year-old.
5. Jason Marquis, RHP	6.8	Marquis was a durable, back-of-the-rotation starter. He finished with nearly 2,000 MLB innings.
6. Kevin McGlinchy, RHP	1.5	McGlinchy had an excellent rookie season, but shoulder issues torpedoed his chances of a long career.
7. Rafael Furcal, SS	39.4	The 2000 NL Rookie of the Year, Furcal had exceptional speed and one of the best arms in the infield.
8. Micah Bowie, LHP	-0.9	Bowie ended up serving as a fill-in lefty reliever for a variety of teams.
9. Wes Helms, 3B	-1.7	Helms had a long career as a platoon corner infielder. He had 10 seasons of playing 80-plus MLB games.
10. Marcus Giles, 2B	16.8	Giles always had power, but he worked extremely hard to turn himself into a playable second baseman.

Chipper Jones was considered a surprise No. 1 pick in 1990, but he soon proved the Braves' wisdom.

CHIPPER JONES, SS

PROPER NAME: Larry Wayne Jones. **BORN:** April 24, 1972 in DeLand, Fla.
HT: 6-4. **WT:** 210. **BATS:** B. **THROWS:** R. **SCHOOL:** Bolles HS, Jacksonville.
FIRST PRO CONTRACT: Selected by Braves in first round (first overall) of 1990 draft;
signed June 4, 1990.

Franchises' destinies can sometimes turn on one decision. If the Braves had selected Todd
Van Poppel, as expected, with the No. 1 pick in the 1990 draft, it would not have kept them
from making a series of World Series appearances—they went to the World Series in 1991
and 1992 before either player could have been expected to make any impact. But it's hard to
imagine the Braves rolling off 14 division titles in 15 years if Paul Snyder and Bobby Cox hadn't
chosen Chipper Jones with the first pick in the 1990 draft. Jones went on to become only the
second No. 1 pick to earn a spot in the Hall of Fame. Jones is one of the best switch-hitters in
MLB history and is second in Braves history in most offensive categories, trailing only Hank
Aaron. When it comes to the Atlanta Braves, he's the best hitter the city has ever seen. Baseball
America extensively covered Jones' rise to that point.

CAREER STATISTICS

Year	Club (League)	Class	AVG	G	AB	R	H	2B	3B	HR	RBI	BB	SO	SB	OBP	SLG
1990	Braves (GCL)	R	.229	44	140	20	32	1	1	1	18	14	25	5	.321	.271
1991	Macon (SAL)	A	.326	136	473	104	154	24	11	15	98	69	70	40	.407	.518
1992	Durham (CAR)	HiA	.277	70	264	43	73	22	1	4	31	31	34	10	.353	.413
	Greenville (SL)	AA	.346	67	266	43	92	17	11	9	42	11	32	14	.367	.594
1993	Richmond (IL)	AAA	.325	139	536	97	174	31	12	13	89	57	70	23	.387	.500
	Atlanta (NL)	MAJ	.667	8	3	2	2	1	0	0	0	1	1	0	.750	1.000
1994	Did not play--Injured															
1995	Atlanta (NL)	MAJ	.265	140	524	87	139	22	3	23	86	73	99	8	.353	.450
1996	Atlanta (NL)	MAJ	.309	157	598	114	185	32	5	30	110	87	88	14	.393	.530
1997	Atlanta (NL)	MAJ	.295	157	597	100	176	41	3	21	111	76	88	20	.371	.479
1998	Atlanta (NL)	MAJ	.313	160	601	123	188	29	5	34	107	96	93	16	.404	.547
1999	Atlanta (NL)	MAJ	.319	157	567	116	181	41	1	45	110	126	94	25	.441	.633
2000	Atlanta (NL)	MAJ	.311	156	579	118	180	38	1	36	111	95	64	14	.404	.566
2001	Atlanta (NL)	MAJ	.330	159	572	113	189	33	5	38	102	98	82	9	.427	.605
2002	Atlanta (NL)	MAJ	.327	158	548	90	179	35	1	26	100	107	89	8	.435	.536
2003	Atlanta (NL)	MAJ	.305	153	555	103	169	33	2	27	106	94	83	2	.402	.517
2004	Rome (SAL)	LoA	.000	1	4	0	0	0	0	0	0	0	0	0	.000	.000
	Atlanta (NL)	MAJ	.248	137	472	69	117	20	1	30	96	84	96	2	.362	.485
2005	Rome (SAL)	LoA	.500	3	6	1	3	0	0	0	2	3	1	0	.667	.500
	Atlanta (NL)	MAJ	.296	109	358	66	106	30	0	21	72	72	56	5	.412	.556
2006	Mississippi (SL)	AA	.167	2	6	1	1	0	0	0	0	0	2	0	.167	.167
	Atlanta (NL)	MAJ	.324	110	411	87	133	28	3	26	86	61	73	6	.409	.596
2007	Atlanta (NL)	MAJ	.337	134	513	108	173	42	4	29	102	82	75	5	.425	.604
2008	Atlanta (NL)	MAJ	.364	128	439	82	160	24	1	22	75	90	61	4	.470	.574
2009	Atlanta (NL)	MAJ	.264	143	488	80	129	23	2	18	71	101	89	4	.388	.430
2010	Atlanta (NL)	MAJ	.265	95	317	47	84	21	0	10	46	61	47	5	.381	.426
2011	Rome (SAL)	LoA	.333	2	3	0	1	0	0	0	1	2	1	0	.500	.333
	Atlanta (NL)	MAJ	.275	126	455	56	125	33	1	18	70	51	80	2	.344	.470
2012	Rome (SAL)	LoA	.250	2	4	0	1	0	0	0	1	2	1	0	.500	.250
	Atlanta (NL)	MAJ	.287	112	387	58	111	23	0	14	62	57	51	1	.377	.455
Major League Totals			.303	2499	8984	1619	2726	549	38	468	1623	1512	1409	150	.401	.529
Minor League Totals			.312	466	1702	309	531	95	36	42	282	189	236	92	.379	.484

A man who was born to hit

JULY 1990

ATLANTA LEADS OFF SELECTIONS WITH JONES

by SEAN KERNAN

Not in his wildest dreams did Chipper Jones expect to be the No. 1 pick in baseball's annual draft.

But that's the way things unfolded June 6 when the Atlanta Braves picked Larry Wayne Jones Jr., a.k.a. Chipper, to bat leadoff in the 1990 draft lineup.

"If I am the first pick, there's nobody in the world who's going to be more surprised than me," Jones said less than 48 hours before the draft.

Surprise!

Even after a Sunday night pow-wow with Braves scouting director Paul Snyder and scout Tony DeMacio, Jones still was uncertain. Not until the phone call came, at 1:23 p.m. on Draft Day, did Jones know for sure he was No. 1.

By Monday evening Atlanta had turned a double play, drafting the 6-foot-3, 185-pound switch-hitter and signing him on the same day. The signing eliminated any chance, slight as it was, that Jones would go to college baseball factory Miami, where he signed a letter of intent in April.

"We were in the ballpark right away," Jones said of contract negotiations. "We said what we wanted, and they said what they wanted to give, and I said why don't we split the difference both ways."

Evidently, they did.

Larry Jones, Chipper's father, said terms of the contract are "extremely fair," covering $68,000 for his college education and a signing bonus which considerably tops the previous record for a high school player. A year ago, the Braves signed prep catcher Tyler Houston to a then-record $241,000.

Jones' bonus was believed to be $275,000. Throw in the college money, a life insurance policy and other perks and the total package approaches $400,000.

Jones, a Pierson native who played for hometown Taylor High his freshman year, gained notoriety at The Bolles School, a private boarding school in Jacksonville, and through the DeLand (Fla.) American Legion program. He becomes the first Florida player ever drafted No. 1 overall in the draft's 26 years.

A shortstop and pitcher in high school, Jones led Bolles to the 2A state championship a year ago, and to a runner-up finish this season. He batted .488 with 10 doubles, five home runs and 25 RBIs, scoring 44 runs and stealing 14 bases. On the mound, he was 7-3, 1.00.

"Good middle infielders are hard to find," said Braves general manager Bobby Cox. "I think we have found a good one. About eight people in our organization have seen him, and they all came to the same conclusion. He's pretty much a polished ballplayer at this time."

The Braves scouted Jones extensively, and Cox himself made three trips to see him. Jones' career will begin at Bradenton of the Rookie-level Gulf Coast League.

He said he realized his good fortune came in large part because Texas high school righthander Todd Van Poppel had brushed off the Braves.

"I know there are some people who will say I was the Braves' second choice," Jones said. "But it's better than being the ninth or 10th. If Todd Van Poppel doesn't want to play for the Atlanta Braves, I'm more than happy to take his place."

In the long run, the Braves may have gotten the player they need most.

"We're very happy with the guy we got," Snyder said. "All somebody has to do is look at our overall pitching, our shortstops and our hitting. When you do that, it's pretty apparent we need help at shortstop and with hitting." ■

JULY 1990

KEEPING UP WITH THE JONESES
(Notably Chipper)
by SEAN KERNAN

Chipper Jones can remember the first time he stepped inside a major league stadium. It's easy because the No. 1 pick in the 1990 draft had been to a big league park only twice, on successive days in July 1987.

"I remember being in awe," Jones says of his visit to Atlanta-Fulton County Stadium. "I just looked around. It was so-o-o big. One thing that really stands out is, I thought 'Wouldn't it be great if some day I could help fill all those empty seats.'"

Today, the Braves share those hopeful thoughts.

The sure-handed shortstop graduated from high school June 2 under his given name, Larry Wayne Jones Jr. When the Braves opened the draft, they selected Larry Wayne Jones Jr. Those monitoring the selection process knew Atlanta was talking about Chipper.

A slight underdog, but a real possibility for the high-pressure, high-exposure No. 1 slot, Chipper Jones was selected by Baseball America to be tracked during the final days before the draft, on Draft Day and after the big day.

FRIDAY, JUNE 1

It's graduation eve and Chipper Jones plans to go to the movies.

Before the 18-year-old sets off on his date with girlfriend Leslie Braddock, a junior at The Bolles School in Jacksonville, there's some last-minute shopping to be done.

One of the traditions at Bolles, a private boarding school, is that males graduate wearing a blue blazer, white shirt, tie and white pants. The problem is, the only white pants owned by this country boy from Pierson, about 90 miles southwest of Jacksonville, are part of a baseball uniform. So, it's off to several clothing stores.

Finally Chipper and Lesie head off to see "Steel Magnolia." But this is a quick date. Tomorrow there's an important doubleheader: graduation and the junior-senior prom.

There's another reason for Chipper's early return to his family's hotel suite. The Braves are on the tube.

As soon as he walks in, Chipper changes the channel from a game involving the Los Angeles Dodgers, the entire family's favorite team until now, to a Braves game. He flops his 6-foot-3, 185-pound body on the floor and starts watching America's team, which in three days may well become Jones' team.

The draft? Well, Chipper says that can wait until Monday.

"I'm more nervous about graduation and prom than I am about the draft," says Chipper, who only talks about the draft when someone else brings up the subject. "I'll probably start getting nervous at home on Sunday night. I think my father is more nervous than I am. He'll probably be waking me up at five in the morning Monday."

Larry Jones, Chipper's father, says an early wakeup call would be the perfect way to start the day.

"Oh, no. Not unless you want me to hit you," Chipper jokes, holding up his right hand, which hours earlier had been in a cast.

Lynne, Chipper's mother, good-naturedly scolds her son.

"Not with your hands," she says, pausing. "Use your feet if you want, but protect those hands."

The Joneses, including paternal grandmother Esther, laugh in unison. Everyone remembers Chipper's hand injury, a metacarpal fracture suffered in a one-punch fight with a teammate the day before Bolles played for the Florida 2-A championship.

Chipper pitched the next day, losing 3-2 to Miami Westminster. His hand was placed in a cast two days after his first fight since grade school.

A couple of other times during the night his father makes reference to the fight, calling his son Sugar Ray Jones. Chipper takes the heat in stride. He's been kidded a lot since the fight, which he says taught him a "major lesson."

Ironically, the fight actually boosted Chipper's stock. Scouts privately admitted they appreciated this brief, fiery display. Soon after scouts were assured the hairline fracture wouldn't hinder Chipper's abilities, their praise for him reached new heights.

But the No. 1 pick? No way. Chipper wasn't buying the stories that prep righthander Todd Van Poppel of Arlington, Texas, wasn't going to sign a pro contract. And neither were his parents.

As much as the trio hoped Chipper was going to be the first player selected, no one believed it would happen. The general feeling was that rumors would continue to fly, setting up Chipper for a big fall when Van Poppel was selected No. 1 and Chipper fifth (by the Pittsburgh Pirates) or sixth (by the Seattle Mariners).

"If I'm the No. 1 pick, there isn't going to be anyone in the world more surprised than me," Chipper says. "I'm not going to get myself hyped up and have a letdown."

SATURDAY, JUNE 2

Graduation day is filled with pomp and circumstance at Bolles, good-luck wishes from friends, parents and teachers. And then there's the prom, a perfect distraction.

Still Chipper is constantly reminded of the coming draft. The commencement speaker is Florida Sen. Connie Mack, grandson of the legendary baseball manager and owner.

And there's the valedictory address given by William Davis Jr., a brilliant 18-year-old with academic numbers even more impressive than Chipper's baseball stats.

"What other school can boast a student who scored a 1,600 on the SAT," Davis says in reference to himself, "and a sure first-round major league draft choice?"

Good question.

Chipper's numbers (.485-5-25, 10 doubles, 44 runs and 14 stolen bases) were impressive in their own right. A three-time all-state performer, Chipper left Bolles as the Florida high school player of the year.

With diploma and a couple of trophies and plaques in hand after the graduation ceremony, it's time for Chipper to reminisce and even to say goodbye to some friends and their parents.

Tom Patrick, father of Chipper's roommate, says he hopes the Bolles Bulldog becomes a Brave. Ron Patrick, one-third of a nearly inseparable trio that included Chipper and Bolles basketball standout B.J. Thompson, often found himself the butt of jokes by the other two.

Braves Buck Draft History

July 1990

The Braves reversed recent draft history by selecting only 10 pitchers among their 52 picks. "We decided to go after some bat guys this year," said Braves scouting director Paul Snyder. "We feel comfortable enough with what we've done to improve our pitching in recent years to address other needs, especially shortstop."

Breaking a 17-year abstinence from taking shortstops with a first-round pick, the Braves selected switch-hitting Chipper Jones with the first overall choice of the draft.

"He's a three-tool guy at a position where we have a weakness in our system," Snyder said. "His overall makeup, the fact that he went away to school and his maturity as a player were all factors. He's a blue-chip player."

Jones becomes the first shortstop selected by the Braves in the first round since Pat Rockett in 1973.

"I expect to be up here in three years," Jones said June 9 after a tour of the Braves clubhouse. "I know there are things I have to work on to improve. I just want to go play right now."

After the signing difficulties and maturity problems experienced with their first-rounder in 1989, catcher Tyler Houston, the Braves welcomed Jones' attitude.

"He might be a little ambitious," said minor league director Bobby Dews, who projected Jones as needing at least four years. "But he wants it badly. With his attitude, he might surprise all of us."

—*JOE STRAUSS*

A shortstop in the minors, Chipper Jones found his long-term home when he moved over to third base.

But the quarterback bound for Princeton gets a few laughs on graduation day, talking about Chipper's old Ford Escort, which he often parked at Bolles amid the sea of late-model sports cars.

"The White Elephant was a classic," Patrick recalls, bringing a John Elway-type smile to Chipper's face. "I think they buried that car somewhere in Pierson after Chipper got the (1990 Ford) Probe. The White Elephant was one of those cars with a sticker that said, Don't Laugh, It's Paid For. It was distinctly Chipper and everybody associated the White Elephant with Chipper."

The laughs about the Jonesmobile help lift the anxiety Chipper feels about the draft. He has kept it to himself and a few friends.

"It's been a tough week for him," says Thompson, a Jacksonville resident who always had room for Chipper at his house. "He did have a couple of peaceful days this week and he was able to kick back at our house. It was sort of a hideout for him."

After a quick change of clothing, Chipper is back in more comfortable duds: a Bolles baseball hat and shirt. He and his family stop at the home of teammate Al Verlander for an afternoon party, during which Chipper hears the same question over and over: "Where do you want to go?"

The real answer probably is "To the prom," though Chipper respectfully and routinely responds, "Atlanta, but I'll be happy with whatever team takes me."

Shortly, it's time for Chipper to don the tuxedo, but not before some words of caution from his father. "Son," Larry says, wrapping his arms around his boy's shoulders, "have a good time tonight, but remember don't do anything you might be ashamed of. You have an awful lot to lose."

The prom, complete with limousine service and dinner, is a memorable evening for Chipper and Leslie, who gives her boyfriend a fitting graduation gift, a book titled "The History of Baseball."

SUNDAY, JUNE 3

This is the day Chipper is most thankful for the solid support of his mother, father and grandparents.

The telephone calls, which began Saturday evening when Pittsburgh scout Dave Holliday rang several times and reporters kept trying to reach Chipper, continue Sunday morning. Holliday opens the parade, inquiring about getting an X-ray of Chipper's hand.

Soon Murphy's Law takes over. The phone goes dead, and Larry rushes off to Taylor High, where he's a teacher and football coach, to call Southern Bell. Esther Jones, Chipper's grandmother, stays home and the phone comes back to life just in time for a call from the Braves, who say they're considering Chipper for the No. 1 pick and want to meet for a "signability study."

When Larry returns, he contacts the Braves and makes dinner plans for 6 p.m. in Daytona Beach, 30 miles away.

Around nine the Dodgers (ninth pick) and Expos (11th) call, saying if Chipper is available they will take him. By then word is filtering out of Texas that Van Poppel has turned down a final offer from Braves general manager Bobby Cox and owner Ted Turner in a face-to-face meeting.

When Larry Jones ponders his son's future in Pierson, Chipper is in Jacksonville trying to get an X-ray of his hand, not an easy task on a Sunday afternoon. About 3 p.m., with the X-ray mission accomplished, Chipper is on his way home.

When he gets there two hours later, he barely has time for a shower. Then he and his parents are off to Daytona for a dinner engagement with Braves scouting director Paul Snyder and scout Tony DeMacio. Cox was scheduled to make the trip, but is tired from the dealings in Texas.

The group, including Chipper's parents, heads to an Italian restaurant for some small talk and a big dinner. Then they all return to Pierson for the really important discussions. If things go well, Atlanta will choose Chipper.

But the phone keeps ringing, interrupting the talks. Most of the calls are from the press and from other teams, including the University of Miami, where Chipper had signed to play college ball.

Hurricanes assistant coach Turtle Thomas calls about 9:45 p.m., wanting to know if there are any Braves running around the house. Not only are the Braves there, but by the time Synder and DeMacio leave just after 11 p.m., they have tomahawked Miami's chances of seeing Jones in a Miami uniform.

Preparation on the part of Chipper's parents and the player's heartfelt desire to play pro ball results in smooth sailing in the signability session. Larry has a solid baseball background. Chipper wants to sign and the business-minded Lynne has been in contact with the Major League Baseball Players Association.

And Bill Johnson, a family friend, who's an attorney in Orlando, have given the Joneses some free advice. (Under NCAA rules, if Chipper has signed with an agent he would have lost his amateur status. As this story went to press, he still had no official agent.)

The Braves initially offer a $250,000 signing bonus, plus enough money to pay for Chipper's college education. The Joneses come back with a figure around $300,000. Then Chipper, who wants to eliminate any hassles, interjects: "Let's just split the difference."

And that's what they did, settling on a signing bonus of $275,000, a record for a high school player.

The entire process mesmerizes Lynne Jones. "I can't imagine how an 18-year-old who didn't have all the help—your knowledge of baseball and the contract background I've done the past few weeks—could handle this.

So all that's left is to wait for the phone call, and then to turn the handshake agreement into a contract. The Joneses feel good about the results when they go to bed Sunday.

"I was real pleased with how the Braves' management approached us," Lynne Jones said. "I was telling them it was about as painless as a root canal, but really they made it as nice as it could be."

MONDAY, JUNE 4

On the morning of Draft Day, there are no calls. The Braves apparently sent out smoke signals, letting the baseball world know of their decision to go with Chipper. Or maybe it's because the phone company has yet to send a repairman.

"You're the Joneses waiting for the call from the baseball draft?" the repairman asks. "Well, I'll just wait down at the end of the driveway until you get the call, just in case there's a problem."

With tension mounting, the phone rings at 1:08 p.m. The 40 or so friends gathered hold their breath while several photographers snap pictures of Chipper answering the call.

Chipper smiles and shouts, "Mom, it's for you."

Moments later, the phone rings again and Chipper's face lights up. But once again it's a false alarm, causing Bolles coach Don Suriano to shout something uncharacteristic at Chipper.

"You're 0-for-2," Suriano yells, breaking the tension.

Finally, The Call comes at 1:23 p.m.

The phone rings, Jones answers it and gives a thumbs-up sign as he talks to Jim Schultz, Atlanta's director of public relations.

"Yes, I'm doing fine, sir, how are you?" Jones says during the most important conversation of his young life. "Thank you, thank you. I appreciate it."

Proud Papa is right there to slap a Braves cap on his son's head. Somehow there just happens to be two more hats around bearing the big script "A," one for Larry and the other for Lynne.

"I just got chill bumps," Chipper says moments later. "It hasn't really hit me yet. It probably won't until this hype settles down."

No chance. Media interviews, including live television segments, keep Chipper and Larry busy throughout the day, and the phone is busy until 15 minutes before midnight.

"I'm out of here after I make these two calls," Chipper says about 7:30 p.m. "Last night was the first time I really thought the Braves were interested in me," he tells one reporter.

Chipper Jones hit .325/.387/.500 for Richmond in 1993.

"I can't see putting myself in the same category as Ken Griffey Jr. I'm just in heaven right now and my father has been in the clouds ever since last night."

As Chipper prepares to slip out to meet buddies from Pierson for a graduation party at a hunting campe about two miles from his house, Dad gives some instructions to the family's newest breadwinner.

"Be home no later than midnight," Larry says.

Chipper negotiates for a later curfew, but he isn't as successful as he was with the Braves. There's no splitting the difference with his dad.

"I don't care if you are the No. 1 draft pick in the country," Larry says, giving his son a huge hug. "You're still my son."

The Braves don't waste any time. They tell Chipper they want to bring him and his family to Atlanta to meet team personnel, players and media and watch a few games.

But even before heading to Atlanta three days after the draft, Chipper receives his first endorsement offer, from a board-game company that wants to take his picture for a card in return for $1,500.

The phone continues to ring. One of the calls is from Miami's Thomas.

"He was real complimentary, saying that I deserve everything I got," Chipper says. "I feel real bad because Coach Thomas, when he was at Georgia Tech, was the first person to send me a college letter. I still have it."

On Wednesday, Chipper gives his hand a test by taking batting practice with a wood bat at Taylor High. Although not initially expected to be a pro power hitter, he belts a few out of the yard and swings until he gets blisters. It's a session he needs to build some confidence before going to Atlanta on Thursday.

"Everything about him is above-average," Cox tells the media. "All he has to do is go play."

And that's about all Chipper wants to do. First in the minors, and in two or three years, in the majors.

The Braves send him to the lowest level of their farm system, Bradenton (Gulf Coast) to finish recuperating from the broken hand and begin his professional career. If it all goes well, he'll advance to Pulaski (Appalachian) in a few weeks.

"I'm really glad it's over. For the last month the phone hasn't stopped ringing," Chipper says. "I just want to get settled and playing. I just want to put on the jersey.

"I guess my biggest thrill will be when I walk out on the field and see that humongous stadium. Even if it isn't filled up, it will probably be 10 times as many people than I've played in front of."

And in time, maybe all the seats will be field, fulfilling the dreams of both the Braves and Chipper Jones. ■

EDITOR'S NOTE: Just as he had predicted, Jones made his home MLB debut a little over three years later. On Sept. 14, 1993 in his first at-bat at Atlanta-Fulton County Stadium he singled as a pinch hitter replacing Jeff Blauser. There were 48,975 fans in attendance. Coming off of back-to-back World Series appearances and on their way to 104 wins in 1993, the Braves' stadium was filled.

AUGUST 1991

JONES HAS THROWING DIFFICULTIES

by SEAN KERNAN

CHARLESTON, S.C. — Macon Braves shortstop Chipper Jones prepared to take the field for the South Atlantic League all-star game in Savannah. Though the crowd included hometown friends and relatives who had driven up from Florida, Jones sounded as if he wished he were back in Macon fielding grounders.

"I have absolutely no confidence in my throwing," said Jones, the first player chosen in the 1990 draft. "It's gotten to the point where I couldn't tell you where the ball is going to end up when I get it."

Jones, 19, made 33 errors in the season's first half, mostly on throws to first.

"In high school, I relied solely on my arm and had the utmost confidence in it," he said. "Here, players are much faster and there's more to it than just a strong arm, not that I've lost any confidence in my arm strength. I haven't. It's the accuracy that's the problem.

"When I was growing up, Steve Sax had the problem throwing from second to first. I would think, 'How can a guy not throw the ball such a short distance?' Until you have to adjust your game to do it, you can't understand what it's like."

Macon manager Ron Majtyka wasn't overly concerned.

"Chipper is a youngster," Majtyka said. "He's still getting used to playing baseball every day. He's going to be fine when he gets some experience, and he's played some great shortstop for us as it is. This is just a matter of concentration."

Jones improved both in the field and at the plate in June. At the end of May, he was batting .244-2-25 with 28 errors. Through the first four weeks of June, he made only five errors, hit three home runs and drove in 18 runs while raising his average to .274.

"I just need to be real loose in the field," he said. "I have no difficulty being relaxed at the plate, but i tend to tighten up on defense, and you can't make plays like that."

Jones on the gobs of autograph seekers: "It's nice to be wanted, though not necessarily after after I go 0-for-4. The adults with five or six cards to sign bother me sometimes, but I try to accommodate as many people as I can."

On sharing an apartment with catcher Tyler Houston, Atlanta's first-round pick in 1989: "We're not the best of friends, and we're not enemies. We get along. We have a friendly competition going after each game where we compare what we've done. It's good, because I need to be pushed and I think he does, too." ∎

JONES REMAINS CHIPPER

April 1991

WEST PALM BEACH, Fla. — The tall short-stop has just finished taking extra ground balls after the regular minor league workouts when Willie Stargell spots him. "Hey Chipper, you're a real comer," shouts Stargell, Atlanta's minor league hitting instructor. "A real cucumber." Stargell starts laughing, and when he recovers he says, "You know, Chipper, I'm starting to like you a little bit." Chipper Jones smiles and heads for the clubhouse. Atlanta selected him with the No. 1 pick in the 1990 draft, and what should have been an honor has been tainted by second-guessing.

Righthander Todd Van Poppel was considered the best prospect in the draft, but told the Braves he wouldn't sign. So Atlanta took Jones, who hit just .229-1-18 in the Rookie-level Gulf Coast League while Van Poppel signed with Oakland and established himself as the best prospect in baseball. Jones, who turns 19 April 24, says he knows a lot of people think the Braves should have taken Van Poppel.

"It doesn't bother me," he says. "I know what kind of guy Todd is, what kind of player Todd is, and to be mentioned in the same breath is an honor."

The Braves didn't pull Jones' name out of a hat. A star shortstop at The Bolles School in Jacksonville, Fla., he would have gone in the first six picks even if Atlanta bypassed him. And when he reported to the GCL, he was still bothered by the aftereffects of a broken wrist sustained late in his senior season.

He won't use the wrist as an excuse, but Jones will say he's happy to finally be at full strength this spring. He spent the last six weeks of the offseason in training. His father threw him two hours of batting practice every day, and Jones also lifted weights, ran and took ground balls.

Chuck LaMar, Atlanta's new minor league and scouting director, says Jones has looked good at the plate this spring. His defense has been a little spotty, thus the extra ground balls.

Jones worked out with players designated for extended spring training, not the usual locale of a No.1 draft pick. He has taken it in stride, though, and says the Braves told several players they were placing them a classification lower than they should be. The idea was to light a fire under them, Jones says, and it has worked in his case. He planned on making the Class A Macon roster.

"Naturally, I would be disappointed if I didn't make it," he says as he squints into the late afternoon sun. "If I went to extended spring training, it would work as a motivation tool. I wouldn't be there long."

—JOE STRAUSS

NOVEMBER 1993

JONES HOPES TO STICK IN MAJORS

by BILL BALLEW

When Chipper Jones sat in front of his makeshift locker in the Braves' clubhouse in September, his back was less than 10 feet from the lockers of shortstop Jeff Blauser and third baseman Terry Pendleton.

And while neither veteran gave the heralded rookie the cold shoulder, both are well aware that the first overall pick in the 1990 draft is about to challenge for their jobs.

Exactly which position Jones will hold for the Braves is still undecided. He has played shortstop throughout his minor league apprenticeship, but errors have haunted him during his four seasons on the farm.

"I had a good year offensively and was kind of iffy on defense again," said Jones, who batted .325-13-89 at Triple-A Richmond. "It was a prototypical Chipper Jones year. I know I need to find the consistency on defense before I'm going to be a mainstay up here."

While he made some impressive defensive plays, Jones paced the International League with 43 errors. Many of his miscues came late in games when the outcome had been virtually determined.

"The majority were careless errors or those compounded by a previous error in a game," Richmond manager Grady Little said. "Many times, his concentration would still be on that first one, which would lead to another one."

While the onslaught of errors created another wave of rumors that the Braves might move Jones to third base, Chuck LaMar, Atlanta's director of scouting and player development, has said several times that Jones will continue to play shortstop. Jones isn't averse to making a move, though he wants to know as soon as possible if that's the Braves' plan.

"I read the papers and I hear what people say and I ask the same questions," Jones said. "I don't want there to be any surprises going into next year. I don't want them to come to me next spring about going to Richmond for another year and playing third base. That's not going to get it with me.

"When some of this came up during the season, I told Chuck if they are going to move me I want to know now. Because if I'm going to move, I want to play winter ball. I don't want there to be any surprises going into my first year of having a legitimate shot of making the major league club."

Despite the assurances of remaining at short, Jones went to instructional league after the major league season concluded to concentrate on his fielding. Though shortstop will be his primary emphasis, he'll also work at second base and third base.

Such efforts will further fine-tune the maturing 21-year-old. He impressed manager Bobby Cox with his small contributions, including two hits in three at-bats, in his first taste of the big leagues this year. The only remaining questions are when and where Jones will be in the major leagues.

"I've had a successful minor league career, but you really haven't accomplished anything until you reach this level," Jones said. ∎

AUGUST 1994

NECESSARY ARROGANCE

by **WILL LINGO**

A beautiful, 70-degree day. Clear, blue sky. Spring training. Yankees and Braves in Fort Lauderdale.

A 3-1 count. The Braves' young phenom at the plate. Terry Mulholland on the mound. Could this day get any better?

"I'd hit a home run off him earlier on a 3-1 pitch, and I was looking to try to get him again," the phenom says. "I took a big swing at a bad pitch."

Try to beat it out. Focus on the front of the bag. Run!

The shortstop scoops up the routine grounder and fires to first. The throw's off line. A peek out of the corner of the eye. It's definitely going to take the first baseman off the bag.

Change of plan. Go to the outside of the bag. Avoid the tag. Plant the left foot, move to the right.

The left spike catches the dirt. The hightop catches the ankle, but it can't reach up to save that knee.

Pop.

"I felt like I had broken my leg," Jones says. He hoped as hard as he could that he'd sprained his knee, that maybe he'd be out for only a month.

"I came off the field pretty much under my own power, and the pain went away in five minutes," he says. "When we got to the clubhouse, I picked up my right knee and it looked OK.

"I picked up my left knee, and it was pretty gruesome."

The trainers broke the obvious news to him: This is a big problem. It will require major surgery, you're out for the year.

"I mean, I broke down right there," says Jones, who's not ashamed to admit he cried.

What made it harder for Jones is that he's the one who was supposed to make the majors this year.

"I felt like I had at least a portion of the left field job won," says Jones, who had been groomed as a shortstop but played so well in the spring that the Braves had to find a place to get him in the lineup.

"I was ready to step in and play every day at this level. I thought I was playing the best ball of my life, and I had worked really hard. I just was really disappointed this happened. It's really detrimental to your mental stability."

Jones is in a big rush. Rehab is boring, playing is fun. He doesn't want to sit and wait when he thinks he's ready to play—which in his mind will be soon. Very soon.

Because he would have made the Braves' Opening Day roster, Jones has done most of his rehab work in Atlanta. He has a locker with the team and he'll start traveling with them in August.

Still he remembers rough days at the beginning.

"All the young guys I came up with were all doing so well," he says. He didn't resent their success, but he lamented that he couldn't be out there working and competing with them.

"It's kind of got me down, I won't lie to you about that. But I decided to use their success as a motivational tool."

So he worked like a dog in rehab, strengthening his knee and his confidence. He started working the day after surgery, and he's concentrated on riding a stationary bike, climbing the Stairmaster and lifting weights.

"Every leg exercise you can imagine. I've done it in the last three months," Jones says. "This is basically all I have done."

He started jogging at the beginning of July and hitting soon after that. Doctors also said the easy swing of golf would be good for his knee. So Jones shaved a couple of strikes off his golf score, which is essential to survive in the Braves' clubhouse.

"I've played a lot, but I play about half as much as the pitchers," he says. "I'd say I am middle of the pack. I've still got a long way to go."

The four-month anniversary of his surgery was Aug. 4 and Jones is ready to pronounce himself fit.

"I can honestly say that I will physically be able to play between four and five months after the surgery," he says. "My only request after the injury was that if the doctors and the knee say I'm ready to play come Sept. 1, let me pinch-hit."

Let's see, a young switch-hitter on the bench with a little speed and a little pop. Who couldn't use that down the stretch?

The Braves, that's who. General manager John Schuerholz draws on every emphatic expression he knows to make it clear that he doesn't want Jones on the field this season.

"No matter how good he looks or how good he feels, he can't get that ligament ready for baseball any faster," Schuerholz says. "Based on the information from our doctors, it seems very unlikely we would use him this season."

In the reconstructive knee surgery Jones had, a ligament is transplanted to replace the ACL. Doctors say it takes at least nine months to get good blood flow established, to regenerate the ligament, to get it ready for the stress of playing.

Thus, strike or no strike, don't look for Chipper Jones in 1994. "For what purpose?" Schuerholz asks. "Would it make sense to jeopardize a 10-year career for one month?"

Schuerholz visualizes a press conference. Jones has reinjured his knee after a late-season appearance with the Braves. Jones says it's all right, that he wanted to help the team win. But Mr. Schuerholz, why did you let the kid play?

"What answer would I give?" Schuerholz asks. "The point is to get the guy back for the rest of his life, not for one at-bat in September."

Hey, maybe this rehab even has some benefits. Jones has added muscle through his extensive weightlifting program, something he admits he needed.

"It's obvious I need to get stronger in order to compete at the big league level. I'm stronger now that I was in spring training," Jones says.

With more size and strength, Jones thinks he can get to the 20 home runs and 20 stolen bases people envision, and still hit .300.

Jones is upbeat, firmly focused on where he'll be this time next year, not grousing about where he is today.

Well, maybe a little bit. Jones aches for the roar of the crowd, the feeling of a sweet swing for a big hit, the success of winning. Rehab is working toward a goal, but . . .

"You don't get the end result every day," Jones says. "It's just the same monotonous thing, day after day. It's really boring."

The drive that made him a great player to begin with makes him a great candidate to recover from the injuries. Call if necessary arrogance. Trusting your body and your ability.

"I've never been one to lack in self-confidence," Jones said. "This is by no means a career-threatening injury. No matter what happened, I would have been back next year. But I refused to let myself think that way.

Soon the Braves will let Jones run the bases full-out. Don't look for him to practice his move to avoid a tag at first base.

"I've probably done that move a hundred times in my lifetime," he says, "but it's not worth going through this kind of thing again to raise your batting average two points."

So we won't look for that. But how will we know if the knee is all the way back.

"The first time I hit a ball into the gap," Jones says. "If I get a triple out of it, I'm back. If I'm not able to, then I'll be a little disappointed." ◼

EDITOR'S NOTE: The Braves didn't have to worry about Jones playing that September. The players strike ended the MLB season on Aug. 11. Jones didn't hit his first triple in 1995 until August, so maybe he was a little disappointed, but no one else was. Jones hit .265/.353/.450 with 23 home runs and 86 RBIs. He finished second in Rookie of the Year voting. Two years later, he hit the 20 home runs and stole 20 bases that people had envisioned.

Chipped Teeth For Chipper

May 1993

Richmond Braves (International) shortstop Larry Wayne "Chipper" Jones might want to find another way to live up to his nickname. Jones was upset about striking out with a runner on third in the first inning of a game against Charlotte. Returning to the dugout, Jones chucked his bat into a wooden bat rack. The bat flew back, and the knob hit him in the mouth, chipping his two top front teeth in an inverted "V."

Jones had to come out of the game. His replacement, Jose Oliva, was mired in an 0-for-16 slump, but he promptly smashed two home runs in a game Richmond won 4-3.

"I'm kind of glad it happened," Jones said. "Jose came in and hit two jacks. At least I can take consolation that the guy filling in for me picked up the slack and basically won the game.

"I was more mad about not getting the RBI. I've got to learn to cage that temper a little bit."

Jones had his teeth repaired by a dentist in a bonding procedure the next afternoon. Then he went out and collected four hits, including his second home run.

—JOE STRAUSS

Chipper Jones hit .300 or better in 10 different MLB seasons.

KEN BABBITT

NOVEMBER 1995

QUESTIONS, EXPECTATIONS DON'T HAMPER JONES

by BILL BALLEW

Chipper Jones didn't begin thinking about winning Rookie-of-the-Year honors last spring.

His thoughts weren't launched before a severe knee injury in 1994 or even during his first year at Triple-A Richmond, when he won the International League's version of the award in 1993.

No, the Atlanta third baseman initially envisioned picking up the trophy in 1990, his first year of professional baseball.

"It's been a goal of mine since I saw David Justice win the award in 1990," says Jones, the first overall pick in that year's draft. "It would be great if I'd win it. But whether or not I do really doesn't matter now because I am very proud of some of the things I have accomplished."

As he should be. Few players, not to mention rookies, entered 1995 with so many expectations when so many unknowns existed. With just eight games of major league experience, Jones was asked to change positions and replace veteran Terry Pendleton's glove and bat at third base. On top of that, Jones was coming off major surgery to repair a torn anterior cruciate ligament in his left knee, which had forced him to miss the entire 1994 season.

Jones relished the opportunity and exploded onto the National League scene. By season's end he was perhaps the NL East champions' most consistent player. That performance may have him running neck-and-neck with the Dodgers Hideo Nomo for NL rookie honors, but Atlanta manager Bobby Cox has no doubts about who deserves the award.

"Chipper's unreal. He really is," Cox says. "He's played great in the field, come through in practically every crucial situation at the plate. He was rusty a little bit in the spring and the first few games up here, but after that it's like he's never missed a beat. To me, it's Chipper all the way."

Surprisingly, the surgically repaired knee never affected Jones during the season. After nearly a year of strenuous rehabilitation, he experienced some soreness during the first two weeks of spring training before the muscles responded to the stress and strain of playing baseball daily.

Jones has grown to believe that the knee injury has made him an even stronger player. He points to his 23 regular season home runs, four more than he hit during his best year in the minors.

"With all the weightlifting I've done for the last year or so with my injury, I've gotten a lot stronger and I think my power numbers are showing it," says Jones, 23. "I'm also stronger later in the year. I went through a little down period at the beginning of

September where my bat speed was slow. But I've gotten my second wind and feel better than I ever have in October."

He proved that by homering twice in the Divisional Series opener against Colorado, with the second blast winning the game for Atlanta in the top of the ninth. That underscored his clutch performance all season, which sometimes gets lost in his so-so batting average. Jones' RBI total was second best on the team, despite having to hit behind Marquis Grisson and Jeff Blauser, who collectively had the lowest on-base percentage of any Nos 1-2 hitters in the NL.

"I haven't hit for as high an average as I had hoped," Jones says, "and that's probably the one part of my game that I'm disappointed with. It's something I'm very confident I can improve on.

Chipper Jones ended up playing 1,992 games at third.

"But to be able to go out there day in and day out and drive in some big runs like I have this year is something to be proud of, especially for a guy in his first year. I know I'm hitting in the middle of the lineup and a lot of things are expected of me, but I feel I've overcome a lot of those lofty expectations."

Another area where Jones has room for improvement is defense. He made 25 errors at the hot corner, the second-highest total among NL third baseman.

However, this year was the first time he played the position. He also made several highlight real plays in the field, including a crucial gem in the playoff opener game against Colorado.

"Adjusting to the position change the way I did early in the season was a big surprise to me," Jones says. "And with the exception of a few games over the last couple of weeks, I've been pretty consistent with the leather all year.

"I think all Bobby and the pitching staff asked me to do was make the routine play. I'm going to make my share of spectacular plays throughout the year, but it's the ball that's hit directly at you that you have to make 95 percent of the time."

Suffice it to say that no one is crying about the absence of Pendleton, the free agent Braves general manager John Schuerholz discarded after the 1994 season. In fact, Jones has gone beyond the call of duty by serving as one of the vocal leaders for an Atlanta club that features veterans who prefer to lead by example.

It's the vote of confidence in return from his teammates, not from those who elect the NL Rookie-of-the-Year, that matters most.

"If at the end of the playoffs my teammates come up to me and say that I did my job and they respect me as a ballplayer then that means more to me than any piece of hardware with my name on it," Jones says. "Individual goals come second with me, especially now." ■

DECEMBER 1995

JONES OVER VAN POPPEL PAYS OFF FOR SNYDER

by BILL BALLEW

Paul Snyder had the baseball world watching him in 1990, when the Braves scouting director owned the draft's No. 1 pick. Texas prep sensation Todd Van Poppel was considered the best talent available, but all spring he had made overtures about pitching at the University of Texas. Also, although he never came out and said it, Van Poppel didn't want to play for the Braves, who at the time were baseball's perennial loser. "I had been out to Texas three times to see the Van Poppels and I could not get an answer to, 'Would you sign if you were drafted?'" Snyder says. "That's all I was trying to find out. I never did get an answer."

Frustrated by that, then general manager Bobby Cox traveled to Texas himself to see if he could get an answer. He got it, though it came through actions rather than words.

"I arranged for Bobby to meet with both Todd and his father," Snyder says. "When Bobby got there, the dad was present, but there was no Todd. Bobby called back and said 'Paul, I think you guys know what we've got to do.'"

Van Poppel's bluff worked. He wound up signing with Oakland for what was at that time the most lucrative draft deal ever.

Atlanta went in another direction. A high school shortstop—Larry Wayne Jones, better known as Chipper—joined the organization as the No. 1 overall pick.

Five years later, Atlanta is quite pleased with the way everything worked out. While Van Poppel has had significant growing pains, Jones finished his first major league season as an integral part of the Braves' World Series title.

Jones wound up being the signature pick of Snyder's first stint as Braves scouting director from 1980-90.

"At that time, we had a divided room," Synder says. "Half felt Todd was the best prospect for the Braves. The other side felt the same way about Chipper. But when you broke it down, we knew we had some pitching on the way. We didn't have middle infielders coming. But at no time did we ever consider Chipper a secondary pick."

Snyder had seen Jones three times before the draft. What impressed him wasn't just his drive but his determination. During one of Snyder's visits, he watched as the switch-hitting Jones defied his coach's demands that he bat exclusively from the right side.

"On his first swing as a lefty, he hit a frozen rope over the right field fence and onto the street," Synder says. "You could tell that there was never a doubt in his mind about whether or not he would play in the big leagues."

What's more, the pick pleased Braves owner Ted Turner in a couple of ways.

"The beauty part of it was, Ted back then considered the seven Southern states Braves' territory," Snyder says. "We've always tried to do whatever we can in this area, but Chipper was the first chance we had to get a guy that high that was out of Ted's states. You can't ask for anything better than that." ∎

Chipper Jones hit .229 in his Gulf Coast League debut. He never hit below .245 in any other pro season.

Chipper Jones scouting reports

ATLANTA BRAVES
NO. 2. PROSPECT AFTER 1990 SEASON

If being the No. 1 player selected overall last June wasn't pressure enough, Jones had added attention created by the Van Poppel situation. The mental drain took its toll on Jones.

The Braves got a kid intent on playing baseball; a potential switch-hitter with speed and pop, and a strong-armed, smooth-gloved shortstop. In other words, a total package.

Jones was allowed to bat righthanded most of his debut season, but the idea of switch-hitting isn't foreign, and became a full-time endeavor in the instructional league. Though his high school coach made him hit righthanded all the time, he did swing from both sides in American Legion ball for two summers.

ATLANTA BRAVES
NO. 1. PROSPECT AFTER 1991 SEASON

It wasn't any secret that the Braves' primary interest with the No. 1 pick in the 1990 draft was Texas schoolboy pitcher Todd Van Poppel.

After several discussions with the Van Poppel family, though, Cox and then-scouting director Paul Snyder became convinced he wouldn't sign if drafted by the Braves, no matter how much the offer. No big deal. The one thing the Braves were heavy on was strong-armed pitching prospects.

So they turned their attention to Jones, the player they had keyed in on the hardest from the start. Jones struggled in his debut season but whatever questions might have cropped up in 1990 were erased with Jones' strong showing last year.

With the broken hand he had sustained before the 1990 draft fully healed, Jones was everything the Braves could have wanted. He won Atlanta's minor league triple crown, hitting .323-15-98. He also displayed good base-stealing speed, swiping 40 bases.

His defense is a little ragged, but time should smooth that out. Jones has range, soft hands and arm strength, but needs to get all those areas under control to substantially cut down on the 56 errors he committed last year at Class A Macon. Thirty-three came in his first 68 games, mostly on throws.

Even if the errors continue and Jones may be moved to second or third base, it won't be a great concern because Jones has plenty of offense to make him a legitimate big leaguer at any position.

Chipper Jones made 32 errors in 1992, but that was a massive improvement over the 56 errors he made in 1991.

ATLANTA BRAVES
NO. 1. PROSPECT AFTER 1992 SEASON

Two months into (the 1992) season, Jones was hitting just .277-4-31 in 264 at-bats for Class A Durham. So what prompted the Braves to promote him to Double-A Greenville?

The answer is he simply has talent bursting out of his double-knits. His ability feeds on challenge, his confidence on success.

So how did the experiment go? All Jones did for the rest of the season was set the Southern League afire, establishing a Greenville record for triples in his limited stay. The phenomenal performance, especially for a player so young, solidified his status as a top position player prospect in baseball. Many on-lookers believed he could have entered Atlanta's pennant race without missing a step.

The No. 1 pick in the 1990 draft, Jones has the bat to become an offensive shortstop with a reputation between a Travis Fryman and Cal Ripken. He could hit a consistent .300 with up to 25-30 home runs, and can run enough to steal 20-25 bases. The fact that he's a switch-hitter with command of both swings only adds to the intrigue.

Like Fryman and Ripken, Jones will end his minor league career with defensive numbers that don't testify to his true ability. He has coordination in his hands and wrists when it comes to fielding the ball, but they don't quite follow his every command when the time comes to throw. Most of his 32 errors last season came on throws, but that total was down from 56 in 1991.

Talk of moving Jones to second or third base has been abandoned, because his instincts are expected to help him grow out of any defensive stumbles that await. Forget any more time in Double-A. The Braves don't care if he hits .220 at Richmond for three months—they know he'll learn and use those lessons to punish major league pitchers.

ATLANTA BRAVES
NO. 1. PROSPECT AFTER 1994 SEASON

The youngest player in Triple-A in 1993, Jones continued to show why the Braves used the first overall pick in the 1990 draft to acquire his services. Handling another jump in classification for the third straight season, the immensely confident shortstop earned Rookie-of-the-Year honors in the International League and led a talented Richmond club in eight offensive categories.

Most young players' defensive skills reach major league standards before their offense catches up. Jones is an exception, wielding a potent stick that scouts believe will produce consistent .300-20-80 seasons in the majors. A natural line drive hitter with exceptional bat control, Jones could resurrect the days of slugging third baseman if he continues to grow.

Jones has good hands and a strong arm, yet was plagued by errors again in 1993. Many of his 43 errors either occurred late in games or after he made an error earlier, both of which could be remedied with stronger concentration. He was tried at second base in instructional league, but feels more comfortable on the left side of the infield.

Though he may begin the season back in Richmond, Jones will battle for a major league job in spring training and will play in Atlanta at some point in 1994.

ATLANTA BRAVES
NO. 1. PROSPECT AFTER 1995 SEASON

Jones tore the anterior-cruciate ligament in his knee during spring training last year after earning a platoon job in left field. It's the only reason the first overall pick the 1990 draft is back in the Top 10, rather than entering his second year in Atlanta. His dedication to rehab could have had Jones back on the field last September, but the extra time has enabled his knee to get even stronger. In his last showing, he earned 1993 Rookie-of-the-Year honors in the International League after leading a prospect-laden Richmond club in eight offensive categories.

Jones always has wielded a potent bat. His tremendous bat control and discriminating eye result in high batting averages and excellent run production. A natural line drive hitter, he always has had solid power output and should produce .300-20-80 numbers annually in the majors as he gains experience and maturity.

Jones' arm gained a reputation for being errant early in his career. While he has improved, he must continue to make the routine play as well as the spectacular. His size could force a move to third base, and he has a bit of outfield experience from last spring.

If veteran shortstop Jeff Blauser isn't re-signed, the starting job is Jones' to lose. Should Blauser return, Jones still will play most every day.

Andruw Jones hit 30 or more home runs in seven different seasons.

ANDRUW JONES, OF

BIOGRAPHY

PROPER NAME: Andruw Rudolf Jones. **BORN:** April 23, 1977 in Willemstad, Curacao.
HT.: 6-1. **WT.:** 225. **BATS:** R. **THROWS:** R.
FIRST PRO CONTRACT: Signed as international free agent by Braves, July 2, 1993.

Nostalgia is deceitful. Given the passage of time, the good old days always seem better, because turmoils are forgotten while the joyous moments remain. But projecting ahead based on potential can be just as dangerous. And when it comes to potential, it's hard to remember a prospect who had more of it than Andruw Jones. The center fielder burst upon the national scene with a 1995 season for low Class A Macon that seemed simply too good for an 18-year-old. So the next year, he was even better, going from high Class A Durham to World Series stardom in the span of six months. At that moment, Jones seemed destined to become one of the best players of all-time. He was MLB ready as a teeenager, blessed with speed, power and amazing range in center field. In the end, Jones did not fully reach that potential. It's possible no one could have matched those lofty expectations. The speed slowly ebbed away in his 20s. The power was always there, as was the defense. So instead of an all-time great, the Braves enjoyed one of the best center fielders of his generation.

CAREER STATISTICS

Year	Club (League)	Class	AVG	G	AB	R	H	2B	3B	HR	RBI	BB	SO	SB	OBP	SLG
1994	Braves (GCL)	R	.221	27	95	22	21	5	1	2	10	16	19	5	.345	.358
	Danville (APP)	R	.336	36	143	20	48	9	2	1	16	9	25	16	.385	.448
1995	Macon (SAL)	LoA	.277	139	537	104	149	41	5	25	100	70	122	56	.372	.512
1996	Durham (CAR)	HiA	.313	66	243	65	76	14	3	17	43	42	54	16	.419	.605
	Greenville (SL)	AA	.369	38	157	39	58	10	1	12	37	17	34	12	.432	.675
	Richmond (IL)	AAA	.378	12	45	11	17	3	1	5	12	1	9	2	.391	.822
	Atlanta (NL)	MAJ	.217	31	106	11	23	7	1	5	13	7	29	3	.265	.443
1997	Atlanta (NL)	MAJ	.231	153	399	60	92	18	1	18	70	56	107	20	.329	.416
1998	Atlanta (NL)	MAJ	.271	159	582	89	158	33	8	31	90	40	129	27	.321	.515
1999	Atlanta (NL)	MAJ	.275	162	592	97	163	35	5	26	84	76	103	24	.365	.483
2000	Atlanta (NL)	MAJ	.303	161	656	122	199	36	6	36	104	59	100	21	.366	.541
2001	Atlanta (NL)	MAJ	.251	161	625	104	157	25	2	34	104	56	142	11	.312	.461
2002	Atlanta (NL)	MAJ	.264	154	560	91	148	34	0	35	94	83	135	8	.366	.513
2003	Atlanta (NL)	MAJ	.277	156	595	101	165	28	2	36	116	53	125	4	.338	.513
2004	Atlanta (NL)	MAJ	.261	154	570	85	149	34	4	29	91	71	147	6	.345	.488
2005	Atlanta (NL)	MAJ	.263	160	586	95	154	24	3	51	128	64	112	5	.347	.575
2006	Atlanta (NL)	MAJ	.262	156	565	107	148	29	0	41	129	82	127	4	.363	.531
2007	Atlanta (NL)	MAJ	.222	154	572	83	127	27	2	26	94	70	138	5	.311	.413
2008	Las Vegas (PCL)	AAA	.323	11	31	7	10	0	0	4	11	3	5	2	.361	.710
	Los Angeles (NL)	MAJ	.158	75	209	21	33	8	1	3	14	27	76	0	.256	.249
2009	Frisco (TL)	AA	.222	3	9	0	2	0	0	0	0	3	1	1	.417	.222
	Texas (AL)	MAJ	.214	82	281	43	60	18	0	17	43	45	72	5	.323	.459
2010	Chicago (AL)	MAJ	.230	107	278	41	64	12	1	19	48	45	73	9	.341	.486
2011	New York (AL)	MAJ	.247	77	190	27	47	8	0	13	33	29	62	0	.356	.495
2012	New York (AL)	MAJ	.197	94	233	27	46	7	0	14	34	28	71	0	.294	.408
Major League Totals			.254	2196	7599	1204	1933	383	36	434	1289	891	1748	152	.337	.486
Minor League Totals			.302	332	1260	268	381	82	13	66	229	161	269	110	.388	.545

A center field wizard with power to spare

FEBRUARY 1995

BRAVES STOCK UP ON GLOBAL TALENT

by BILL BALLEW

Discovered by scout Givanni Viceisza in October 1992, as a 15-year-old Andruw Jones caused jaws to drop when Paul Snyder and Braves Latin American supervisor Carlos Rios traveled to the Netherlands Antilles to evaluate him. His seemingly effortless motions led Snyder to say, "Any one of the scouts' wives would have been in awe."

"Roberto Clemente," Snyder says when asked who he first thought of when he saw Jones. "I remember watching Clemente in 1960. He got a base hit, rounded first base and put on the brakes but remained on his feet while going back to the base.

"That's exactly what Andruw did. Great body control, could slide on his spikes if he wanted to. Then when I watched him throw and hit and everything else, it was obvious he was a 21-year-old in a 15-year-old's body in terms of baseball talent."

Snyder also learned quickly where Jones got his athletic ability. On his way to see Jones for the first time, Snyder picked up Sherton Saturnino, a Curacao native and the perennial favorite in the Braves' annual 60-yard dash during minor league spring training.

"I get to the field for Andruw and Sherton to run, and Andruw's dad is taking off his pants. He's got a baseball uniform on underneath," Snyder says. "I asked him what he was doing, and he said 'I'm going to run, too.'

"Well Sherton ran his 6.5, Andruw ran a 6.73, and darned if his 46-year-old dad didn't run a 7.16. It was the most incredible thing I have seen. I looked down at him and he has ankles like a man has wrists. Andruw's the same way, which is what you're looking for when you're searching for speed."

The only thing that kept the Braves from signing Jones immediately was his age. International players must be 16 as of Sept. 1 of the year they sign.

Clark says Viceisza might have been the difference in Jones ever being discovered.

"If Givanni hadn't brought him in, we may never have seen him," Clark says, "because they play a very limited and sporadic program down there as far as leagues and tournaments go." ■

IT'S HARD TO KEEP UP WITH JONES

by WILL LINGO

Curacao is one of those tiny islands in the Caribbean that looks like a crumb on your map of the world.

But look closer, and you'll see a rich island culture. Colonized by the Netherlands, it features buildings that look like they've been transported whole from Amsterdam.

The beauty is further enhanced by many of the buildings' pastel colors. Legend has it that the former white color of the buildings gave the island's governor headaches, so he put a tax on all white buildings and the citizens broke out the colorful paint.

The larger of the two main islands that make up the Netherland Antilles (Bonaire is the other), Curacao sits just 40 miles north of Venezuela. Trade winds keep the climate mild. It's a favorite stop of cruise ships.

But the best thing about Curacao? The people.

Curacao comes from the Spainish word for heart. "It feels like when you get there, the people open their arms to you, open their hearts for you," says Pete Manzano, a broadcaster for the Atlanta Braves International Radio Network. "What is particular about the island of Curacao is the people."

Oh, and one other thing, the thing that has Manzano passing off his broadcasting dutires and coming to Macon for a special broadcast back to Curacao:

"At this moment, they have the most powerful player in the minor leagues."

Andruw Vs. Vladimir

July 1995

Macon center fielder Andruw Jones, the 18-year-old star of the talent-rich Braves system, might be the top prospect in the league, but Albany center fielder Vladimir Guerrero is No. 1A. Or perhaps it's the other way around. Guerrero, 19, is the latest in a line of Expos minor league stars. He was hitting .335-10-37 and has the best outfield arm in the league. In one inning at Albany Guerrero threw out a runner at third and another at home.

"He's going to be a star in the major leagues," said Expos general manager Kevin Malone, in Albany for the league all-star game. "If we don't think this league is a challenge for him in the second half, we won't hesitate to move him up."

Macon manager Nelson Norman says Jones, who was hitting .286-16-64 with 26 stolen bases, saw only two fastballs over the plate in the first half after he hit 11 home runs in the first three weeks. Both of those were thrown by Columbus righthander Jaret Wright, and Jones hit both out of Golden Park in Columbus.

—GENE SAPAKOFF

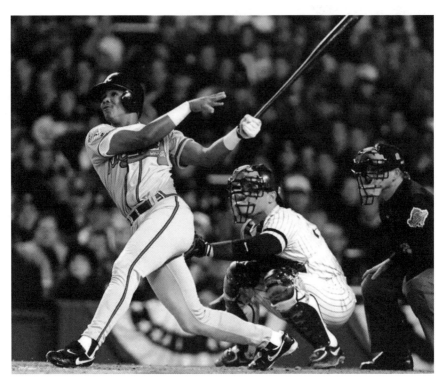

Andruw Jones remains the youngest player to ever hit a home run in the World Series.

We couldn't agree more. The population of 150,000 has produced a very special person who spent his summer in Macon. His name is Andruw Jones.

We might as well get the numbers of out of the way now. Jones hit 25 home runs, drove in 100 runs and stole 56 bases.

For a while, people were saying there had never been a season like that in the minors. Then in the last 40 years. At last check, it hadn't happened since 1961, when Jose Cardenal did it in the old Class D Sophomore League.

But go beyond the numbers. They're not what makes Jones special, anyway.

"It makes me happy because people from Curacao will be happy with me," says Jones, still just 18. "But I don't really worry too much because I just play the game, just get more experience, because experience you learn more and you get better."

A frightening thought for opponents. But is Jones really that big a hero in Curacao?

"Is Hideo Nomo the main figure in Japan?" Manzano says. "At this moment he's probably the main figure in Curacao."

"I hope he doesn't get hurt. That's about the only thing that could hurt his career. He could be one of the best, if not the best player in the major leagues, in five or six years.

This year he's the best in the minor leagues, Baseball America's 1995 Minor League Player of the Year.

"He just has so much natural ability," says Nelson Norman, his manager at Macon. "There is something there that you don't see at this age. You look at him and you can see something there that other players don't have."

And he has the determination that pushes his talent over the top. "Sometimes I'm just going to bat and go hit the ball hard," Jones says. "But I think when I go to the plate and say I'm going to get a hit now no matter, nobody can get me out. I will get a base hit."

No doubt the Braves saw something special when they found Jones. But he actually missed several Braves tryouts before he finally went to one and showed his stuff.

"My manager told me to go, but I don't know, I didn't go," Jones says. "The fourth time I went, and they looked at me and they said, oh, I've got good talent and I can be a superstar in the major leagues."

That might not be idle talk. Though Jones was only 15 and couldn't sign a contract until he turned 16, the Braves knew what they had and snapped him up.

So at age 15, it was time to leave home for the United States, a potentially frightening experience that Jones welcomed. It was a chance to fulfill his dream.

"Curacao is kind of like the United States, but it's not so fun here that it's like back home," Jones says. "Home is more fun. I think probably because it's my island. I was born there. People speak your language and you can communicate more. It's fun here because I love to play baseball."

Jones communicates well in English, but it's clear sometimes that he's searching for just the right word and can't find it. Understandable, because English is his third language.

On Curacao, as well as on nearby Aruba and Bonaire, the residents speak Papiamento, an amalgam of English, Spanish and Dutch. Jones also speaks Spanish fluently, and he uses that to communicate with Hispanic players and coaches. He could speak Dutch or Indie in a pinch, too.

In baseball's developing international age, Jones is a human melting pot. Jones' team in Macon had a manager and two players from the Dominican Republic, two players from Australia and one from Puerto Rico. Plus another teammate from Curacao, Sherton Saturnino, whom the Braves signed in 1990.

Saturnino and Jones are roommates on the road and speak to each other in Papiamento. Saturnino has helped Jones in his first full professional season, but as its final days wound down, Saturnino could tell Jones was ready to go home.

"He's been talking about going home every day," Saturnino says, "but he won't tell you that he's homesick."

On Jones' locker in Macon, where other players photos of their loved ones or baseball heroes, he had his ticket home.

"It has not been hard because I had already gone out and played baseball in other islands and other countries," Jones says. "But after a couple of months . . . you just kind of go home in the night after games, and you start thinking you start feeling a little bit you want to see your mom or your dad, all those people."

After they get home, the players from Curacao who play professionally in the United States will practice together through the winter. And in that group, who's the best? Saturnino doesn't have to think about it at all.

"Right now we've got Andruw. He does everything like that," he says, snapping his fingers. "He does a lot of good things, but he's still young. I think he's got everything."

Most observers agree. A sure sign is that when baseball people talk about Jones, they don't talk about his tools. They assume you must know he has them all.

In a short conversation with Paul Snyder, for instance, the Braves' director of scouting talks about none of Jones' specific skills. But he mentions the following names: Grissom, Griffey, Aaron.

And then his favorite story when he's asked about his first impression of Jones. Snyder already had seen Jones work out, and he watched him in a game later that day.

"It was his first time at bat, and he hit a ball to right-center. He came around first at full speed, saw the outfielder come up with the ball and just hit the brakes. He skidded standing up," Snyder says. "The only other time I had seen something like that was in 1960 in Philadephia at Shibe Park."

The player? Roberto Clemente.

"It just gave me a special feeling," Snyder says. "I knew that he was something special.

"I'm not smart enough to tell you where it's going to stop. It doesn't matter whether he has a bat or glove in his hands. He stands out."

Conventional wisdom is that Jones will skip over Class A Durham next year and head to Double-A Greenville, presumably putting him on a timetable to be in center field in Atlanta in 1998. Snyder says throw that timetable away.

"He doesn't have one," Snyder says. "I think that would be a mistake on our part. Our biggest fear is that he'll get bored. We just want to keep him reaching."

Jones knows he needs some time, but he doesn't think he'll need much.

"I just want to get to the big leagues right now, but you got to have more experience," he says. "This is the first full season I got. And maybe two more full seasons, or maybe one more full season. I will be ready to hit against major league pitchers."

His youth, it seems, is all that works against him. He's inexperienced and still has some growing up to do.

That plainly scares the Braves to death. They know he has the tools. They just don't want anything to screw up his thing from Point A (minor league phenom) to Point B (major league star).

"The biggest danger is that he's going to start believing what you guys write about him," Snyder says. "But he's done an excellent job of keeping everything in perspective."

Jones was fined this year for failing to run out ground balls, for instance, but by all accounts and by all appearances, that was just an occasional lapse brought on by being 18. His omnipresent smile and enthusiasm for the game show through most of the time.

"He does everything so easy, sometimes he thinks he can get away with things," says Rod Gilbreath, the Braves assistant farm director, who paid Jones a late-season visit in Macon. "He likes to do things his way."

A good illustration of Jones' youthful acts of rebellion is his pants, which Jones prefers to wear pulled down to his ankles. But Braves organization policy requires that players show at least part of their stockings.

So when Jones tore his long pants sliding in a game, Norman told the clubhouse attendant not to fix them.

"He will test you," he says. "He's so young, you've got to stay on him all the time. An 18-year-old can get carried away real quick."

Andruw Jones will not stray too far afield. His father Henry will see to that. From talking to Jones and the people who work with him, Henry is the most important figure in his son's life.

When Andruw is at home, Henry throws batting practice to him and other players, and hits him fly balls all winter. Henry is renowned as an outfielder, but he never had an interest in being a professional.

But most importantly, Henry keeps Andruw straight. "Andruw was raised the same way I was," Norman said. "His dad kept him on a short leash."

Norman points to a piece of paper on the bulletin board in his office. It's Henry Jones' phone number. "He told me, 'If Andruw gives you any trouble, you give me a call. I'll be in Macon the next day and you tell Andruw things will not be good for him.' "

Norman never had to make that call. "I just use it as a threat," he says.

Jones doesn't think of his father's discipline, though. He thinks of his father's love and approval.

"I think he's real happy with me," Jones says. "I've got an opportunity to live my dream that I've played for all my life. I've just got to keep working hard and just make it."

So as the tourists pass through the postcard-pretty streets of Wilmestad on Curacao this winter, as other youngsters play soccer, the most powerful player in the minor leagues will continue to stoke the dream that burns inside him, the dream ignited by his father.

"When I was young I always tell my father I just wanted to play professional baseball," he says. "I just wanted to make professional baseball, just wanted to be a professional baseball player.

"That's the thing. I think I was just born for baseball." ■

OOOH, ANDRUW
ANDRUW JONES FOLLOWED UP HIS MINOR LEAGUE PLAYER-OF-THE-YEAR SEASON WITH AN EVEN BETTER YEAR

by WILL LINGO

Sorry Andruw Jones. You're only 19, but we've run out of ways to talk about how good you are.

It would seem that zipping through the Braves system so quickly wouldn't give people enough time to know you were coming, much less time to build up so much hype.

But there it is. The world we live in, apparently.

The stories have all been told. And then again to make sure nobody missed them. Running the 40-yard dash with your father in Curacao? Heard it. That booming home run you hit in (insert your city name here)? Heard it twice.

Even one of the better baseball-prospect stories of recent years, the one where Braves scouting director Paul Snyder saw you round first and skid to a stop standing up, isn't quite as good when you know the punch line. Snyder hasn't seen anything like that since he watched . . . Roberto Clemente.

The praise has been heaped on you. The Braves try desperately not to blow too much sunshine up their prospects' skirts, but even they have to admit you're pretty doggone good.

"You know people are special," Snyder says. "You know they overcome a lot of things. But if I said I knew this was going to happen so quickly, I'd be lying."

Do you seriously think numbers can begin to tell us a story? There's a reason you can't spell numbers without N-U-M-B. After a while, they cease to have meaning to people.

So those folks who were impressed by last year's .277-25-100 (with 56 steals) season at Class A Macon just didn't look up from their Cream of Wheat when they noticed you were batting .313 at Class A Durham or .369 at Double-A Greenville, or even .378 at Triple-A Richmond.

Maybe they did finally notice when you batted .461 in July, which is illegal in some states. And when you got called up to Atlanta and hit five home runs in your first 17 major league games, it was time to pay attention. And, hey, you're Baseball America's Minor League Player of the Year for the second straight season.

But all we can hope for anyone who reads a story, or hears the praise, or sees the numbers, is to take the next step and watch you play. Ah, there's the missing element. Just watch and enjoy.

"I don't think anybody who's seen him hasn't thought he has been legit," Braves shortstop Chipper Jones said. "He's got the good face. You can just look at him and you can tell. He's got the smooth actions, the good body. He's the one that baseball comes easy to."

He looks so good, in fact, that a question appears on the horizon. Who is the best Jones on this team?

"I'm not going to answer that question," Chipper says with a smile.

For now, the question is moot. In his second full season, Chipper Jones is already The Man, mentioned in MVP talk. Andruw Jones is a role player.

If there is any doubt about that, just look as they run onto the lush green of Wrigley Field. On the back of Chipper's jersey: "JONES." On the back of Andruw's jersey; "A. JONES." So while Andruw is a Jones, Chipper is the Jones.

Maybe that's the best thing the Braves could have done. While Andruw was clearly ready to get a taste of the majors and was ruining the curve for all other minor leaguers, maybe they wanted to show him that he still hasn't done all they want him to do.

And meanwhile, he gets much better meal money.

That's clear enough, as Jones unfolds a couple of large bills to give to the clubbie before a game. Sliding into the locker room with Chipper Jones and Ryan Klesko, Jones looks pretty impressed with himself. And why not? A 19-year-old in the big leagues. That's a pretty long way from last year in Macon, when he ate at McDonald's and lived in the home of one of his teammates, John Rocker, who's from Macon and spent the season in Class A.

Dear John: Hope things went well for you this year. I'm in Chicago now with the

Andruw Jones is one of only two players to win a pair of Baseball America Minor League Player of the Year awards.

Braves. We're staying at the Palmer House Hilton. Not as nice as the La Quinta Inn in Augusta, but it's a living. Ha ha. Love, Andruw.

"Everything is nicer here," Jones says. "The hotels, the travel, everything."

A long way from Macon indeed. Hard to believe it was just a year ago that Jones sent the historians poring through their record books with that 25 homer-100 RBI-50 steal combo.

Maybe even harder to believe was that Jones moved up just one step after that, to high Class A Durham.

"They told me I was not ready for Double-A," Jones says. "So I said I would just go there, do my job, play hard and see what happens."

What happened was .313-17-43 with 16 steals and 65 runs in half a season. In a lineup that featured power prospect Ron Wright (since traded to the Pirates) and up-and-coming third baseman Wes Helms, Jones was the unquestioned star while maintaining order in center field.

"We could have done a lot of things with that team," he says. Fortunately for Carolina League pitchers, at midseason the Braves moved the trio en masse to Greenville. That was the end of the group tour, though. Jones made the rest of the trip alone.

He started slowly in Greenville, but when he caught up to Double-A pitching, he obliterated it.

"At Macon and Durham, the pitching was about the same, and a lot of the guys I played against were the same guys I played against last year," he says. "Going to Greenville, that was the biggest adjustment I made. There were a lot of better pitchers."

Jones talks a lot about adjustments. Coming to the United States from Curacao in the Netherland Antilles. Learning to hit curveballs last year and learning to hit consistent quality pitching this year. Life is all about adjustments. We all should be so well adjusted.

"I started to make my adjustments, and after that they told me they were going to move me to a higher level," Jones says.

Apparently no adjustments were needed there. Forty-five quick at-bats were all the Braves needed to see at Triple-A Richmond.

"When I got to Triple-A, everybody was telling me 'You might have a chance to go to Atlanta,'" Jones says. "I didn't really think about it.

"I played about five games in center field and then they moved me to right field, and I started thinking, 'Something's going on.'"

Something was going on. The Braves decided that Jones had learned enough. It was time to bring him to Atlanta, even before rosters were expanded.

The decision was surprising only in its swiftness. No one doubts that Jones can play in the major leagues, or that he can excel. But in the grand plan, everyone thought he would spend another full season in the minors before being handed over to the world.

With the Braves conducting a year-long talent search in right field after Dave Justice was hurt, though, they would have been foolish not to give a long look to Jones.

When Braves general manager John Schuerholz had a teleconference in August to talk about whether Jones was ready for the majors, the sentiment was clear. Minor league managers and all the executives in the scouting and farm departments agreed that he should be promoted.

"No one thought that he would run into a wall," Schuerholz says. "No one brought it up. Ordinarily, that would come up with you discuss promoting a young player. But this time it never arose."

Jones actually already had run into a wall in Greenville. When he did, he knocked down a section of the center-field fence, but he made the catch.

So it was on to Atlanta for Jones, and he probably has gotten a good dose of humility there. He's strictly a part-time player, and he has just 15 hits in his first 61 at-bats for a downright human .246 average.

Those 15 were exciting though. Just five were singles. Five were home runs, four were doubles and one was a triple. When he stops chasing those high fastballs and lays off the evil breaking stuff, watch out.

Manager Bobby Cox likes what he sees so far. He says right up front that Jones isn't ready to be an everyday player in the big leagues, but you aren't sure you believe him.

"He can really swing the lumber," Cox says. "And really, we only brought him up a couple of weeks early. We would have brought him up in September anyway because he can steal a base."

With so many stars around, Jones can blend in. And when Braves executives see Jones walking out to the outfield with Marquis Grissom and Dwight Smith, they have to feel good about what's rubbing off.

No offense to Pedro Swann, of course, but learning in Atlanta has got to be better for Jones than learning in Richmond. Like a gifted student, challenging him gets the most out of his potential.

During batting practice at Wrigley, Jones is down to his last cut. He takes it over the left field bleachers, over the fence and onto Waveland Avenue. Everyone in the ballpark and on the field pauses for a gaze.

The adjustments continue, though they're fine adjustments that most players never get far enough to make. While it's nice to have your transition into the major leagues eased by playing for such a talented team, it's sometimes difficult when you're used to being a star.

"Here everything is harder, much harder, everyone is good," Jones says. "Other people have got to play, it's not just me. I'm used to playing every day, but they've got to play everybody."

Chipper, the other Jones in this clubhouse, knows that bridling like that can be a good thing. Chipper knows firsthand that a little bit, or maybe even a lot, of cockiness never hurt anybody.

"He's definitely got the necessary arrogance," Chipper says. "When I first saw him, he had a lot of ketchup and mustard on him. But he's grown up and gotten rid of that kind of stuff. It's not going to be easy, but he's been quick to make the adjustment everywhere else.

"He's good. He knows he's good, and he knows everybody knows he's good."

A year ago, the Braves' 18-year-old phenom was already the Minor League Player of the Year, and they had to worry about how to get him through the minor leagues without him going bad.

Jones solved that problem quite quickly by blitzing though the system too quickly to pick up any bad habits.

To be sure, he's still a teenager. Last year, though, the organization was worried about how low his uniform pants came down. This year, it's whether he needs to play winter ball if he stays with the major leaguers throughout the postseason.

The Braves want him to play. Jones would rather go home, as he has the last two winters.

"I don't want to play winter ball," he says. "But whatever the Braves want to do, I'll do. I don't worry about that stuff anymore."

Now he has to worry about becoming the best player on a team filled with all-stars. He's on his way.

When asked who the best Jones on the team is, Andruw points without hesitation toward Chipper. "Right now, he is. But maybe next year . . ."

Given what we've seen in the last 12 months and the 12 before that, we wouldn't bet against it. ■

When he was in the South Atlantic League, Andruw Jones was voted the best batting prospect, power prospect, baserunner and defensive outfielder.

Andruw Jones scouting reports

1994 GULF COAST LEAGUE
NO. 2 PROSPECT

Jones hit .221 and left for the Rookie-level Appalachian League after only 27 games, but the 17-year-old Curacao product's tools—hitting, power, speed, outfield play and arm—were above average across the board.

"He can do everything," Braves manager Jim Saul said. "He will go quickly to the big leagues."

1994 APPALACHIAN LEAGUE
NO. 2 PROSPECT

Another 17-year-old making his pro debut, Jones jumped from the Rookie-level Gulf Coast League in midseason. He's a five-tool player whose best weapon is his speed, stealing bases and covering a lot of ground in the outfield. He also has a strong, accurate arm.

Jones showed some ability to turn on fastballs and should hit for average with a bit of power. He can lay down a bunt when necessary.

1995 SOUTH ATLANTIC LEAGUE
NO.1 PROSPECT

Jones was just 17 in April when he took the SAL lead in home runs. At 18, the kid from Curacao pulled off a rare quadruple when he was named best batting prospect, best power prospect, best baserunner and best defensive outfielder in the SAL in a survey of league managers. He was also named the league's most exciting player.

Some managers and a few of Jones' teammates questioned his approach, which at times seems casual. But Jones was coachable and durable. He led the SAL in runs because of his aggressive baserunning, stolen bases because of his excellent first step and extra-base hits because of his power. He also ranked among the top four in doubles, home runs and RBIs.

"What's not to like?" Albany manager Doug Sisson said. "He can go as far as his desire will take him."

1996 CAROLINA LEAGUE
NO. 1 PROSPECT

Jones, who won Baseball America's Minor League Player of the Year award the last two years, didn't stay in Durham long enough to win any of the CL's postseason awards. But nobody came close to keeping up with this Jones.

Physically there's little Jones can't do, though his unparalleled offensive skills tend to over-shadow his defense. The Braves knew it was only a matter of time before Jones' talent forced them to promote him to Atlanta, though it's unlikely they thought he would start the year in Durham and reach the majors by August.

"It's kind of hard just picking one thing with him," Bulls manager Randy Ingle said. "He does everything well above average. I guess the thing I liked was his patience. With his reputation, he didn't get a lot of pitches to hit, but he was able to lay off. That's very impressive for a 19-year-old."

1996 SOUTHERN LEAGUE
NO. 1 PROSPECT

Just 19 years old, Jones was spectacular at the plate and in the field. He played center field for Greenville, but was switched to right field in Richmond to get him ready for the outfield vacancy in Atlanta.

Jones impressed everyone with his all-around game. He showed he could hit for a high aver-age, flashed his power, displayed his speed and got to anything in his vicinity in the outfield.

"What's not to like?" Orlando manager Bruce Kimm said. "The kid has shown everything."

"He's one of the best prospects I've ever seen in the minor leagues," Greenville manager Jeff Cox said. "He's just so multi-talented. He is all-star caliber in every facet of the game."

ATLANTA BRAVES
NO. 2. PROSPECT AFTER 1994 SEASON

In his first year of pro ball, Jones was rated among the Top 10 Prospects in two Rookie leagues. He was named the No. 2 prospect in the Appalachian League after making the jump from the Gulf Coast League, where he was ranked No. 3.

Jones is one of the most gifted athletes in the minor leagues. A true five-tool player, he's a burner who uses his speed and instincts in the outfield and on the bases. His arm is among the best in the organization.

Jones simply needs to play. His lack of professional experience is the only thing keeping him from being an impact player at higher levels.

Jones should start 1995 at Class A Macon. No one in Atlanta would be surprised if he rises through the organization rapidly. They quietly compare him to Roberto Clemente.

ATLANTA BRAVES
NO. 1. PROSPECT AFTER 1995 SEASON

Baseball America's 1995 Minor League Player of the Year, Jones (his first name is pronounced AHN-drew) was 17 when he started the 1995 season—young even by South Atlantic League standards. But he still dominated the loop and earned recognition from managers as the top prospect. The Curacao native also was named the league's best batting prospect, best power prospect, best baserunner and best defensive outfielder. He led the minors with 71 extra-base hits, led the SAL in runs and stolen bases and ranked among the top four in doubles, home runs and RBIs.

Jones is the quintessential five-tool talent. One of the most physically mature 18-year-olds scouts have seen, Jones doesn't seem awed or overwhelmed by any aspect of the game. He makes adjustments between pitches and can hit practically any fastball sent his way. He also has a plus arm and goes into the gaps aggressively, thinking little of his safety while making diving or leaping catches. His all-out style and impressive array of talents have drawn comparisons to a young Cesar Cedeno, one of the best teenage players of the last 30 years.

Despite what his 56 stolen bases might indicate, Jones' running ability rates as average. His tremendous quickness makes up for a lack of world-class speed. Jones needs to become more patient at the plate and can't allow his rapid success to go to his head. The Braves believe those matters will improve naturally as he continues to play every day against better competition.

Jones is the type of player who can explode through an organization. Several scouts believe he could have succeeded with few problems at Double-A Greenville in 1995. Nevertheless, the Braves want to make sure Jones receives the proper maturing at every step before promoting him. Durham and/or Greenville await in 1996, with the majors an outside possibility for late 1997.

ATLANTA BRAVES
NO. 1. PROSPECT AFTER 1996 SEASON

No one in baseball was on a faster track than Andruw Jones in 1996. He concluded his rise from high Class A to the majors by becoming only the second player in history to hit home runs in his first two World Series at-bats. He also won his second straight Minor League Player of the Year award.

The quintessential five-tool talent, Jones could become a 40-40 threat. He owns amazing speed and power, and has the strongest outfield arms in the system.

Jones will become a better baserunner as he learns how to use his speed. He still falls prey to breaking balls when out of rhythm at the plate.

The Braves are trying to clear the way for Jones to start in left field. At worst he'll platoon in left and right.

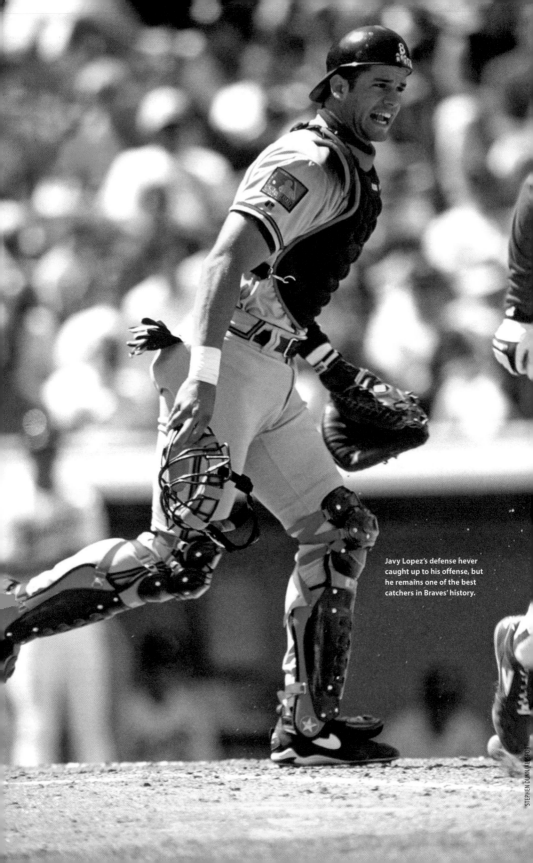

Javy Lopez's defense never caught up to his offense, but he remains one of the best catchers in Braves' history.

JAVY LOPEZ, C

BIOGRAPHY

PROPER NAME: Javier Lopez. **BORN:** Nov. 5, 1970 in Ponce, Puerto Rico.
HT.: 6-3. **WT.:** 230. **BATS:** R. **THROWS:** R.
FIRST PRO CONTRACT: Signed as international free agent, Nov. 6, 1987.

It's hard to develop a catcher. Over the 20 years before Lopez arrived in Atlanta, Bruce Benedict, Ozzie Virgil and Greg Olson were the only Braves catchers to have any staying power at the position. That changed when Lopez arrived. From 1994 to 2003, Lopez gave the Braves one of the better offensive catchers in the National League.

CAREER STATISTICS

Year	Club (League)	Class	AVG	G	AB	R	H	2B	3B	HR	RBI	BB	SO	SB	OBP	SLG
1988	Braves (GCL)	Rk	.191	31	94	8	18	4	0	1	9	3	19	1	.214	.266
1989	Pulaski (APP)	Rk	.261	51	153	27	40	8	1	3	27	5	35	3	.284	.386
1990	Burlington (MID)	LoA	.265	116	422	48	112	17	3	11	55	14	84	0	.297	.398
1991	Durham (CAR)	HiA	.245	113	384	43	94	14	2	11	51	25	88	10	.294	.378
1992	Atlanta (NL)	MLB	.375	9	16	3	6	2	0	0	2	0	1	0	.375	.500
1992	Greenville (SL)	AA	.321	115	442	63	142	28	3	16	60	24	47	7	.362	.507
1993	Atlanta (NL)	MLB	.375	8	16	1	6	1	1	1	2	0	2	0	.412	.750
1993	Richmond (IL)	AAA	.305	100	380	56	116	23	2	17	74	12	53	1	.334	.511
1994	Atlanta (NL)	MAJ	.245	80	277	27	68	9	0	13	35	17	61	0	.299	.419
1995	Atlanta (NL)	MAJ	.315	100	333	37	105	11	4	14	51	14	57	0	.344	.498
1996	Atlanta (NL)	MAJ	.282	138	489	56	138	19	1	23	69	28	84	1	.322	.466
1997	Atlanta (NL)	MAJ	.295	123	414	52	122	28	1	23	68	40	82	1	.361	.534
1998	Atlanta (NL)	MAJ	.284	133	489	73	139	21	1	34	106	30	85	5	.328	.540
1999	Atlanta (NL)	MAJ	.317	65	246	34	78	18	1	11	45	20	41	0	.375	.533
2000	Atlanta (NL)	MAJ	.287	134	481	60	138	21	1	24	89	35	80	0	.337	.484
2001	Atlanta (NL)	MAJ	.267	128	438	45	117	16	1	17	66	28	82	1	.322	.425
2002	Atlanta (NL)	MAJ	.233	109	347	31	81	15	0	11	52	26	63	0	.299	.372
2003	Atlanta (NL)	MAJ	.328	129	457	89	150	29	3	43	109	33	90	0	.378	.687
2004	Baltimore (AL)	MAJ	.316	150	579	83	183	33	3	23	86	47	97	0	.370	.503
2005	Baltimore (AL)	MAJ	.278	103	395	47	110	24	1	15	49	19	68	0	.322	.458
2006	Baltimore (AL)	MAJ	.265	76	279	30	74	15	1	8	31	18	60	0	.314	.412
	Boston (AL)	MAJ	.190	18	63	6	12	5	0	0	4	2	16	0	.215	.270
Minor League Totals			.279	532	1897	247	530	96	11	60	280	84	330	22	.315	.436
Major League Totals			.287	1503	5319	674	1527	267	19	260	864	357	969	8	.337	.491

Javy Lopez was behind the plate for the deciding game of the only World Series title in Atlanta Braves history.

Javy Lopez
scouting reports

ATLANTA BRAVES
NO. 4 PROSPECT AFTER 1990 SEASON

While Tyler Houston's main weapon is his bat, Lopez will get a long, hard look based on his ability to catch and throw. As a 19-year-old, he has already shown a big league arm.

But Lopez has a ways to go. He has been slowed by limited English and a reluctance to admit he doesn't understand what is being said. Lopez has to make it clear that he's in charge of the game.

It is going to be a slow process with the bat. Though he hit .265 at Burlington last summer, the more telling numbers are only 14 walks in 116 games. Lopez should have average power, and has to accept that if he can just get on base—where he is not a clogger—he will be contributing enough.

ATLANTA BRAVES
NO. 6 PROSPECT AFTER 1991 SEASON

The Braves put an emphasis on drafting catchers in the last few years, but Lopez—signed as a free agent—is ahead of them all. He has more power and arm strength than any catcher in the system, including Tyler Houston, the second player overall drafted in 1989.

Lopez has size, meaning he should be durable, but has had to work on his footwork and agility. His biggest asset may be his willingness to work. He is a good listener, willing to make the adjustments instructors suggest. His improvement, particularly behind the plate, has been steady the last two years, and he's ready for Double-A.

He isn't intimidated as a hitter, but needs to cut his stroke down a bit to allow for more selectivity.

ATLANTA BRAVES
NO. 2 PROSPECT AFTER 1992 SEASON

Along the same lines as Chipper Jones, the Braves envision Lopez as an all-around talent whose value is enhanced by his position. A hard worker with enthusiasm, Lopez set out in 1992 to excel both offensively and defensively, and the returns were favorable. He's everything the Braves wanted but never got out of Tyler Houston, the No. 2 pick in the 1989 draft.

Lopez' offense still is ahead of his glove. Though his batting average last year was spectacular, he's expected to drop to the .250-.260 range and keep the power, like most catchers. Speed will not be a major asset.

Behind the plate, Lopez packs a strong arm and has improved his receiving skills. His pitch-calling has been an area of concern, but he helped Greenville to a Southern League-leading 2.62 ERA last year.

Ryan Klesko struggled in his first stint with Triple-A Richmond in 1992. That helped push the Braves to trade for Fred McGriff in 1993.

RYAN KLESKO, 1B/OF

PROPER NAME: Ryan Anthony Klesko. **BORN:** June 12, 1971 in Westminster, Calif.
HT.: 6-3. **WT.:** 220. **BATS:** L. **THROWS:** L. **SCHOOL:** Westminster (Calif.) HS.
CAREER TRANSACTIONS: Selected by Braves in fifth round of 1989 draft; signed June 18, 1989.

Klesko had to continually adapt throughout his baseball career. A high school pitcher, he became a draft prospect as a slugging first basemen. Then the Fred McGriff trade in 1993 meant Klesko had to adapt again, moving to left field because McGriff was entrenched at first base. Through it all, Klesko just kept hitting. He never ended up having the 40-plus home run season that seemed possible on his climb through the minors, but he did average nearly 30 home runs per season with the Braves.

CAREER STATISTICS

Year	Club (League)	Class	AVG	G	AB	R	H	2B	3B	HR	RBI	BB	SO	SB	OBP	SLG
1989	Braves (GCL)	R	.404	17	57	14	23	5	4	1	16	6	6	4	.453	.684
	Sumter (SAL)	A	.289	25	90	17	26	6	0	1	12	11	14	1	.363	.389
1990	Sumter (SAL)	A	.368	63	231	41	85	15	1	10	38	31	30	13	.437	.571
	Durham (CAR)	A	.274	77	292	40	80	16	1	7	47	32	53	10	.343	.408
1991	Greenville (SL)	AA	.291	126	419	64	122	22	3	14	67	75	60	14	.404	.458
1992	Richmond (IL)	AAA	.251	123	418	63	105	22	2	17	59	41	72	3	.323	.435
	Atlanta (NL)	MAJ	.000	13	14	0	0	0	0	0	1	0	5	0	.067	.000
1993	Richmond (IL)	AAA	.274	98	343	59	94	14	2	22	74	47	69	4	.361	.519
	Atlanta (NL)	MAJ	.353	22	17	3	6	1	0	2	5	3	4	0	.450	.765
1994	Atlanta (NL)	MAJ	.278	92	245	42	68	13	3	17	47	26	48	1	.344	.563
1995	Greenville (SL)	AA	.231	4	13	1	3	0	0	1	4	2	1	0	.333	.462
	Atlanta (NL)	MAJ	.310	107	329	48	102	25	2	23	70	47	72	5	.396	.608
1996	Atlanta (NL)	MAJ	.282	153	528	90	149	21	4	34	93	68	129	6	.364	.530
1997	Atlanta (NL)	MAJ	.261	143	467	67	122	23	6	24	84	48	130	4	.334	.490
1998	Atlanta (NL)	MAJ	.274	129	427	69	117	29	1	18	70	56	66	5	.359	.473
1999	Atlanta (NL)	MAJ	.297	133	404	55	120	28	2	21	80	53	69	5	.376	.532
2000	San Diego (NL)	MAJ	.283	145	494	88	140	33	2	26	92	91	81	23	.393	.516
2001	San Diego (NL)	MAJ	.286	146	538	105	154	34	6	30	113	88	89	23	.384	.539
2002	San Diego (NL)	MAJ	.300	146	540	90	162	39	1	29	95	76	86	6	.388	.537
2003	San Diego (NL)	MAJ	.252	121	397	47	100	18	0	21	67	65	83	2	.354	.456
2004	San Diego (NL)	MAJ	.291	127	402	58	117	32	2	9	66	73	67	3	.399	.448
2005	San Diego (NL)	MAJ	.248	137	443	61	110	19	1	18	58	75	80	3	.358	.418
2006	Lake Elsinore (CAL)	HiA	.273	8	22	2	6	2	0	0	1	5	5	0	.407	.364
	San Diego (NL)	MAJ	.750	6	4	0	3	1	0	0	2	2	0	0	.833	1.000
2007	San Francisco (NL)	MAJ	.260	116	362	51	94	27	3	6	44	46	68	5	.344	.401
Major League Totals			**.279**	**1736**	**5611**	**874**	**1564**	**343**	**33**	**278**	**987**	**817**	**1077**	**91**	**.370**	**.500**
Minor League Totals			**.289**	**541**	**1885**	**301**	**544**	**102**	**13**	**73**	**318**	**250**	**310**	**49**	**.372**	**.473**

Ryan Klesko ran reasonably well for a big slugger, which is why he was able to handle a move to left field.

Ryan Klesko
scouting reports

ATLANTA BRAVES
NO. 1 PROSPECT AFTER 1990 SEASON

Back in the fall of 1988, when scouts were making up their preliminary lists for the coming June draft, Klesko was considered a sure-fire first round pick as a lefthanded pitcher. By draft time though, Klesko has fallen from grace, a victim of a season-long arm injury. That, plus a scholarship offer from Arizona State University, made Klesko a major gamble.

The Braves decided to roll the dice. They drafted him in the fifth round and spent $135,000 to sign him. Even if he couldn't pitch, scouts were impressed with the way Klesko, who played first base when he wasn't on the mound, could swing the bat.

It took a year for Klesko to accept that he wasn't going to pitch. The Braves went so far as to bring him to Atlanta after instructional league in 1989 and let him meet face-to-face with team doctors who were emphatic that his elbow was not up to the demands of pitching.

Klesko's franchise-player potential has surfaced so quickly that this winter, after his first full pro season at the Class A level, Klesko earned a job in Puerto Rico. He has exceptional plate discipline, bat quickness and power. He's that rare young player who has shown the ability to pull the ball and clear fences, but also has shown the knowledge that he can't pull everything. He's willing to go to left field and strong enough to damage there.

There is a learning process going on defensively. In high school, first base merely was a spot to fill between pitching assignments. But Klesko is the type of athlete who will be adequate, at least, by the time he makes it to the big leagues. His meal ticket, though, will be the bat, not the glove.

ATLANTA BRAVES
NO. 2 PROSPECT AFTER 1991 SEASON

Klesko's final numbers were impressive, but what pleased the Braves about his 1991 season was the way he overcome an early-season struggle (11-for-58, no home runs, four RBIs in April). He also had a subpar winter in Puerto Rico, but the Braves chalked that up to a pulled muscle and the flu.

Klesko has the Kirk Gibson-type gung ho approach to the game and is a legitimate middle-of-the-lineup power hitter. Klesko has to learn patience because pitchers will not challenge him in key situations.

Klesko has above-average speed and at least early in his career will be a threat on the basepaths. His biggest challenge will be to put as much effort into improving his defense as he does his hitting.

ATLANTA BRAVES
NO. 2 PROSPECT AFTER 1992 SEASON

After being named the Southern League MVP at age 20, Klesko struggled in his first several months in Triple-A last season. But his passionate determination helped him rebound and put up respectable numbers. He moved on to the Arizona Fall League and became its top prospect.

Klesko's raw power should become his calling card in Atlanta. Scouts say he won't hit for high average or steal bases, but Klesko makes enough contact and has encouraging speed for a first baseman.

Klesko loves hitting so much, however, that his defense is not as sharp as Atlanta hoped. He'll expect to make the Braves roster out of spring training, but he'll almost definitely spend the first half of the season in Richmond.

ATLANTA BRAVES
NO. 2 PROSPECT AFTER 1993 SEASON

After two years in Triple-A, Klesko has proven he's ready for the majors. When the Braves acquired first baseman Fred McGriff, Klesko reacted by making the most of his opportunities during two brief stints in Atlanta, hitting .353 in 17 at-bats with two home runs.

Klesko was the premier power hitter in the International League in 1993. While he sometimes tries to hit the ball into the next county, Klesko makes solid contact and doesn't strike out much.

A former high school pitcher, Klesko continues to improve at first base, but still lacks fluidness around the bag. The Braves believe his superb athletic ability and good arm could enable him to become an above-average left fielder.

Whether it's left field or first base, Klesko will play somewhere in Atlanta in 1994.

MARCUS GILES, 2B

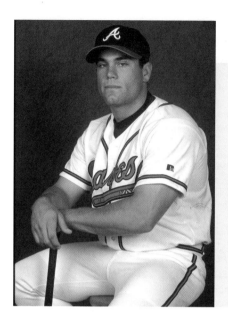

In 1998, the Braves sent shortstop Troy Cameron, the club's first-round pick in 1997, and Giles, the club's 52nd-round pick in 1996, to low Class A Macon. Talk to the two players for five minutes and it was hard not to think that Giles was the first-rounder. He carried himself with a confidence and swagger that stemmed from his desire to prove he wasn't going to be overlooked. A brutal second baseman early in his minor league career, Giles spent countless hours working with coach (and former Braves second baseman) Glenn Hubbard in the hot Georgia summer sun to turn himself into a playable second baseman. Giles had a few excellent years as Atlanta's second baseman, although his career ended soon after he reached free agency in 2006.

RANKED AS BRAVES NO. 3 PROSPECT AFTER 1999 SEASON

Giles earned his second league MVP award in as many seasons after leading the Carolina League in batting average, hits and doubles while placing second with a .513 slugging percentage and 60 extra-base hits at Class A Myrtle Beach. He is the younger brother of Pirates outfielder Brian Giles. A line-drive hitter with a quick, compact stroke, Giles creates an explosion when the ball meets his bat. While he did not hit as many home runs as he had at Class A Macon in 1998 (37), he continued to drive the ball to the gaps and drive in runs. His defense also improved; he made just seven errors. Weaknesses: Giles is not blessed with tremendous quickness or soft hands but has the work ethic necessary to overcome such shortcomings. He has cut down on his strikeouts and must continue that trend. Giles has overcome long odds to make himself a prospect. He will climb one step closer to the majors in 2000 by starting at Greenville.

RANKED AS BRAVES NO. 1 PROSPECT AFTER 2000 SEASON

The MVP in the Class A South Atlantic and Carolina leagues in 1998-99, Giles struggled early last season in Double-A before making adjustments to higher quality pitching. He found his groove in June and wound up with another productive season while playing in the Southern League all-star game, Double-A all-star game and the Futures Game. Giles is a pure offensive player. He has a short, compact stroke that packs a line-drive punch to all fields. While he continues to hear criticism about his defense, his glovework is consistent and better than advertised. Giles' range is only average, though he makes plays on every ball he reaches. His speed is also average, but his knowledge of the basepaths enabled him to steal a career-high 25 bases last season. Those who hit play in the major leagues. As long as Giles continues to produce and improve his defense, he'll join his brother Brian, an all-star outfielder with Pittsburgh, at the game's top level. Marcus' trek continues this spring in Triple-A.

MARK WOHLERS, RHP

Mark Wohlers was a fireballer in a time when a 95-plus mph fastball was a rarity. A failed starter, Wohlers quickly found new life as a reliever. He recorded the last out of Atlanta's lone World Series crown in 1995 (and saved all four of Atlanta's wins in that series). Unfortunately for Wohlers, he was also the pitcher who gave up the home run to Jim Leyritz, the key blow that shifted the momentum in the Yankees' win over the Braves in the 1996 World Series.

RANKED AS BRAVES NO. 5 PROSPECT AFTER 1990 SEASON

Two years into his pro career, Wohlers was headed nowhere. Try 41 pro pitching appearances, an 8-11, 5.33 record, 174 innings, 150 strikeouts and 137 walks. Two starts into 1990, manager Ned Yost and Sumter pitching coach Matt West decided it was time Wohlers moved to the bullpen. From pitching afraid and forcing himself to pitch from behind, Wohlers became the aggressor. He had a durable enough arm to make 51 appearances between Sumter and Double-A Greenville. Armed with a fastball that will reach 95 mph and a hard breaking ball, Wohlers found that two pitches were plenty once he became a reliever.

RANKED AS BRAVES NO. 3 PROSPECT AFTER 1991 SEASON

Wohlers' future is in his hands. He has to learn to use his slider in key situations. It was a consistent 85-mph pitch in the minors, but he became timid using it when he was called up to help the Braves in their pennant drive. When he throws the slider with conviction, hitters can't sit back on a 95-plus mph fastball that rides up and in on righthanders. After Wohlers stumbled as a starter in his first 1.5 pro seasons, the Braves decided to put him in the bullpen, mainly to help his control. His career took off. In the last two years, he has shown late-inning command. He converted 32 of 35 save chances last year.

The Braves have done an excellent job of signing and developing shortstops, but some, like Elvis Andrus, ended up spending their MLB careers elsewhere.

TOM PRIDDY

The end of one era, an attempt to start another

Coming out of the 1990s, the Atlanta Braves were quite clearly the dominant team of the National League.

Atlanta had won five NL pennants in the previous nine years, and in one of those years there was no pennant winner. Atlanta had won more than 100 games on four different occasions.

But all good things must come to an end. Since being swept by the Yankees in the 1999 World Series, Atlanta had not made it back to the World Series in the next two decades. The Braves were still one of the best teams in baseball in the first half of the 2000s. Atlanta won five straight division titles from 2000-2005, and the club won 101 games twice over that stretch.

What they just couldn't seem to do was find any playoff success. In 2000, the Braves had the second-best record in the National League, but they were outscored 24-10 in a three-game NLDS sweep by the Cardinals. In 2001, the Braves managed to win their NLDS series over the Astros, but they were beaten in five games in the NLCS by eventual champion Arizona.

The Braves lost in five games to the Giants in the 2002 NLDS. In 2003 and 2004, the Braves again were knocked out in a five-game NLDS.

In 2005, the Braves' playoff futility tormented Braves fans in innovative ways. Atlanta led Houston 6-1 heading to the bottom of the eighth inning in a winner-take-all Game 5 of the NLDS. But Lance Berkman hit a grand slam off Kyle Farnsworth in the eighth to cut the lead to one run. With two outs in the bottom of the ninth, Brad Ausmus hit another homer off Farnsworth to send the game to extra innings.

Atlanta managed to get a runner into scoring position in the 10th, 11th, 12th, 14th and 17th innings, but never managed to score. Houston did not have nearly as many scoring opportunities in extra innings, but Chris Burke hit a walk-off home run off of Joey Devine in the bottom of the 18th.

That was both the high point and the low point of the Braves organization for the remainder of the decade. It seemed to be the harbinger of more success. Instead, it proved to be the last gasp of a declining team.

That 2005 "Baby Braves" team seemed to be the start of another run. The Braves'

The Braves won the NL East title in 2005 despite breaking in 18 rookies over the course of the season. Of those rookies only Brian McCann ended up having a long career with the Braves.

stars of the 1990s had started to fade away—Tom Glavine left in free agency after the 2002 season; Greg Maddux returned to Chicago as a free agent after the 2003 season. Coming out of the 2005 season, Chipper Jones was going to be 34. Andruw Jones was getting ready for his final all-star season and would be gone from Atlanta one year later. John Smoltz was 39.

But Atlanta had managed to seemingly turn over the roster while maintaining success. Atlanta's 2005 club fielded as many as seven rookies at one time (while also sometimes fielding full lineups of homegrown players). With Brian McCann, Jeff Francouer, Kelly Johnson, Wilson Betemit, Ryan Langerhans, Adam LaRoche, Kyle Davies and Andy Marte, the Braves seemed to have the core of team with staying power. An offseason trade of prospects had brought in Tim Hudson as well.

It wasn't to be. A number of those young players (like Marte and Langerhans) proved incapable of being big league regulars. Francouer and Davies were better as rookies than they would ever be going forward. Looking back, McCann was the only one of those young stars who became a franchise cornerstone.

The talent in the farm system began to dip in the late 2000s, and trading prospects for established major leaguers hurt as well. At the trade deadline in 2007, the Braves traded Elvis Andrus, Neftali Feliz, Jarrod Saltalamacchia and Beau Jones to acquire Mark Teixeira.

The move was supposed to help the Braves climb out of second place in the NL East. Instead, they slumped in the final months of the season and finished third in the division at 84-78.

Just a year after he was acquired, Teixeira was traded away, but the return the Braves received for dealing him (Casey Kotchman and Stephen Marek) didn't come close to matching what they had given up.

That was a rare misstep. Through the Braves' run from 1991-2005 when the Braves traded prospects, they would give up less than they got back, especially when the team traded from its deep well of pitching prospects.

Over the years, the Braves traded pitching prospects Yorkis Perez, Nate Minchey, Donnie Elliott, Chris Seelbach, Rob Bell, Micah Bowie, Jason Shiell, Jimmy Osting, Luis Rivera, Jose Cappel-

Few prospect trades have come back to bite the Braves, but they would have love to kept Adam Wainwright.

lan, Merkin Valdez, Esteban Yan, Damian Moss, Dan Meyer, Adam Wainwright and Jason Schmidt in deals to add solid major league talent.

Those pitching prospects brought back key players like Fred McGriff, Marquis Grissom, Russ Ortiz, Tim Hudson and J.D. Drew.

Of all those well-regarded pitching prospects, Wainwright and Schmidt were the only deals that came back to haunt the Braves.

"He's the master," Marlins assistant GM Dan Jennings told Baseball America in 2005. "The most important thing a GM can do is evaluate your own. Atlanta has proven year after year they do it better than anyone."

Schuerholz may have won deal after deal, but he says that it was always a fair deal.

"When I make a judgement about whether we should keep this kid or whether we should trade him or not, it's because of the judgements that I rely on from my scouting and player development people," Schuerholz told Baseball America in 2005. "It's quid-pro-quo—(other teams) know their guys better, we know our guys better. So we trade fairly, honestly."

The Braves were not awful from 2006-2009. Twice they finished with a winning record. But they did finish the decade by failing to make the playoffs for four straight seasons—a drought that remains as long as any playoff drought the Braves have had since the 1980s.

But by 2009, a farm system that included Freddie Freeman, Jason Heyward, Julio Teheran and Craig Kimbrel gave some indications that the 2010s could begin better than the 2000s ended. ∎

BA Braves Top 10 Prospects year by year

2000

Player, Pos.	WAR	What happened
1. Rafael Furcal, SS	39.4	The 2000 NL Rookie of the Year, Furcal had exceptional speed and one of the best arms in the infield.
2. George Lombard, OF	-0.9	One of the top running back recruits in 1994, Lombard had short stints of six seasons in the majors.
3. Marcus Giles, 2B	16.8	Giles always had power, but he worked extremely hard to turn himself into a playable second baseman.
4. Scott Sobkowiak, RHP	0	Sobkowiak made one big league appearance in 2001, but his career ended up being shorter than expected.
5. Luis Rivera, RHP	0.4	A great pitching prospect, shoulder injuries meant his career was finished as a 22-year-old.
6. Jason Marquis, RHP	6.8	Marquis epitomized what teams look for in a durable, back-of-the-rotation starter.
7. Junior Brignac, OF	—	The Braves loved Brignac's athleticism, but he didn't hit enough. He reached Double-A for 62 games.
8. Jimmy Osting, LHP	-0.3	Osting saw his career slowed by Tommy John surgery, but he did make brief MLB appearances.
9. Pat Manning, 2B	—	A third-round pick in 1999, Manning didn't hit enough to be a big leaguer. He topped out in high Class A.
10. Brett Evert, RHP	—	Evert impressed with his excellent breaking ball, but his career topped out in Triple-A.

2001

Player, Pos.	WAR	What happened
1. Wilson Betemit, SS	2.8	Betemit ended up being a useful, versatile infielder over an 11-year MLB career.
2. Matt McClendon, RHP	—	McClendon seemed to have put everything together, but his command disappeared in 2001, ruining his career.
3. Marcus Giles, 2B	16.8	Giles always had power, but he worked extremely hard to turn himself into a playable second baseman.
4. Matt Belisle, RHP	7.3	Belisle was traded to the Reds to bring Kent Mercker back to the Braves. He went on to pitch 15 MLB seasons.
5. Jason Marquis, RHP	6.8	Marquis epitomized what teams look for in a durable, back-of-the-rotation starter.
6. William Sylvester, RHP	—	Sylvester was a generally effective minor league reliever, but he never got the call to the majors.
7. Adam Wainwright, RHP	40.2	One year of J.D. Drew and Eli Marrero was not worth dealing Wainwright.
8. Wes Helms, 3B	-1.7	Helms had a long career as a platoon corner infielder. He had 10 seasons of playing 80-plus games.
9. Christian Parra, RHP	—	As quickly as the undrafted Parra appeared on the scene, injuries just as quickly ended his career.
10. Scott Sobkowiak, RHP	0	Sobkowiak made one big league appearance in 2001, but his career ended up being shorter than expected.

2002

Player, Pos.	WAR	What happened
1. Wilson Betemit, SS	2.8	Betemit ended up being a useful, versatile infielder over an 11-year MLB career.
2. Adam Wainwright, RHP	40.2	One year of J.D. Drew and Eli Marrero was not worth dealing Wainwright.
3. Kelly Johnson, SS	17.9	Johnson was the Braves' everyday second baseman for three years before leaving in free agency.
4. Brett Evert, RHP	—	Evert impressed with his excellent breaking ball, but his career topped out in Triple-A.
5. Carlos Duran, OF	—	Duran last played in the United States in 2006, but he spent another decade playing baseball in Italy.
6. Matt Belisle, RHP	7.3	Belisle was traded to the Reds to bring Kent Mercker back to the Braves. He went on to pitch 15 MLB seasons.
7. Zach Miner, RHP	3.7	The Braves traded Miner to Detroit, where he spent four seasons as a swingman for Detroit.
8. Gonzalo Lopez, RHP	—	Injuries meant that Lopez had four seasons in a six-year stretch where he was limited to less than 15 innings.
9. Bubba Nelson, RHP	—	Nelson was impressive as a starter in his first two full pro seasons, but he didn't take to a move to the bullpen.
10. Jung Bong, LHP	-0.9	After a shoulder injury, Bung ended up returning to pitch in South Korea.

2003

Player, Pos.	WAR	What happened
1. Adam Wainwright, RHP	40.2	One year of J.D. Drew and Eli Marrero was not worth dealing Wainwright.
2. Wilson Betemit, SS	2.8	Betemit ended up being a useful, versatile infielder over an 11-year MLB career.
3. Andy Marte, 3B	-1.1	Marte's failure to find an MLB role was a shock. He tragically died in a Jan. 2017 car accident.
4. Bubba Nelson, RHP	—	Nelson was impressive as a starter in his first two full pro seasons, but he didn't take to a move to the bullpen.
5. Macay McBride, LHP	-0.2	McBride reached the majors as a 22-year-old, but he was out of baseball with an elbow injury soon afterwards.
6. Jeff Francoeur, OF	6.7	Francoeur had a truly remarkable debut. He didn't live up to those hopes, but he did play nearly 1,500 games.
7. Carlos Duran, OF	—	Duran last played in the United States in 2006, but he spent another decade playing baseball in Italy.
8. Scott Thorman, 1B	-1	A slugger from Ontario, Thorman didn't hit for enough power or average to have a lengthy MLB career.
9. Brett Evert, RHP	—	Evert impressed with his excellent breaking ball, but his career topped out in Triple-A.
10. Gonzalo Lopez, RHP	—	Injuries meant that Lopez had four seasons in a six-year stretch where he was limited to less than 15 innings.

2004

Player, Pos.	WAR	What happened
1. Andy Marte, 3B	-1.1	Marte's failure to find an MLB role was a shock. He tragically died in a Jan. 2017 car accident
2. Jeff Francoeur, OF	6.7	Francoeur had a truly remarkable debut. He didn't live up to those hopes, but he did play nearly 1,500 games.
3. Bubba Nelson, RHP	—	Nelson was impressive as a starter in his first two full pro seasons, but he didn't take to a move to the bullpen.
4. Dan Meyer, LHP	-0.9	Meyer was important because he was traded to Oakland (with two others) to acquire Tim Hudson.
5. Adam LaRoche, 1B	14.2	LaRoche had a long, 12-year MLB career as a steady, if unspectacular, first baseman with solid power.
6. Macay McBride, LHP	-0.2	McBride reached the majors as a 22-year-old, but he was out of baseball with an elbow injury soon afterwards.
7. Brian McCann, C	31.8	McCann made seven all-star appearances thanks to a very consistent bat and solid defense.
8. Kyle Davies, RHP	0	Davies never wowed, but his apparent talent kept earning him extra chances to figure it out.
9. Anthony Lerew, RHP	-1	Lerew gained five mph on his fastball in the minors, but never found MLB success. His best work came in Korea.
10. Kelly Johnson, SS	17.9	Johnson was the Braves' everyday second baseman for three years before leaving in free agency.

2005

Player, Pos.	WAR	What happened
1. Jeff Francoeur, OF	6.7	Francoeur had a truly remarkable debut. He didn't live up to those hopes, but he did play nearly 1,500 games.
2. Andy Marte, 3B	-1.1	Marte's failure to find an MLB role was a shock. He tragically died in a Jan. 2017 car accident.
3. Brian McCann, C	31.8	McCann made seven all-star appearances thanks to a very consistent bat and solid defense.
4. Kyle Davies, RHP	0	Davies never wowed, but his apparent talent kept earning him extra chances to figure it out.
5. Anthony Lerew, RHP	-1	Lerew gained five mph on his fastball in the minors, but never found MLB success. His best work came in Korea.
6. Jake Stevens, LHP	—	After an impressive MiLB start, Stevens' stuff started to back up and he never regained that early form.
7. Luis Hernandez, SS	—	Hernandez's free-swinging ways caught up to him, and the Braves let him leave as a minor league free agent.
8. Kelly Johnson, OF	17.9	Johnson was the Braves' everyday second baseman for three years before leaving in free agency.
9. Jarrod Saltalamacchia, C	5.8	The Braves had to choose between Saltalamacchia and McCann. They chose correctly.
10. Blaine Boyer, RHP	-1.8	Boyer struggled early, but he was a useful reliever later on. He played 12 seasons and made 447 appearances.

2006

Player, Pos.	WAR	What happened
1. Jarrod Saltalamacchia, C	5.8	The Braves had to choose between Saltalamacchia and McCann. They chose correctly.
2. Elvis Andrus, SS	31.7	Atlanta spent big to acquire Mark Teixeira in 2007. Andrus is the prospect they wish they hadn't dealt.
3. Yunel Escobar, SS	27	Escobar's presence helped lead to trading Andrus. Then Andrelton Simmons' arrival helped push Escobar out.
4. Anthony Lerew, RHP	-1	Lerew gained five mph on his fastball in the minors, but never found MLB success. His best work came in Korea.
5. Joey Devine, RHP	2	Devine moved quickly to the big leagues, but two Tommy John surgeries kept him from long-term success.
6. Chuck James, LHP	2.4	James had two solid years in Atlanta's rotation, but shoulder surgery knocked him out of the majors.
7. Brandon Jones, OF	-0.3	Jones didn't do enough in his one lengthy MLB stint to avoid being placed on waivers.
8. Eric Campbell, 3B	—	Campbell won the Sally League home run title, but he was suspended multiple times for disciplinary reasons.
9. Beau Jones, LHP	—	Jones' control troubles hampered his development. He was traded in the Mark Teixeira deal.
10. Matt Harrison, LHP	8.9	Another player traded in the Teixeira swap, Harrison spent eight years with the Rangers.

2007

Player, Pos.	WAR	What happened
1. Jarrod Saltalamacchia, C	5.8	The Braves had to choose between Saltalamacchia and McCann, they chose correctly.
2. Elvis Andrus, SS	31.7	Atlanta spent big to acquire Mark Teixeira in 2007. Andrus is the prospect they wish they hadn't dealt.
3. Matt Harrison, LHP	8.9	Another player traded in the Teixeira swap, Harrison spent eight years with the Rangers.
4. Brandon Jones, OF	-0.3	Jones didn't do enough in his one lengthy MLB stint to avoid being placed on waivers.
5. Van Pope, 3B	—	Pope's arm and range made him an impressive third base prospect defensively, but he didn't hit enough.
6. Eric Campbell, 3B	—	Campbell won the Sally League home run title, but he was suspended multiple times for disciplinary reasons.
7. Scott Thorman, 1B/OF	-1	A slugger from Ontario, Thorman didn't hit for enough power or average to have a lengthy MLB career.
8. Jo-Jo Reyes, LHP	-3.8	Despite some solid minor league success, Reyes could never find success in the majors (13-26, 6.06).
9. Joey Devine, RHP	2	Devine moved quickly to the big leagues, but two Tommy John surgeries kept him from long-term success.
10. Yunel Escobar, INF	27	Escobar's presence helped lead to trading Andrus. Then Andrelton Simmons' arrival helped push Escobar out.

2008

Player, Pos.	WAR	What happened
1. Jordan Schafer, OF	-2.2	Schafer had great physical tools. He could run and he has a great arm, but he didn't hit enough.
2. Jason Heyward, OF	36.9	Heyward had an amazing start to his career, but his age-20 season has been his best so far.
3. Jair Jurrjens, RHP	10.4	Jurrjens had a great start to his Braves career, but injuries led to ineffectiveness by the time he turned 26.
4. Brandon Jones, OF	-0.3	Jones didn't do enough in his one lengthy MLB stint to avoid being placed on waivers.
5. Gorkys Hernandez, OF	-1	A light-hitting but speedy defensive whiz, Hernandez managed to find a career as an backup outfielder.
6. Brent Lillibridge, SS	-0.9	Lillibridge played for six teams in six years in the majors as an up-and-down, backup infielder.
7. Cole Rohrbough, LHP	—	A high-priced draft-and-follow, Rohrbough hurt his shoulder in 2009 and never regained effectiveness.
8. Jeff Locke, LHP	-1.2	Locke was traded (with Gorkys Hernandez and Charlie Morton) to the Pirates for Nate McLouth.
9. Tommy Hanson, RHP	4.8	Outstanding as a rookie, Hanson's ERA rose in each of his five MLB seasons. He died in 2015.
10. Julio Teheran, RHP	20.2	Teheran has been a steady, reliable, mid-rotation starter for a decade. He's a two-time all-star.

2009

Player, Pos.	WAR	What happened
1. Tommy Hanson, RHP	4.8	Outstanding as a rookie, Hanson's ERA rose in each of his five MLB seasons. He died in 2015
2. Jason Heyward, OF	36.9	Heyward had an amazing start to his career, but his age-20 season has been his best so far.
3. Jordan Schafer, OF	-2.2	Schafer had great physical tools. He could run and he has a great arm, but he didn't hit enough.
4. Gorkys Hernandez, OF	-1	A light-hitting but speedy defensive whiz, Hernandez managed to find a career as an backup outfielder.
5. Freddie Freeman, 1B	37.4	The best first baseman in Atlanta Braves history, there's a solid case that he's the best in Braves history.
6. Cole Rohrbough, LHP	—	A high-priced draft-and-follow, Rohrbough hurt his shoulder in 2009 and never regained effectiveness.
7. Jeff Locke, LHP	-1.2	Locke was traded (with Gorkys Hernandez and Charlie Morton) to the Pirates for Nate McLouth.
8. Julio Teheran, RHP	20.2	Teheran has been a steady, reliable, mid-rotation starter for a decade. He's a two-time all-star.
9. Kris Medlen, RHP	8.3	Medlen handled starting and relieving in Atlanta. He was sensational in 2012 and quite good in 2013.
10. Craig Kimbrel, RHP	19.6	The best reliever of the 2010s, Kimbrel had a 1.43 ERA in five seasons with Atlanta.

jason Heyward seemed to be the Braves' next franchise cornerstone when he debuted in 2010. He ended up being traded after just five seasons in Atlanta.

SETLIFF

JASON HEYWARD, OF

BIOGRAPHY

PROPER NAME: Jason Adenolith Heyward. **BORN:** Aug. 9, 1989 in Ridgewood, N.J.
HT.: 6-5. **WT.:** 240. **BATS:** L. **THROWS:** L. **SCHOOL:** Henry County HS, McDonough, Ga.
FIRST PRO CONTRACT: Selected by Braves in first round (14th overall) of 2007 draft; signed Aug. 12, 2007.

On his rise to the majors, Freddie Freeman was supposed to be the wingman. While he was having an impressive climb through the Braves' farm system, Jason Heyward was one step ahead of him and was even more impressive. Heyward's combination of jaw-dropping power and plate discipline wowed most everyone while leaving a trail of dented cars in the parking lot of the Braves' spring training facility. With the Braves, Heyward finished second in the NL Rookie of the Year voting in 2010. In 2012, he hit 27 home runs and swiped 21 bases. and he later won two Gold Gloves while with the Braves. But his career still feels like a little bit of a disappointment considering just how impressive he was on his rise to the majors. The Braves ended up trading Heyward for a pair of pitchers one year before he hit free agency. One of them, Shelby Miller, was then traded to the D-backs in a deal that brought Dansby Swanson in return. So while Heyward is long gone from Atlanta, his legacy lives on.

CAREER STATISTICS

Year	Club (League)	Class	AVG	G	AB	R	H	2B	3B	HR	RBI	BB	SO	SB	OBP	SLG
2007	Braves (GCL)	R	.296	8	27	1	8	4	0	1	5	2	4	1	.355	.556
	Danville (APP)	R	.313	4	16	3	5	1	0	0	1	1	5	0	.353	.375
2008	Rome (SAL)	LoA	.323	120	449	88	145	27	6	11	52	49	74	15	.388	.483
	M. Beach (CAR)	HiA	.182	7	22	3	4	2	0	0	4	2	4	0	.240	.273
2009	M. Beach (CAR)	HiA	.296	49	189	34	56	12	0	10	31	21	30	4	.369	.519
	Mississippi (SL)	AA	.352	47	162	32	57	13	4	7	30	28	19	5	.446	.611
	Gwinnett (IL)	AAA	.364	3	11	3	4	0	0	0	2	2	2	1	.462	.364
2010	Atlanta (NL)	MAJ	.277	142	520	83	144	29	5	18	72	91	128	11	.393	.456
2011	Gwinnett (IL)	AAA	.167	2	6	1	1	1	0	0	0	1	1	0	.286	.333
	Atlanta (NL)	MAJ	.227	128	396	50	90	18	2	14	42	51	93	9	.319	.389
2012	Atlanta (NL)	MAJ	.269	158	587	93	158	30	6	27	82	58	152	21	.335	.479
2013	Gwinnett (IL)	AAA	.300	6	20	1	6	1	0	0	6	4	7	1	.423	.350
	Atlanta (NL)	MAJ	.254	104	382	67	97	22	1	14	38	48	73	2	.349	.427
2014	Atlanta (NL)	MAJ	.271	149	573	74	155	26	3	11	58	67	98	20	.351	.384
2015	St. Louis (NL)	MAJ	.293	154	547	79	160	33	4	13	60	56	90	23	.359	.439
2016	Chicago (NL)	MAJ	.230	142	530	61	122	27	1	7	49	54	93	11	.306	.325
2017	South Bend (MWL)	LoA	.571	3	7	2	4	0	0	0	2	1	0	0	.625	.571
	Chicago (NL)	MAJ	.259	126	432	59	112	15	4	11	59	41	67	4	.326	.389
2018	Chicago (NL)	MAJ	.270	127	440	67	119	23	4	8	57	42	60	1	.335	.395
2019	Chicago (NL)	MAJ	.256	144	504	78	129	20	4	21	62	68	106	8	.347	.437
Major League Totals			.262	1374	4911	711	1286	243	34	144	579	576	960	110	.343	.413
Minor League Totals			.319	249	909	168	290	61	10	29	133	111	146	27	.393	.504

A great glove, big power and plenty of patience

APRIL 2009

TALENT OF HEYWARD, STANTON BELIE THEIR YOUTH

by BEN BADLER

KISSIMMEE, FLA. — Jason Heyward and Mike Stanton were only 18 last season. It sure didn't seem like it, though.

No, 18-year-olds tend not to be nearly six and a half feet tall and 225 pounds, with good speed. They tend not to tear through their first full seasons in pro ball the way Stanton did from the right side of the plate and Heyward did from the left. And if they do have those attributes, they tend not to carry themselves with the soft-spoken humility that Stanton and Heyward exhibit.

The two would have plenty to brag about, if they chose to. Stanton's 2008 performance was one of the best in recent memory for a teenager in low Class A. Among teenagers with at least 250 plate appearances at that level in the last 15 years, Stanton's .992 OPS is tied for the highest. Heyward batted .323/.388/.483 with 11 home runs last season, also in the South Atlantic League, with the Braves' Rome affiliate. He then earned a promotion to high Class A Myrtle Beach for seven games in August, shortly after his 19th birthday, and seven more in the Carolina League playoffs.

"Even at an early age, when he put on a Braves uniform, he looked like he physically fit with the types of bodies that we see with major league players," Braves farm director Kurt Kemp said. "And then when you looked at all the areas of his game—his natural hitting ability, his raw power, how well he throws, how well he runs for a man of his size and the work that he does as an outfielder—there was just not anything that you didn't like about him."

Along with the Blue Jays' Travis Snider, Heyward and Stanton are two of the best corner outfield prospects in baseball. Heyward ranks fifth overall on Baseball America's Top 100 Prospects list, while Stanton is No. 16. Heyward's scouting report as an amateur beamed about five legitimate tools, with the strike-zone discipline, pitch recognition and instincts that would allow those tools to play in game action.

There was one concern, why wouldn't he swing the bat more often?

"Senior year, I did walk a good bit more than I ever have in my whole time playing baseball," Heyward said. "They definitely pitched around me a little bit. You could tell, when we were up by five or six runs, they'd put me on base. That's kind of expected in high school, but then there were teams that tried to challenge me, and that's when I tried to make them pay. It didn't happen the majority of the time, but I tried to make it happen."

Scouts tell stories of how they went in to see Heyward multiple times, only to come away without seeing him swing in a game. How can a team invest millions in a high school player when no one gets to see him hit?

"He had a lot better plate discipline than people realized," one American League scouting director said, "and people confused that with him not being aggressive. He made a fool of some people by being more disciplined than they gave him credit for."

As a senior at Henry County High in McDonough, Ga., Heyward batted .520, with 29 hits—including eight home runs—in only 50 at-bats. He was at the plate many more times, of course. His high school coach Jason Shadden estimated from his records that Heyward walked nearly 40 times his senior season and struck out only five.

"I'm friends with a lot of coaches in the county, and they would tell me before the game they're not going to throw to him," Shadden said. "As far as his approach at the plate, he's the most disciplined hitter I think I've ever seen and I've ever coached, period. I've never seen anybody who's got an eye as good as he did. He saw the ball better than anybody and he could fight any pitch off until he got the one that he wanted.

"He was so disciplined at the plate there were times that he'd let one go by and I'm like, 'Dadgum man. Come on, swing it.' You know, 3-2, he's got the count worked out, and then he makes it hurt that way too. There weren't a lot of times when he lost composure or anything like that. He knew the game, he was a smart player—he just knew the game. He knew what he needed to do, so telling him anything was just reminding him."

For many young hitters, getting pitched around so much could turn into a recipe for bad habits, swinging at pitches out of the strike zone or at least out of a player's hitting zone. It didn't seem to change Heyward.

"It's definitely tempting for any hitter who's not getting pitched to, because it's hard to get only one pitch to see a game to get a good swing off of," Heyward said. "You've got to be ready to go because at the big league level, you're not going to get a cookie every time. It's a little tempting, but I had to stay within myself, and that's what everyone wanted to see—me not getting too aggressive and staying within myself."

"Certain guys have a pretty good feel from a young age about the strike zone," Braves hitting coordinator Leon Roberts said. "They've been coached pretty good when they were young—Little League, junior high, high school, summer ball, whatever. What happens is, somebody has sort of looked after him or impressed upon him how to hit good pitches and take bad pitches, and through time he's developed a pretty good eye and a pretty good strike zone."

Heyward hit a growth spurt that made it clear he had big things ahead of him.

"Oh, my freshman year in high school," Heyward said. "When I was in eighth grade, I was 5-9. Freshman year of high school I was 6-1 and a half. So then it just took off from there. By the time I finished high school, I was 6-4. There was a little growing in there."

Heyward came into professional baseball needing little refinement. He still took those close pitches on the corners of the plate that frustrated scouts who saw him in high school. Except now, the pro scouts who came in left impressed with Heyward's ability to lay off those pitches.

"The first time I saw him was a couple years ago during instructional ball when I was a hitting coach in Triple-A," Roberts said. "I came down to help a little bit with hitting in instructional ball. I saw a big, strong physical specimen. Pretty good eye, OK swing, but a pretty good package to start with.

"Some of the strides I've seen him make is understanding how to hit, how to hit for a little bit of power, how to use the whole field, how to hit off lefthanded pitching, how to take a walk when he looks pretty dangerous with them trying to pitch around him—little things like that."

The Braves have made tweaks, but they have mostly left Heyward as is.

"We're drafted in the positions we are for a reason, and they don't try to do too much to change that," Heyward said. "But they also want to keep us going in a positive direction to keep improving. They haven't really tampered with me too much, but when I get away from what I normally do, they'll say, 'Hey, let's get back to this. Let's do this and what you're successful at.' "

His plus-plus power hasn't shown up on the stat sheet yet, but that might have more to do with his environments than his skill level. His home ballpark in Rome last year suppresses power, with an average distance down the foul lines that's longer than any other SAL park. Eight of his 11 home runs last year came on the road, and his OPS was 76 points higher on the road.

"He is just a terrific young man, first and foremost," Kemp said. "He comes from a great family and he has been from day one respectful, hard-working—all of the good qualities that you like to see in a young man, he possesses those things. He has never acted as if he was a first-round draft choice, but he works as hard as any draft choice that we have. He was a first-round draft choice, but he takes instruction as well as any player that we have." ∎

OCTOBER 2009

MINOR LEAGUE PLAYER OF THE YEAR

by MATT WINKELJOHN

ATLANTA — The parallels between players are impossible to miss, yet it doesn't take long for Braves officials to try and distance Jason Heyward from former Braves phenom Jeff Francoeur.

Braves general manager Frank Wren and farm director Kurt Kemp are comfortable with the suggestion that Heyward, who just turned 20, is on track to one day be the face of the franchise, or at least join catcher Brian McCann in sharing the role as the career of Chipper Jones winds down in Atlanta.

They just don't want to say that Heyward is following in Francoeur's footsteps—even if Francoeur blazed this very path four short years ago—lest there be some insinuation that he might follow that trail all the way off an ugly ledge like the one that came earlier this summer. That's when Francoeur, in desperate need of new scenery, was traded to the Mets.

So they speak in a respectful yet hesitant way, mindful that there is only so much they can do to manage perceptions. It's natural for people to wonder if Francoeur left behind a cautionary tale, which the Braves used to create a new template that they're applying to Heyward.

"The answer to that, I would say, is no," Kemp said. "I can't give you an example of something we would do differently. I think we have to fairly give Jason Heyward a chance to be Jason Heyward. I think he is his own person, with his own personal makeup. . . with the similarity that they're both hometown guys."

Heyward did not receive a September callup when rosters expanded, even though he may appear as ready as Francoeur was when he moved up in the middle of 2005. All Francoeur did was finish runner-up in voting for National League rookie of the year in half a season. That was Francoeur's third full professional season, however, while this is Heyward's second.

And unlike Francoeur, who struggled in his first exposure to Double-A in 2004, Heyward has thrived. In fact, he improved after moving up from high Class A Myrtle Beach to Double-A Mississippi, batting .336/.434/.605 with seven home runs there after batting .296/.369/.519 with 10 homers for the Pelicans.

Taken together—his .314/.399/.557 overall performance in his second full season, plus his ascension into the role of future franchise cornerstone—Heyward was an easy choice as Baseball America's Minor League Player of the Year, a singular distinction for a singular talent.

The comparisons are natural enough. Both players were hometown phenoms coming out of high school (Francoeur from Parkview High in the northern suburb of Lilburn, Heyward from Henry County High in McDonough, south of Atlanta). Both were drafted in the first round, both play right field and have cannon arms, and both have been beyond precocious as minor leaguers.

"I'm not sure that we can dictate or legislate (perceptions)," Wren said. "I think that's going to happen on its own. We can try to prepare Jason Heyward for what's coming. I think one of the things that we have going for us is Jason is a very level-headed kid. I think he's able to handle just about anything.

"That's not to infer that Jeff wasn't. I just don't know that we can manage it to the degree that we would like."

What it boils down to is staying power, and developing more of it. When you produce as Heyward has, even as Francoeur still can, the debate about skills seems moot.

Heyward has lightning-quick bat speed, his defense and arm strength are above-average, he runs well, and at 6-foot-4, 225 pounds he could still grow more. He's been compared to Dave Parker, Willie McCovey, Fred McGriff and . . . you get the drift.

Yet many more players have the skills to make it to the majors than have the gray matter to excel over time once there, to hold the pieces together through the swoons that are inevitable parts of the game.

On these topics, Wren, Kemp and Mississippi manager Phillip Wellman are happy to opine about Heyward. He'll get your attention with his numbers (he had hit into one double play in 182 Double-A plate appearances, and a mere 10 in 977 career minor league plate appearances). The panting commences, however, on the topic of Heyward's intangibles.

Jason Heyward didn't get to hit much in high school because pitchers pitched around him so often.

"One of the measures you have is how do they handle the failures that are part of this game because it's going to happen to everybody," Kemp said. "The physical game—playing every single night, being able to manage your body with rest, the way you eat, your conditioning.

"It's a different sport than, say, football where you pump it up once a week and then come back down and practice six days. How do you handle failure, keep it on an emotional even keel? We all know he has outstanding physical ability, but all of the other things along with it, his mental makeup, his approach, his work ethic, those peripheral things that go into his makeup are Jason's and Jason's alone."

Heyward's ability to keep himself in the moment rather than rush himself impresses many. While he is uncommonly diligent in preparation, right down to his offseason strength and hitting coaches, he takes a simple overall approach: pressure be damned.

"Mentally, for one you've got to always understand it's just a game," Heyward said. "The struggles you have, it's an opportunity to learn, make an adjustment. You take it as it comes at you. I trust my swing, my abilities, my hands. The mindset going in, the way you get more comfortable, is knowing you're going to get another opportunity."

Mississippi manager Phillip Wellman said Heyward is neither especially vocal nor timid. In a word, steady.

"We're always looking for weaknesses we can develop. In all honesty, I've spent two months looking for things we can work on, and it sounds crazy, but I can't find any," Wellman said. "That's a credit to his ability to make adjustments. He's very cerebral. He'll strike out twice on changeups, and I'll say, 'Now maybe there's something.' And the next time up, he'll hit a 2-0 changeup 500 feet.

"Playing on a team with 23-, 24- and 25-year-olds, I think he's been given that respect because of the way he handles himself, like a professional. For a kid who just turned 20, he's very mature.

"It's obvious that he's been raised in a great environment. Both parents went to Dartmouth. I have a daughter who is 20, and he doesn't have those silly tendencies. He's articulate and well mannered. The apple didn't fall far from the tree, and he's obviously got a great tree."

In spite of the surface similarities between Heyward and Francoeur, when you break it down, differences are there. The biggest by far comes in their approach at the plate. Francoeur is one of the game's great free swingers, with just 132 career walks in 2,819 plate appearances. He has struck out 503 times.

Heyward? Not so much.

In fact, scouts had difficulty pinning down his skills as a hitter when he was in high school because so many opponents pitched around him—and he rarely went fishing for balls out of the zone. For this, Braves scouting director Roy Clark will be eternally grateful, because it allowed Heyward to slip to the 14th overall pick in the 2007 draft.

Heyward's value has changed since then, but his patience has not. In fact, it has improved as he moved to Double-A. In his first 188 minor league games, Heyward walked 75 times and struck out 117. In 44 games with Mississippi, he walked 27 times and struck out 16. As pitchers get more cerebral, so does he.

"Good hitters do a good job of commanding their strike zone, swing at strikes and take the balls. He had an advanced ability, baseball maturity, strike-zone discipline," Kemp said. "I talked with him a little bit about that at Mississippi, how different pitchers were. You can see the maturity just in his answers.

"A certain number of teams that are going to see him more than once have a different plan for him. He understands he has to get good pitches to hit. He has a good hitting plan, making adjustments at-bat to at-bat."

Simplistic though it may be, the biggest difference between Francoeur and Heyward could be that Francoeur takes a football mentality to the plate: attack, attack, attack. Heyward's plan: wait, bait and bash.

No surprise.

At Parkview, Francoeur was one of the top high school football players in Georgia, signing a letter of intent to play at Clemson after helping lead his school to consecutive state titles in the big school classification.

That may have worked against him.

High school football is a very big deal in the Peach State, and because of that Francoeur drew plenty of publicity before even graduating. Hence, heightened expectations when the Braves called him up.

Not every hometown player will arrive with such a heavy weight on his shoulders.

"I think every player is different," Wren said. "Take Brian McCann (also a metro Atlanta product). He was in a different spot than Jeff Francoeur. I think part of the situation with Jeff is people had heard of him while he was playing high school football in Atlanta. Probably prior to us drafting Jason Heyward, very few fans had heard of him. One got a great deal of media coverage and one did not."

Yet if you're looking for something instructive to have come out of Francoeur's path through the Braves organization, something team officials are using to light the way for Heyward, you might be searching for a while.

"You can look at somebody like Chipper Jones, a former first-round draft choice who came in with high expectations and has carved out a very nice career," Kemp said. "He's not a hometown guy, but I'd rather look at it as a comparison of two first-rounders than two hometown guys."

There's one other notable difference between Heyward and these other players that people may be shy about pointing out: Heyward is black. Should he one day surpass the nebulous threshold that defines a franchise player for the Braves, he could be a megawatt black baseball star in one of the nation's most desirable cities for African-Americans. The

Braves haven't produced their own black star since David Justice was drafted in 1985.

One need only look at the NFL's Falcons to see how big a deal it was to have a black quarterback in Michael Vick before he got into trouble with the law. When Vick disappeared from the NFL for a couple of years, the Falcons' season-ticket base sank like a rock.

The number of African-American players in the major leagues dwindled in recent years to 8.2 percent two years ago (though it was above 10 percent last year) versus about 28 percent in 1977, when the Yankees won the World Series with a lineup that usually featured six black players.

Heyward could offer a booster shot in this regard. Yes, Heyward's agent, Victor Menocal, has given this plenty of thought.

"We definitely feel that with all respect to McCann and those guys, that Jason can be the face of that organization in the future," Menocal said. "He wants to give back to the community.

"I think with the percentage of African-Americans in the major leagues now being low, that definitely is important to Jason. Obviously being in Atlanta, I think it will help. If you look at him and you have the likes of Hank Aaron, Terry Pendleton and David Justice before him, he's the up and coming prospect."

You might expect a barely 20-year-old kid just two-plus years out of high school to stumble and stutter when asked about the prospects of being a hometown hero and franchise player, and how the juxtaposition of all that and being an African-American in Atlanta might bring pressures for which there is no training.

Heyward has thought about it. He has not dwelled upon it.

"As far as playing for the hometown, that's a privilege and something not everybody gets to do," he said. "There are some things that are going to come from a business standpoint that will make it tougher than others. But whether it's my hometown or wherever, I've got to go out and it's just baseball; it's a game. I've got to remember why I started playing the game, because I have fun.

"The stage gets bigger, more people get to watch you, or you're on TV. That stuff's all fun, but players get to go out there and have fun and represent themselves."

Wren may not want to compare Heyward to other players. He's less hesitant about the implications of having a potential black hometown superstar, even if he doesn't quite sound like he's started building a marketing plan around the idea.

"It is undeniable that we have lost a large number of African-American players to other sports," he said. "I think it helps us as a sport to have African-Americans as star players. I think that will help African-American players in the Atlanta area want to be baseball players. But I've never heard our fans talk about a player's race or ethnicity. They're just Braves, and we want to have good players."

For all the oohing and aahing over Heyward's patient, measured approach, he had an interesting answer when asked if he believes he's on track—his track.

"I didn't really have a schedule mapped out as far as what team I would be on when," he said. "I just set out to have myself ready to play the best I can in the majors in 2009. I do feel like if they say, 'Hey Jason, come up,' I've done the best I could."

Heyward has done quite well, but there is no guarantee he'll hit the big leagues this year.

Kemp said when the Braves put together Heyward's developmental plan after he signed for $1.7 million in 2007, the goal was for him to spend all or most of the 2008 season in one place rather than move him up quickly. They wanted to give him a chance to settle into a routine and formulate his own methods for dealing with the rigors of baseball as a day-in/day-out job rather than a hobby.

He was in low Class A Rome most of the '08 season, moving to Myrtle Beach only for a few games and the playoffs at the end of the summer. This season, the Braves moved him to Mississippi in July, and at some point soon—whether for a cameo in September or next year—he's certain to make the jump to Atlanta.

Kemp doesn't think the jump will faze Heyward.

"I think about that. I think the really good ones cherish that, look forward to being on the big stage," Kemp sad. "You saw the way he fit in spring training. Sometimes when we do that, guys have kind of a wild look to them for a while. Jason in spring training fit in right away.

"I think the really good ones really look forward to the challenge of facing the best, and being the best, and I see that in Jason. I think he's looking forward to the day when that happens. I don't think he's going to put any additional pressure on himself."

Wren wouldn't touch the subject of a callup, but he offered the kind of summary judgment every player would like to have on his scouting report:

"I don't think there's any doubt that he is that kind of guy. He's the kind of guy who can change a game," Wren said. "We could put him at any of the three outfield spots at the major league level, and he could play them. He has speed . . . If you watch him from first to third, even if you were a novice, you're going to be impressed.

"He has bat speed. I would venture to say there were not many guys in our camp this spring that hit the ball as hard as Jason. And he's a good baseball player. It's one of the higher compliments. It sounds simplistic, but to people in the industry it's the highest compliment. He is a good baseball player." ∎

OCTOBER 2010

HEYWARD WINS TOUGH ROOKIE OF THE YEAR RACE

by DAVID O'BRIEN

ATLANTA — Five years after their teams squared off for the Georgia Class AAAA state championship, Jason Heyward and Buster Posey found themselves on a considerably larger stage.

Heyward's Braves and Posey's Giants met in a best-of-five National League Division Series, and suddenly a lot of writers from around the country were asking the two Georgia guys about that best-of-three series in 2005.

If you happened to have been at that high school championship series, could you even have imagined you were watching two players who would finish first and second in Baseball America's Rookie of the Year voting five years later?

Could you have imagined that you were watching a level of talent that major league franchises can hope to get only once every decade, or maybe only once every generation? Because that's how special most observers believe Heyward and Posey are.

Heyward occupied right field for the Braves from Opening Day this season and hit .277/.393/.456 with 18 homers, 72 RBIs and 11 stolen bases in 142 games, playing through a thumb injury that diminished his power for about six weeks and eventually required a disabled list stint that kept him out of the All-Star Game after he had been elected as a starter.

Posey, who wasn't called up until the end of May and in fact ranked as BA's top prospect in the Triple-A Pacific Coast League this season, hit .305/.357/.505 with 18 homers and 67 RBIs in 108 games, including a ridiculous .417 with seven homers, 24 RBIs and a 1.067 OPS in July in just his second full month in the majors.

Heyward hit a tape-measure homer in his first at-bat on Opening Day, had 10 homers and 38 RBIs in his first two months before the thumb injury, and led major league rookies with 91 walks and a .393 on-base percentage that was the sixth-highest ever for a player who began a season younger than 21. His OBP and walks both ranked fourth in the NL overall. Posey, who played at Florida State after his high school career, has only three years of catching experience yet is lauded for his skills and leadership of a pitching staff that led the majors with a 3.36 ERA.

Among Braves with at least 50 at-bats with runners in scoring position, Heyward's .306 average in those situations was the team's second-best, and his .927 OPS was the team leader. Posey led the Giants with a .312 average and .923 OPS with runners in scoring position.

Both players became almost instantly beloved by their teams' fans and managers, not only for their production on the field but for the way they conducted themselves on and off it. "Young kid, 20 years old, full of energy and talent," Braves manager Bobby Cox said early in the season, citing Heyward's positive effect on clubhouse chemistry. "It really is energizing to have somebody like that for the veterans, to have someone come along and help immediately."

Giants manager Bruce Bochy, for his part, said of Posey at the end of the season: "What this kid has done for us, the way he's handled the staff, playing every day and being a catcher, I know how hard that is. It's the toughest thing in ball. Your legs are worn down and yet he was able to find a way to get through it and handle the staff, and of course, hit a home run (in a playoff-clinching victory over San Diego).

"You talk about a catcher hitting cleanup, you think of a Johnny Bench. That's who comes to mind. You just don't see many of these guys."

By the narrowest of margins, however, Baseball America selects Heyward as its Rookie of the Year for 2010, giving him the nod based on his age—he is almost two and a half years younger than Posey, even though he signed one year earlier—and the way he carried the Braves lineup for most of the season, especially when injuries struck such veterans as Chipper Jones.

This isn't the first time Heyward and Posey have gone head to head. Their schools met in the 2005 Georgia high school playoffs, with Henry County High's Heyward and Lee County High's Posey playing key roles. They both remember the confrontation, although they aren't effusive in recalling the matchup.

"He was a senior," Heyward said of their 2005 state championship series meeting, the first time he said he'd played against Posey. "It was my sophomore year. He played in East Cobb (Baseball), but I didn't play with him there. He was on an older team."

What does Heyward remember about Posey from back then? "He was a very versatile player," he said. "He pitched and he hit well. He always hit well. He was a player you had to watch out for, that you had to be careful if you were playing against him."

And that's about it. Heyward is a no-nonsense sort of guy, a rookie who's old school in believing that rookies should mostly be seen and not heard. It's one of the many traits his teammates love about him, along with his huge ability.

So Heyward doesn't go on at length with stories and anecdotes about Posey and their championship series, which, incidentally, Henry County won two games to one.

Posey's memory of Heyward: "I remember him being really big already as a sophomore," Posey told the San Francisco Chronicle.

Both rookies struggled in the final weeks of the season, Heyward batting .173 with one extra-base hit and one RBI in the Braves' final 14 games, and Posey hitting .143 in his final 11 games. However, half of Posey's six hits in that stretch were home runs, and he hit eight homers in 28 games during September and October.

"I've seen Pose a lot on video and watching games, and he's dynamite," Cox said. "The kid is going to be a great hitter; he already is. And he's got power, an arm that's like a laser going to second base, and he stepped right in down the stretch, catching a really good pitching staff with no problems.

"That says a lot about a kid that's out of south Georgia."

Cox smiled and added, "I don't know how we missed him."

The Braves are known for scouting and drafting a bevy of talented players from Georgia, but they can't draft them all. Besides, they've already got their own Georgia native behind the dish, Brian McCann.

What shouldn't be overlooked, however, is Heyward's season-long contributions with the Braves. He went just 2-for-16 in the Division Series, and got dropped to sixth in the lineup for the final game of the series, the first time he had hit lower than third in the order since the beginning of May. He batted second for most of the season (99 games) and third for 11 games.

And that alone illustrates how important Heyward was to the Braves all season. In a team that was patched together, Heyward was a constant as Atlanta returned to the playoffs for the first time since 2005. Of the nine players the Braves sent out to start Game One of the Division Series, just three—Derek Lowe, McCann and Heyward—started on Opening Day.

"I would say this season—what a starting point. What a year to build on," Heyward said. "Lot of experiences, lot of fun, a lot to take from. And I enjoyed it and most definitely don't take anything for granted, from Opening Day till now."

But even Cox, an unabashed Heyward supporter throughout his final season in the dugout, admitted it was a difficult call for Rookie of the Year.

"That's for you guys to vote on," he said. "Jason Heyward played almost every game. You have to consider his on-base percentage is almost .400, he's got a lot of timely hits, and he's a great right fielder that throws well and defends very well. And he's been there all year.

"But I can make a case for (Posey) just as well." ■

Jason Heyward always showed patience when minor league pitchers tried to pitch around him.

Jason Heyward
scouting reports

ATLANTA BRAVES
NO. 2 PROSPECT AFTER 2007 SEASON

Another high-profile Braves pick from the Atlanta area, Heyward led Henry County to its first state title as a junior and batted .520 with eight home runs in 52 at-bats as a senior. He slipped to Atlanta with the 14th pick, mostly because opponents pitched around him so much in the spring that clubs had difficulty getting a good look at him. Signed for $1.7 million, he homered in his first professional game. Heyward has the physical attributes and instincts to be a star. His raw power is off the charts and his bat speed is nearly as good. He shows impressive plate discipline and pitch recognition. He's a good baserunner and has a plus arm with good carry. Heyward just needs to fine-tune his game. His patience leads to Frank Thomas comparisons, though he could be more productive by turning up his aggressiveness. He's discovering how to use his hands to drive the ball and will improve his batting average by using the entire field. His routes and ability to move back on fly balls need work. Though only 18, Heyward looks like a man among boys. He profiles well as a right fielder and should move quickly through the system, and he will open his first full season in low Class A.

ATLANTA BRAVES
NO. 2 PROSPECT AFTER 2008 SEASON

The 14th overall pick in the 2007 draft, Heyward continues to leave many observers wondering why 13 teams passed on the five-tool outfielder. Signed for $1.7 million, he ranked as the No. 2 prospect in the low Class A South Atlantic League in 2008. He finished third in hitting (.323) and fourth in on-base percentage (.388) as one of the SAL's youngest players at age 18. Heyward is a prototypical right fielder with impressive size, athleticism and makeup. He swings a big bat from the left side, drawing comparisons to the likes of Willie McCovey, Dave Parker and Dave Winfield. Heyward has outstanding plate discipline and pitch recognition for a teenager. He has average speed and is an intelligent baserunner. Defensively, he covers a lot of ground in right field and has a plus arm with excellent carry on his throws. While there is no question he has power in his bat, Heyward went deep only 11 times in 2008. The Braves believe he'll hit more homers once he learns to use his hands more efficiently and looks for pitches to pound. He's still working on getting better jumps on balls hit over his head and improving his routes on balls hit to his right. Heyward will return to high Class A, where he ended 2008, but his mature approach and ability to make rapid adjustments soon will put him on the fast track. Atlanta's No. 3 hitter of the future could make his big league debut in 2010.

ATLANTA BRAVES
NO. 1 PROSPECT AFTER 2009 SEASON

The 14th overall pick in the 2007 draft, Heyward signed for $1.7 million and since has emerged as the top position prospect in baseball. He earned Baseball America's Minor League Player of the Year award after hitting .323/.408/.555 at three minor league stops, including a dominating performance at Double-A Mississippi. An oblique injury slowed him in early May, and he missed the Carolina League-California League All-Star game with a hip injury. Heyward recovered in time to play in the Futures Game and raised the issue about whether the Braves should call him up for the stretch drive shortly after his 20th birthday. He ranked as the No. 1 prospect in the high Class A Carolina and Double-A Southern leagues. The main reason Heyward remained on the draft board so long in 2007 centered on the limited number of times he swung the bat as a high school senior. Opponents rarely pitched to him and he refused to compromise his impressive command of the strike zone. He has continued to demonstrate uncanny patience as he has climbed the ladder in pro ball. That type of feel for the game is just one of the many intangibles Heyward brings to the field . He has a plan every time he steps in the box and makes adjustments between at-bats. Heyward has outstanding bat speed, uses the entire field well and can drive the ball to the opposite field. His short swing is a bit unorthodox, but it works and he should hit for a high average with a lot of power. Despite standing 6-foot-4, Heyward has solid-average speed. He has outstanding instincts on the basepaths and plus range in right field. His impressive body control allows him to make diving catches with relative ease, and his plus arm is one of the strongest in the minors with velocity, carry and accuracy on his throws. He also takes good routes on fly balls. Heyward briefly struggled with quality changeups when he reached Double-A but quickly adapted. Injuries are the other concern. They've limited him to just 876 pro at-bats, and he played in just 99 games in 2009 because of the oblique and hip injuries, plus a jammed heel in August. Then his Arizona Fall League stint was cut short with a hamstring strain that was also causing back inflammation. He needs to prove he's not brittle. Scouts who follow the Braves say Heyward was the best player they saw in the minor leagues last season. With the trade of former golden boy Jeff Francoeur in July and the expected free-agent departure of Garret Anderson, there are openings for Heyward to make his major league debut sooner rather than later. Atlanta wants to be patient, but he has improved every time he has been challenged at a higher level, including a stint in big league camp last spring as a non-roster invitee. Even if he opens 2010 at Triple-A Gwinnett, Heyward will be starting in Atlanta at some point during the year, and he has all the ability to emerge as one of the game's premier players .

Freddie Freeman has finished in the Top 10 in the National League for on-base percentage six times.

FREDDIE FREEMAN, 1B

BIOGRAPHY

PROPER NAME: Frederick Charles Freeman. **BORN:** September 12, 1989 in Fountain Valley, Calif.
HT: 6-5. **WT:** 220. **BATS:** L. **THROWS:** R. **SCHOOL:** El Modena HS, Orange, Calif..
FIRST PRO CONTRACT: Selected by Braves in second round of 2007 draft; signed June 10,
2007.

Because much of his success came at a time when the Braves were rebuilding, it's easy to
overlook just how impressive Freddie Freeman's career has been. Heading into the 2020s with
plenty of career left ahead of him, he already has a strong claim to being the best first baseman in Braves history. He's proven to be one of the better pure hitters in the National League
while providing the power expected from a first baseman. It's been a great career for a player
who many scouts wanted to move to the mound when he was coming out of high school.

CAREER STATISTICS

Year	Club (League)	Class	AVG	G	AB	R	H	2B	3B	HR	RBI	BB	SO	SB	OBP	SLG
2007	Braves (GCL)	R	.268	59	224	24	60	7	0	6	30	7	33	1	.295	.379
2008	Rome (SAL)	LoA	.316	130	491	70	155	33	7	18	95	46	84	5	.378	.521
2009	Myrtle Beach (CAR)	HiA	.302	70	255	43	77	19	0	6	34	26	41	1	.394	.447
	Mississippi (SL)	AA	.248	41	149	15	37	8	0	2	24	11	19	0	.308	.342
2010	Gwinnett (IL)	AAA	.319	124	461	73	147	35	2	18	87	43	84	6	.378	.521
	Atlanta (NL)	MAJ	.167	20	24	3	4	1	0	1	1	0	8	0	.167	.333
2011	Atlanta (NL)	MAJ	.282	157	571	67	161	32	0	21	76	53	142	4	.346	.448
2012	Atlanta (NL)	MAJ	.259	147	540	91	140	33	2	23	94	64	129	2	.340	.456
2013	Gwinnett (IL)	AAA	.500	3	10	3	5	2	0	0	2	1	3	0	.583	.700
	Atlanta (NL)	MAJ	.319	147	551	89	176	27	2	23	109	66	121	1	.396	.501
2014	Atlanta (NL)	MAJ	.288	162	607	93	175	43	4	18	78	90	145	3	.386	.461
2015	Braves (GCL)	R	.182	3	11	2	2	0	0	1	3	0	4	0	.182	.455
	Gwinnett (IL)	AAA	.375	2	8	0	3	1	0	0	2	2	3	0	.500	.500
	Atlanta (NL)	MAJ	.276	118	416	62	115	27	0	18	66	56	98	3	.370	.471
2016	Atlanta (NL)	MAJ	.302	158	589	102	178	43	6	34	91	89	171	6	.400	.569
2017	Gwinnett (IL)	AAA	.667	2	3	1	2	0	0	0	0	2	1	0	.800	.667
	Atlanta (NL)	MAJ	.307	117	440	84	135	35	2	28	71	65	95	8	.403	.586
2018	Atlanta (NL)	MAJ	.309	162	618	94	191	44	4	23	98	76	132	10	.388	.505
2019	Atlanta (NL)	MAJ	.294	156	589	113	173	33	2	38	120	86	125	6	.388	.550
Major League Totals			.293	1344	4945	798	1448	318	22	227	804	645	1166	43	.379	.504
Minor League Totals			.303	434	1612	231	488	105	9	51	277	138	272	13	.365	.474

MARCH 2011

FREEMAN READY TO HELP LEAD BRAVES NEXT YOUTH MOVEMENT

by BILL BALLEW

For the second time in as many seasons, Atlanta general manager Frank Wren entered spring training having penciled a rookie into the starting lineup.

What's more, Wren also opted to walk the proverbial tightrope without a net, meaning the options should Freddie Freeman falter are not considered certainties to stop a freefall at the infield's first turn.

Wren not only realizes the situation but is quite comfortable with it. After all, right fielder Jason Heyward held his own in the same situation in 2010 while earning Baseball America Rookie of the Year honors. And considering the fact that Freeman is cut from the same cloth as Heyward, the Braves' GM sees no reason why another part of the team's foundation and subtle youth movement won't be an ideal fit.

"Freddie is much like Jason in that his maturity is much greater than his experience," Wren said. "Succeeding in the major leagues is much more than having the physical talent to play the game. It's just as important to be able to handle the job from an emotional standpoint, especially when you have millions of people watching and evaluating your performance on a daily basis.

"But from everything we've seen, Freddie is capable of handling the game and the ups and downs that come with it."

Since he was drafted in the second round in 2007, the California native has also shown the consistency and ability to succeed at the game's top level when the time was deemed right. Even though he struggled during a cup of coffee with Atlanta last September by hitting .167/.333/.167, he showed at Triple-A Gwinnett that he has nothing left to prove in the minor leagues.

"There were a lot of ups and downs last season but I feel like I learned a lot," said Freeman, who hit .319/.378/.521 at Gwinnett. "I made several adjustments, particularly in terms of getting my pitch to hit. At the beginning of the year I was swinging at everything, being too aggressive. Once I settled down, everything started to happen for me."

In the process, Freeman became the first Braves' farmhand to win International League rookie of the year honors since Chipper Jones in 1993. The first baseman was a deserving recipient after leading the league with 147 hits and 240 total bases, tying for second in batting average, and placing second with 35 doubles. He also ranked fourth in slugging percentage and fifth with 55 extra-base hits.

Through his first three years in the organization, Freeman and Heyward formed the minors' best tag team while they climbed every step along the organizational ladder together. They were also roommates, which did not change in 2010. With Coolray Field in Gwinnett and Atlanta's Turner Field less than 35 miles apart, they shared an apartment, giving Freeman a first-hand look at what a first-year player experiences in the major leagues.

"We really don't talk about baseball that much," Freeman said. "When one of us was on the road and went 0-for-4, we'd call to see what was going on. The best part was hearing a few stories from Jason that only made me want to get there quicker."

While the dynamic duo was able to carpool in September, Freeman has not looked like the same player who made his major league debut last year. Though quiet as usual, the fuzzy-cheeked first baseman has displayed more confidence upon stepping in against veteran pitchers. He attacked the ball in his spring debut, resulting in three doubles in as many trips to the plate.

"He's going to hit," Jones said. "You look at his swing and his approach and you have no doubt he's going to hit."

Equally impressive is the size Freeman added during the offseason. At 6-foot-5, he has always had a significant presence—both in the batter's box and at first base—while tipping the Toledos at 225 pounds. Yet after a winter in which he hit the weight room four times a week while consuming protein shakes on a daily basis, he added 17 pounds of muscle while maintaining his solid athleticism and cat-like reactions.

"My frame is big enough to carry it," Freeman said of the added weight. "I worked on getting bigger but also on getting quicker, particularly with my fast-twitch muscles. I can tell a difference so far."

Scouts have suggested that Freeman will hit for more power as his body matures. In his three full seasons in the minors, he averaged 49.3 extra-base hits per year, including 14.7 home runs per campaign. Much like Heyward, he's a line-drive hitter who uses the entire field, and is at his best when he's hitting the ball back through the box.

Even though Freeman, 21, has averaged 80 RBIs over the past three seasons, including 87 in 2010, Atlanta manager Fredi Gonzalez does not plan to open the season with the first baseman hitting in the middle of the lineup. With the return of Jones and the arrival of second baseman Dan Uggla, Gonzalez believes the Braves can afford to bat Freeman seventh or even eighth to reduce the amount of pressure on the youngster.

Freeman isn't going to question that thought process, but he's eager to hit wherever Gonzalez puts him. And even with Eric Hinske and Joe Mather as the backups, the Braves are confident a change in plans is not in the offing.

DRAFT REPORT

June 2007

A member of both USA Baseball's youth and junior national teams, Freeman dominated for the youth team in 2005 before struggling in the World Junior Championship last fall (2-for-21) in Cuba. His stock has rebounded this spring, as he helped El Modena High to a playoff berth as both a hitter and pitcher. While his track record with Team USA and in showcases makes him a top-three rounds talent as a power hitter, scouts are increasingly intrigued with Freeman as a pitcher. Just 17, he has excellent size, and while working as El Modena's closer he has shown control of two present plus pitches: a heavy 90-93 mph fastball and a power slider. His feel for pitching and clean arm action belie his pitching inexperience—and his desire to remain a hitter. A Cal State Fullerton signee, Freeman could definitely be a two-way player if he gets to college. Teams that like his arm better may still have to give him a chance to hit first before putting him on the mound.

"I think the most impressive thing about Freddie is the way he has grown and adapted at each of the levels he has played," Braves farm director Kurt Kemp said. "Last year was a great example of that. He was the youngest player in the International League and started off all right, but he kept getting better and better as the season went on. He adapts to the challenges he faces as well as anyone you'll see. He's going to get the chance to do that in the big leagues, and we believe he'll continue to make the adjustments up there." ∎

Freddie Freeman scouting reports

ATLANTA BRAVES
NO.19 PROSPECT AFTER 2007 SEASON

The Braves' willingness to let him hit, along with a signing bonus of $409,500, contributed to Freeman's decision to bypass Cal State Fullerton and sign with Atlanta as the 78th overall pick in the 2007 draft. A former member of USA Baseball's youth and junior national teams, Freeman attracted strong interest from many teams for his abilities on the mound. He showed two plus pitches--a heavy, low-90s fastball and a hard slider--while working as a closer in high school, but Freeman always has preferred mashing the ball as opposed to throwing it. Only 17 when drafted, he has an ideal hitter's frame that projects extremely well. He has above-average power with a smooth stroke from the left side that produces hits that sound different coming off the bat. He shows a good feel for the strike zone and his hands work very well, helping to give him above-average raw power. Though not the fleetest afoot, Freeman handles first base well, displaying good footwork and excellent reactions. He also has an exceedingly strong arm for the position. His performance in spring training will determine whether he opens 2008 in low Class A or in extended spring training.

ATLANTA BRAVES
NO. 5 PROSPECT AFTER 2008 SEASON

Many scouts preferred Freeman as a power pitching prospect, but he wanted to swing the bat and the Braves were glad to oblige when they drafted him in the second round in 2007. The youngest player to sign out of the 2007 draft, he was named Braves minor league player of the year in 2008 after ranking second in the South Atlantic League in slugging (.521) and fourth in RBIs (95). Freeman is an RBI machine who relishes the opportunity to hit with runners on base. He's an aggressive hitter with a swing-first approach, yet he has good pitch recognition and doesn't chase pitches out of the zone. He drives the ball with authority with his sweet, smooth swing and should be able to produce significant home run totals at higher levels. His defense is well-above-average at first base, with some scouts comparing Freeman to Mark Grace but with more power. Freeman's approach doesn't lend itself to drawing a lot of walks. He has below-average speed, though he's by no means a baseclogger. The Braves could have moved Freeman to high Class A last season with relative ease, but they wanted to make certain he had a solid foundation of success as an 18-year-old. He'll move up to Myrtle Beach in 2009, and the Braves won't hold him back if he continues to produce.

ATLANTA BRAVES
NO.2 PROSPECT AFTER 2009 SEASON

The youngest player to sign out of the 2007 draft, Freeman continues to be Robin to Jason Heyward's Batman. He reached Double-A at age 19 last summer and hit .319/.354/.493 in his first month there before lingering soreness in his left wrist hampered his production. He missed the last two weeks, but didn't need surgery and headed to the Arizona Fall League. Freeman has been an RBI machine at every level, thriving with runners in scoring position. He drives the ball with consistency with a sweet, fluid swing, and scouts believe his doubles will become homers as he gains experience and strength. Comparisons to Keith Hernandez and Mark Grace with more power have become commonplace because of his defense, which managers rated the best among first basemen in both the Carolina and Southern leagues last season. Freeman runs well enough for a big man but never will be noted for his speed. His attacking approach at the plate doesn't lend itself to walks, but Atlanta gladly will sacrifice some on-base percentage for RBIs. The Braves will seek a stopgap solution at first base for 2010, with an eye on turning the position over to Freeman the next season. With him and Heyward, the Braves should be set at the right-side corners for the foreseeable future.

ATLANTA BRAVES
NO. 2 PROSPECT AFTER 2010 SEASON

The 78th overall pick in the 2007 draft, Freeman has been among the youngest players in every league he has played. He was the second-youngest starter in the Triple-A International League in 2010, when he was tabbed the circuit's rookie of the year. He led the IL in hits (147) and total bases (240), and managers rated him the loop's best defensive first baseman. Freeman has a smooth, aggressive swing from the left side. He possesses raw power that should generate 20-plus homers annually in the major leagues. He has good plate coverage with a patient approach that leads to consistent contact. He thrives in RBI situations and wants the bat in his hand with the game on the line. Defensively, Freeman has quick feet and above-average range at first base. He does all the little things well around the bag and he even has a cannon for an arm. Though not a blazer, he runs well for his size and shows outstanding instincts on the basepaths. Though his success was limited during his September callup, Freeman swatted his first big league homer against Roy Halladay. He may have an up-and-down 2011 season at the plate, but that roller-coaster ride should come as Atlanta's starting first baseman at age 21.

"The swing is different from Heyward's," Mississippi manager Phillip Wellman said. "They're built differently, but the thing they share is the approach at the plate, a good idea of the strike zone."

"Freddie lives to drive in runs," Rome manager Randy Ingle said. "Every time he goes up to the plate, he's looking to hit. He never looks to walk. He wants to do some damage. His pitch recognition and plate discipline are off the charts, and his production is so good because of his approach."

CraigcKimbrel walked 28 batters in 26 innings at Myrtle Beach in 2009. A year later, he was pitching in the majors.

RODGER WOOD

CRAIG KIMBREL, RHP

BIOGRAPHY

PROPER NAME: Craig Michael Kimbrel. **BORN:** May 28, 1988 in Huntsville, Ala.
HT.: 6-0. **WT.:** 210. **BATS:** R. **THROWS:** R. **SCHOOL:** Wallace State (Ala.) JC.
CAREER TRANSACTIONS: Selected by Braves in third round of 2008 draft; signed June 6, 2008.

Craig Kimbrel is the anomaly that reminds everyone in baseball that development is not always linear. In fact, sometimes it doesn't even make all that much sense. When Kimbrel was coming up through the minors, he had a big arm and almost no one squared him up. There was a legitimate concern, however, that his wildness would limit his effectiveness. Pitching for Myrtle Beach in 2009, Kimbrel once walked five batters in one inning. He walked more than 5.5 batters per nine innings for his minor league career. In the major leagues, Kimbrel soon harnessed his control while continuing to prove to be nearly unhittable. The combination made him one of the best relievers of the 2010s.

CAREER STATISTICS

Year	Club (League)	Class	W	L	ERA	G	GS	CG	SV	IP	H	R	ER	HR	BB	SO	AVG
2008	Danville (APP)	R	1	2	0.47	12	0	0	6	19	5	4	1	0	10	27	.076
	Rome (SAL)	LoA	2	0	0.71	10	0	0	4	13	6	1	1	0	4	26	.140
	Myrtle Beach (CAR)	HiA	0	0	0.00	2	0	0	0	4	5	0	0	0	1	3	.385
2009	Rome (SAL)	LoA	0	0	0.90	16	0	0	10	20	9	2	2	0	6	38	.132
	Myrtle Beach (CAR)	HiA	0	2	5.47	19	0	0	2	26	18	19	16	2	28	45	.200
	Mississippi (SL)	AA	2	1	0.77	12	0	0	6	12	3	1	1	0	7	17	.083
	Gwinnett (IL)	AAA	0	0	0.00	2	0	0	0	2	0	0	0	0	4	3	.000
2010	Gwinnett (IL)	AAA	3	2	1.62	48	0	0	23	56	28	13	10	3	35	83	.148
	Atlanta (NL)	MAJ	4	0	0.44	21	0	0	1	21	9	2	1	0	16	40	.125
2011	Atlanta (NL)	MAJ	4	3	2.10	79	0	0	46	77	48	19	18	3	32	127	.178
2012	Atlanta (NL)	MAJ	3	1	1.01	63	0	0	42	63	27	7	7	3	14	116	.126
2013	-- (WBC)	INT	0	1	4.91	4	0	0	0	4	5	2	2	0	0	3	--
	Atlanta (NL)	MAJ	4	3	1.21	68	0	0	50	67	39	10	9	4	20	98	.166
2014	Atlanta (NL)	MAJ	0	3	1.61	63	0	0	47	62	30	13	11	2	26	95	.142
2015	San Diego (NL)	MAJ	4	2	2.58	61	0	0	39	59	40	19	17	6	22	87	.185
2016	Pawtucket (IL)	AAA	0	0	0.00	1	1	0	0	1	0	0	0	0	0	0	.500
	Boston (AL)	MAJ	2	6	3.40	57	0	0	31	53	28	22	20	4	30	83	.152
2017	Boston (AL)	MAJ	5	0	1.43	67	0	0	35	69	33	11	11	6	14	126	.140
2018	Boston (AL)	MAJ	5	1	2.74	63	0	0	42	62	31	19	19	7	31	96	.146
2019	Iowa (PCL)	AAA	0	0	2.45	4	1	0	0	4	2	1	1	1	1	4	--
	Chicago (NL)	MAJ	0	1	6.86	22	0	0	12	20	21	15	15	9	10	30	--
Major League Totals			**31**	**20**	**2.09**	**564**	**0**	**0**	**345**	**552**	**306**	**137**	**128**	**44**	**215**	**898**	**.154**
Minor League Totals			**8**	**7**	**1.86**	**126**	**2**	**0**	**51**	**155**	**77**	**41**	**32**	**6**	**96**	**246**	**.146**

APRIL 2010

KIMBREL, VENTERS COULD OFFER BRAVES IMMEDIATE RELIEF

by BILL BALLEW

Outfielder Jason Heyward was without question the top story from big league camp this spring, but the 2007 first-round pick was not the only rookie in the hunt for a job at the game's top level.

The Braves entered the final two weeks giving long looks to relievers Craig Kimbrel and Jonny Venters after both put together solid showings against major league hitters.

Kimbrel, 21, impressed Atlanta manager Bobby Cox and pitching coach Roger McDowell in much the same manner he has opened eyes in the minor leagues during his first two pro seasons. A third-round pick in 2008 out of Wallace State (Ala.) CC, Kimbrel possesses a fastball that has been clocked as high as 98 mph and an above-average curveball.

Kimbrel struggled with his control early last year at high Class A Myrtle Beach but regained his rhythm at Rome before making his ascent all the way to Triple-A Gwinnett over the rest of the summer. The 5-foot-11, 200-pound righthander concluded the season with a 2.85 ERA and 18 saves in 60 innings.

"Craig has been much more consistent with his mechanics this spring, which has allowed him to have much better control and command of all his pitches," farm director Kurt Kemp said. "He's impressed our coaches with the way he's willing to consider new ideas and try different things."

Venters, 25, has been working his way up the organizational ladder since he was a draft-and-follow pick out of Indian River (Fla.) CC in 2003. The lefthander suffered a setback when he missed the 2006 season after tearing an elbow ligament that required Tommy John surgery.

Venters was a combined 8-11, 4.42 last year while making 29 starts between Double-A Mississippi and Gwinnett. According to M-Braves' pitching coach Marty Reed, Venters would have been a candidate for a 15-win season had he stayed in the Southern League. The lefthander throws an 88-94 mph fastball with a plus slider and an average curveball and changeup. His biggest challenge has involved throwing strikes and locating all of his pitches consistently. ■

Draft Report

June 2008

Craig Kimbrel leads the list of junior college players in the state. At 6 feet, Kimbrel is an undersized righty with a lightning-quick arm, producing velocity in the mid- to upper 90s. Kimbrel has worked as a starter and closer and profiles to pitch out of the bullpen at the pro level. His slider is still developing as is his command. Kimbrel has overmatched JuCo hitters this spring, and with each strong performance it became less likely he'd be following though on his commitment to Alabama.

Craig Kimbrel scouting reports

ATLANTA BRAVES
NO. 10 PROSPECT AFTER 2008 SEASON

The Braves drafted Kimbrel in the 33rd round in 2007, but he turned down a $125,000 bonus to return to Wallace State (Ala.) CC. He averaged 13.7 strikeouts per nine innings and limited batters to a .140 average as a sophomore, and the Braves signed him for $391,000 as a third-round pick. He was just as dominant in pro ball, concluding his debut with four scoreless innings in high Class A. Though he's undersized, Kimbrel has a strong frame and a lightning-quick arm. Throwing from a low three-quarters delivery, he has a fastball that resides at 92-95 mph and touches 98 with heavy sink. His heater tends to run in on righthanded hitters before exploding to the plate. He has a closer's mentality. Kimbrel needs more consistency with his control and two secondary pitches, both of which project to become average. His slider still gets slurvy and his changeup isn't reliable. Kimbrel made the best impression among Atlanta's 2008 draft class. He has the ingredients to become a major league closer.

ATLANTA BRAVES
NO. 5 PROSPECT AFTER 2009 SEASON

Kimbrel turned down $125,000 as a Braves 33rd-round pick in 2007 before signing for $391,000 as a third-rounder a year later. He overcame a slow start at high Class A Myrtle Beach--he had 18 walks and a 10.97 ERA in 11 innings--to save 18 games and rank second among minor league relievers with 15.5 strikeouts per nine innings. Kimbrel has the stuff and mentality to be a big league closer. He aggressively challenges hitters with his plus-plus fastball, which sits at 93-95 mph, touches 98 and has nasty life. He also throws an above-average breaking ball that he calls a curveball but looks more like a slider. He flashes a deceptive changeup, though he rarely used it in 2009. Kimbrel needs to pitch inside more often with his fastball. Though he showed marked improvement after April, he needs better command of his stuff. He spent most of his time in the AFL trying to hone his changeup. Kimbrel has moved quicker than expected and is Atlanta's closer of the future. More time in Triple-A would benefit him, but he could make his major league debut in the second half of 2010.

ATLANTA BRAVES
NO. 5 PROSPECT AFTER 2010 SEASON

The Braves selected 10 junior college players in the first 15 rounds of the 2008 draft, starting with Kimbrel in the third round. He signed for $391,000 after turning down $125,000 from Atlanta as a 33rd-round pick a year earlier. He ranked third in the International League with 23 saves and reached the big leagues in his second full pro season. He was dynamic during the pennant race, finishing the year with 12 scoreless big league outings while striking out 23 in 12 innings. Kimbrel has averaged 14.8 strikeouts per nine innings as a pro, thanks to his heavy fastball, which sits at 93-96 mph with excellent sink. His slurvy curveball gives him a second plus pitch to complement his heater. After rarely throwing a changeup in 2009, he worked on the pitch prior to last season and mixed it in on occasion. While moving faster than anticipated, Kimbrel has made significant strides with his command and his ability to pitch inside. Reminiscent of a righthanded Billy Wagner, he has the stuff and makeup to finish games. The Braves tried to expose Kimbrel to the job of a major league closer and Wagner's expertise without rushing him in 2010. He responded well, putting himself in position to take over as Atlanta's closer in 2011 following Wagner's retirement.

Brian McCann retired in 2019 after an excellent 15-year MLB career.

BRIAN McCANN, C

BIOGRAPHY

PROPER NAME: Brian Michael McCann. **BORN:** Feb. 20, 1984 in Athens, Ga.
HT.: 6-3. **WT.:** 225. **BATS:** L. **THROWS:** R. **SCHOOL:** Duluth (Ga.) HS.
CAREER TRANSACTIONS: Selected by Braves in second round of 2002 draft; signed July 11, 2002.

Coming into the 2002 draft, McCann was seen as a heady player who knew the game. His father was former Marshall head coach Howard McCann and his brother, Brad McCann, was also a solid prospect. McCann was viewed as a catcher who had a chance to hit and provide solid defense. He lived up to every expectation. McCann arrived in the second half of 2005 to help push the Braves to a playoff berth, then rattled off six consecutive all-star game appearances. Considering the wear and tear that comes with catching, McCann's consistency has been remarkable—he hit 20 home runs or more in nine consecutive seasons.

CAREER STATISTICS

Year	Club (League)	Class	AVG	G	AB	R	H	2B	3B	HR	RBI	BB	SO	SB	OBP	SLG
2002	Braves (GCL)	R	.220	29	100	9	22	5	0	2	11	10	22	0	.295	.330
2003	Rome (SAL)	LoA	.290	115	424	40	123	31	3	12	71	24	73	7	.329	.462
2004	Myrtle Beach (CAR)	HiA	.278	111	385	45	107	35	0	16	66	31	54	2	.337	.494
2005	Mississippi (SL)	AA	.265	48	166	27	44	13	2	6	26	25	26	2	.359	.476
	Atlanta (NL)	MAJ	.278	59	180	20	50	7	0	5	23	18	26	1	.345	.400
2006	Rome (SAL)	LoA	.286	2	7	0	2	0	0	0	0	1	1	0	.375	.286
	Atlanta (NL)	MAJ	.333	130	442	61	147	34	0	24	93	41	54	2	.388	.572
2007	Atlanta (NL)	MAJ	.270	139	504	51	136	38	0	18	92	35	74	0	.320	.452
2008	Atlanta (NL)	MAJ	.301	145	509	68	153	42	1	23	87	57	64	5	.373	.523
2009	Myrtle Beach (CAR)	HiA	.333	2	6	1	2	2	0	0	1	1	2	0	.429	.667
	Gwinnett (IL)	AAA	.333	1	3	0	1	1	0	0	1	1	0	0	.500	.667
	Atlanta (NL)	MAJ	.281	138	488	63	137	35	1	21	94	49	83	4	.349	.486
2010	Atlanta (NL)	MAJ	.269	143	479	63	129	25	0	21	77	74	98	5	.375	.453
2011	Gwinnett (IL)	AAA	.333	2	6	1	2	0	0	1	2	0	1	0	.333	.833
	Atlanta (NL)	MAJ	.270	128	466	51	126	19	0	24	71	57	89	3	.351	.466
2012	Atlanta (NL)	MAJ	.230	121	439	44	101	14	0	20	67	44	76	3	.300	.399
2013	Rome (SAL)	LoA	.357	4	14	4	5	1	0	3	7	2	2	0	.438	1.071
	Gwinnett (IL)	AAA	.333	3	9	1	3	0	0	1	2	1	1	0	.400	.667
	Atlanta (NL)	MAJ	.256	102	356	43	91	13	0	20	57	39	66	0	.336	.461
2014	New York (AL)	MAJ	.232	140	495	57	115	15	1	23	75	32	77	0	.286	.406
2015	New York (AL)	MAJ	.232	135	465	68	108	15	1	26	94	52	97	0	.320	.437
2016	New York (AL)	MAJ	.244	129	426	56	104	13	0	20	58	53	99	1	.336	.415
2017	Houston (AL)	MAJ	.241	97	349	47	84	12	1	18	62	38	58	1	.323	.436
2018	Fresno (PCL)	AAA	.143	2	7	1	1	0	0	0	0	1	2	0	.250	.143
	Corpus Christi (TL)	AA	.200	5	15	1	3	0	0	1	3	2	3	0	.294	.400
	Houston (AL)	MAJ	.212	63	189	22	40	3	0	7	23	19	40	0	.301	.339
2019	Atlanta (NL)	MAJ	.242	83	269	27	65	9	0	11	42	31	51	0	.318	.398
Major League Totals			**.262**	**1752**	**6056**	**741**	**1586**	**294**	**5**	**281**	**1015**	**639**	**1052**	**25**	**.337**	**.451**
Minor League Totals			**.276**	**324**	**1142**	**130**	**315**	**88**	**5**	**42**	**190**	**99**	**187**	**11**	**.336**	**.472**

Brian McCann left Atlanta in free agency after the 2013 season but he returned to Atlanta for his final season in 2019.

Brian McCann scouting reports

ATLANTA BRAVES
NO. 7 PROSPECT AFTER 2003 SEASON

The son of former Marshall head baseball coach Howard McCann and younger brother of Clemson third base prospect Brad McCann, Brian put together a solid first full season in pro ball. He ranked second in the organization in RBIs and fourth in batting. Drafted for his offensive potential, McCann has a pretty swing and plenty of raw power. But he's far from one-dimensional, as he's just a tick behind Brayan Pena as the top defensive catcher in the system. McCann's arm strength is good and his accuracy is improving. The Braves also love his hard-nosed attitude behind the plate. McCann has made strides with his defense, but he's not a sure thing to remain at catcher. He'll need to continue to improve his footwork and agility. He also must stay in shape in order to remain strong throughout the season. He homered just once during the last two months of the season after going deep 11 times in the first three. He has much more offensive upside than projected 2004 starter Johnny Estrada, and the Braves are thrilled with the progress McCann has shown early in his career. He'll spend 2004 in high Class A.

ATLANTA BRAVES
NO. 3 PROSPECT AFTER 2004 SEASON

Despite playing at pitcher-friendly Myrtle Beach, McCann put together one of the best all-around seasons of any catcher in the minors. A Carolina League all-star, he tied for the organization lead in doubles and set a career high for homers. Older brother Brad, a third baseman, signed with the Marlins as a 2004 sixth-round pick, and his father Howard is the former head coach at Marshall. McCann has a sweet lefthanded swing and as much raw power as anyone in the organization. He employs a disciplined approach at the plate and makes solid contact. Drafted primarily for his bat, he has dedicated himself to improving behind the plate and was named the CL's best defensive catcher. He threw out 30 percent of basestealers with his strong, accurate arm and quick release. While pitchers like throwing to McCann, he needs to hone his skills behind the plate, particularly his footwork and agility. Offensively, he could draw more walks. He's a below-average runner. He has drawn comparisons to Eddie Taubensee, but the Braves say McCann has a higher ceiling. He'll spend 2005 at the new Double-A Mississippi affiliate and could reach Atlanta by late 2006.

Rafael Furcal's speed and arm were two of the best in the game when he was in his prime.

RAFAEL FURCAL, SS

BIOGRAPHY

PROPER NAME: Rafael Antoni Furcal. **BORN:** Oct. 24, 1977 in Loma de Cabrera, D.R.
HT.: 5-8. **WT.:** 195. **BATS:** B. **THROWS:** R.
FIRST PRO CONTRACT: Signed as international free agent by Braves, Nov. 9, 1996

When the Braves signed Furcal, he played second base. It didn't take long to realize that playing a player with Furcal's railgun of an arm on that side of second base was a waste. Furcal quickly moved to shortstop, capably handling the position while wowing everyone with one of the strongest arms scouts had seen in several years. Furcal was the seven-time winner of best infield arm in Baseball America's MLB Best Tools survey. His speed also proved to be an excellent asset—he topped 20 steals in nine different MLB seasons. Furcal ended up being named the National League Rookie of the Year and Baseball America's Rookie of the Year in 2000, and he was selected to the NL All-Star team on three different ocassions.

CAREER STATISTICS

Year	Club (League)	Class	AVG	G	AB	R	H	2B	3B	HR	RBI	BB	SO	SB	OBP	SLG
1997	Braves (GCL)	R	.258	50	190	31	49	5	4	1	9	20	21	15	.335	.342
1998	Danville (APP)	R	.328	66	268	56	88	15	4	0	23	36	29	60	.412	.414
1999	Macon (SAL)	LoA	.337	83	335	73	113	15	1	1	29	41	36	73	.417	.397
	Myrtle Beach (CAR)	HiA	.293	43	184	32	54	9	3	0	12	14	42	23	.343	.375
2000	Greenville (SL)	AA	.200	3	10	1	2	0	0	1	3	1	0	0	.273	.500
	Atlanta (NL)	MAJ	.295	131	455	87	134	20	4	4	37	73	80	40	.394	.382
2001	Atlanta (NL)	MAJ	.275	79	324	39	89	19	0	4	30	24	56	22	.321	.370
2002	Atlanta (NL)	MAJ	.275	154	636	95	175	31	8	8	47	43	114	27	.323	.387
2003	Atlanta (NL)	MAJ	.292	156	664	130	194	35	10	15	61	60	76	25	.352	.443
2004	Atlanta (NL)	MAJ	.279	143	563	103	157	24	5	14	59	58	71	29	.344	.414
2005	Atlanta (NL)	MAJ	.284	154	616	100	175	31	11	12	58	62	78	46	.348	.429
2006	Los Angeles (NL)	MAJ	.300	159	654	113	196	32	9	15	63	73	98	37	.369	.445
2007	Inland Empire (CAL)	HiA	.167	2	6	0	1	0	0	0	0	2	1	1	.375	.167
	Los Angeles (NL)	MAJ	.270	138	581	87	157	23	4	6	47	55	68	25	.333	.355
2008	Las Vegas (PCL)	AAA	.333	1	3	0	1	1	0	0	1	0	0	0	.333	.667
	Los Angeles (NL)	MAJ	.357	36	143	34	51	12	2	5	16	20	17	8	.439	.573
2009	Los Angeles (NL)	MAJ	.269	150	613	92	165	28	5	9	47	61	89	12	.335	.375
2010	Inland Empire (CAL)	HiA	.000	2	4	0	0	0	0	0	0	2	2	0	.333	.000
	Albuquerque (PCL)	AAA	.600	2	5	3	3	1	1	1	4	1	0	0	.667	1.800
	Los Angeles (NL)	MAJ	.300	97	383	66	115	23	7	8	43	40	60	22	.366	.460
2011	Albuquerque (PCL)	AAA	.385	4	13	2	5	1	0	1	6	3	1	0	.500	.692
	R. Cucamonga (CAL)	HiA	.318	6	22	10	7	0	0	0	1	3	3	1	.400	.318
	Los Angeles (NL)	MAJ	.197	37	137	15	27	4	0	1	12	11	21	5	.272	.248
	St. Louis (NL)	MAJ	.255	50	196	29	50	11	0	7	16	17	18	4	.316	.418
2012	St. Louis (NL)	MAJ	.264	121	477	69	126	18	3	5	49	44	57	12	.325	.346
2013	Did not play--Injured															
2014	Jacksonville (SL)	AA	.297	10	37	5	11	2	0	0	0	3	2	4	.350	.351
	Jupiter (FSL)	HiA	.316	11	38	6	12	0	0	0	1	5	5	1	.409	.316
	Miami (NL)	MAJ	.171	9	35	4	6	0	1	0	2	2	7	0	.216	.229
	Cibaenas (DL)	WIN	.500	1	4	0	2	1	0	0	0	0	0	0	.500	.750
2015	Wilmington (CAR)	HiA	.188	4	16	2	3	1	0	0	0	1	2	0	.235	.250
	NW Arkansas (TL)	AA	.333	3	9	2	3	0	0	0	2	2	2	0	.417	.333
Major League Totals			**.281**	**1614**	**6477**	**1063**	**1817**	**311**	**69**	**113**	**587**	**643**	**910**	**314**	**.346**	**.402**
Minor League Totals			**.309**	**290**	**1140**	**223**	**352**	**50**	**13**	**5**	**91**	**134**	**146**	**178**	**.386**	**.389**

Rafael Furcal set a league record with 60 steals in the Appalachian League.

Rafael Furcal scouting reports

ATLANTA BRAVES
NO. 7 PROSPECT AFTER 1998 SEASON

Furcal has played two years in the United States and won't turn 19 until Aug. 24. He made as much progress as anyone in the organization at rookie-level Danville in 1998, earning recognition as the Appalachian League's top prospect while shattering the league's stolen-base record.

Moved from second base to shortstop in instructional league, Furcal has three plus tools and will improve a fourth once he settles in at his new position. He has outstanding speed, a strong arm, great range and excellent hitting ability. His all-around talent and instincts to play the game may be his strongest attributes. Since power is not Furcal's forte, he needs to perfect the little man's game with bunt hits and moving runners over. Furcal must improve upon his ability in taking the right angle to get around grounders at shortstop.

Atlanta has longed for an athletic, defensive-minded shortstop. Furcal is their man and figures to be a starter at Macon in 1999.

ATLANTA BRAVES
NO.1 PROSPECT AFTER 1999 SEASON

Furcal has blazed his way through the organization over the past two years. The Dominican infielder jumped on the fast track in 1998, when Appalachian League managers named him the Rookie-level league's top prospect. He batted .328-0-23 with a league-record 60 stolen bases for Danville. His efforts were even more impressive this season, when Furcal ranked as the South Atlantic League's top prospect after leading the circuit in stolen bases in just 83 games. He continued to excel in the Carolina League following a July promotion and served as a catalyst for Class A Myrtle Beach, which wound up sharing the league championship. Add in the fact that Furcal played most of the '99 season at age 18 (his birthday is in late August), and his rapid rise is nothing short of amazing.

Furcal made the move from second base to shortstop with aplomb this season. Equally productive from both sides of the plate, Furcal hits for a high average and has the tools necessary to be an outstanding major league leadoff hitter. His instincts are his most impressive trait. No minor leaguer reads a pitcher better on the basepaths, enabling Furcal to get massive jumps and lead the minors in stolen bases this year. He also always seems to be at the right spot on defense. His glove is consistent, while his range and arm strength are well above-average.

A four-tool player who lacks only power, Furcal needs to refine his skills. Already a good bunter, he will be a nightmare at the plate if he can learn to place bunts. Furcal needs to develop more patience at the plate and draw more walks, which he failed to do after his promotion to Myrtle Beach. The Braves want to see him learn to take the shortest route to ground balls instead of trusting his arm to retire hitters at first on bang-bang plays. Those improvements should happen as he continues to gain experience and face better competition.

Furcal is the next long-term answer at short for Atlanta. He will begin the 2000 campaign at Double-A Greenville, but a mid-season promotion to Triple-A Richmond is a distinct possibility.

JEFF FRANCOEUR, OF

For a while Francoeur owned Atlanta and it was easy to see why. He was a local high school star, known as much for his football exploits as his baseball career at perennial power Parkview HS in Lilburn, Ga. He moved quickly through the minors and hit .300/.336/.549 as a 21-year-old in a half season with the Braves in 2005. At that point it would have been shocking to imagine that Francoeur would be traded just four seasons later. His extreme aggressiveness at the plate became his undoing–his .300 average as a rookie was the last time he hit .300, and he finished his career with a .303 on-base percentage. Francoeur is still well liked in Atlanta and has since joined the Braves broadcast team.

RANKED ATLANTA BRAVES NO. 6 PROSPECT AFTER THE 2002 SEASON

The 23rd overall pick last June, Francoeur made a seamless transition from high school to pro ball. Francoeur impresses scouts as much with his character as he does with his tools. And he's loaded with tools, starting with 6.43-second speed in the 60-yard dash and solid baserunning instincts. He has a plus arm and the ability and instincts to play all three outfield positions. He drives the ball to all fields and makes rapid adjustments. His swing is smooth and features little wasted movement. Experience is the biggest thing lacking for Francoeur. As he focuses on baseball, he'll understand how pitchers are trying to set him up at the plate and how to read them while getting leads.

RANKED ATLANTA BRAVES NO. 1 PROSPECT AFTER THE 2004 SEASON

A two-sport standout in high school, Francoeur was a high school all-America defensive back who turned down the opportunity to play football and baseball at Clemson. Francoeur was on the verge of a promotion to Double-A Greenville last July when he squared around to bunt and the ball ricocheted off the bat up into his face, breaking his right cheekbone. Initially expected to miss the rest of the season after having surgery, Francoeur pushed himself and returned in five weeks. Francoeur is one of the purest five-tool players in the minor leagues. Scouts rave about the way he consistently gets the barrel of the bat on the ball. He uses his hands well in his swing and generates tremendous bat speed, which combined with his natural power should enable him to hit 30-plus home runs annually in the majors. Francoeur used his season at pitcher-friendly Myrtle Beach to his advantage, becoming adept at driving outside pitches the opposite way. Defensively, he made a seamless move from center field to right last year. Managers rated his arm the best among Carolina League outfielders. He has outstanding range and gets good jumps on balls. His knack for being in the right position can be attributed to his speed as well as his baseball instincts and intelligence.

KELLY JOHNSON, 2B

Drafted as a shortstop, Johnson only played 12 innings at his natural position in the major leagues, but the versatile infielder played most everywhere else. He actually arrived in Atlanta as a left fielder, filling a need. After missing the 2006 season because of an elbow injury, he returned as the Braves' everyday second baseman. He returned to the Braves twice more as a free agent and each time he was traded away to the Mets at the trade deadline.

RANKED ATLANTA BRAVES NO. 3 PROSPECT AFTER THE 2001 SEASON

Johnson made the Braves look brilliant in 2001. Little known as a supplemental first-round pick the year before, he blossomed into one of the most dangerous hitters in the South Atlantic League. Johnson ended up second in the league with a .404 on-base percentage and fourth with a .513 slugging percentage. An excellent athlete with a potent stick, Johnson hits the ball hard and has as much raw power as anyone in the organization. He also has above-average speed that enabled him to steal 25 bases. Sally League managers tabbed him as the league's best prospect, best hitter, best power hitter and most exciting player. Johnson might not blossom, though, until he finds a comfortable defensive position. He struggled at shortstop in the season's first half, making numerous careless mistakes, before showing better concentration during the last two months. Johnson tends to ride the emotional roller coaster and can be hard on himself. Scouting director Roy Clark and scout Charlie Smith simply outworked the competition in evaluating Johnson..

RANKED ATLANTA BRAVES NO. 8 PROSPECT AFTER THE 2004 SEASON

A supplemental first-round pick in 2000 who was initially a promising shortstop prospect, Johnson stalled in 2002-03 but got his career going again last season when he repeated Double-A. He also moved from shortstop to the outfield with relative ease, seeing time at all three spots and playing primarily in left field. Johnson has solid all-around tools and a hard-nosed, fearless approach. He spread his stance at the plate and regained the power he showed three years earlier. As an outfielder, he showed a plus arm along with good speed and range. Johnson is still learning to trust himself. He also has to make more consistent contact at the plate and work on the nuances of outfield play. It's easy to forget how young Johnson is. Another dash of maturity could allow him to move more quickly than he has to this point. The Braves have slated Johnson for Triple-A in 2005 and continue to count on him as an eventual contributor in the majors.

KRIS MEDLEN, RHP

Medlen's major league career was one of the odder ones for a Braves pitcher. As an undersized righthander with a dominating curveball, he was a reliever when he was drafted and he didn't make his first pro start until he reached Double-A. He arrived in Atlanta as a reliever, moved to the rotation and quickly blew out his elbow, requiring Tommy John surgery. Medlen made it back as a reliever in 2012, moved back to the rotation on July 31 and finished that season with one of the best stretches of starting pitching the Braves have ever seen. Atlanta won all 12 of his starts to finish that season as he posted a 0.97 ERA over that stretch. Unfortunately for Medlen, his elbow just couldn't seem to handle the workload, he blew his elbow again after a solid 2013 season.

RANKED ATLANTA BRAVES NO. 24 PROSPECT AFTER THE 2007 SEASON

After posting a 0.81 ERA at three stops in the lower minors, Medlen reached Double-A a little more than a year after signing as a 10th-round pick out of the 2006 draft. An aggressive pitcher with a quick and resilient arm, he doubled as a shortstop in junior college. He isn't afraid to challenge hitters with his low-90s fastball and does an excellent job of mixing his sharp curveball, which often serves as his strikeout pitch. He continues to work on his changeup, which shows promise, but he doesn't use it much out of the bullpen. While his size is less than ideal in the eyes of many scouts, Medlen pitches with great confidence and has ideal makeup for a closer. He also repeats his compact delivery well and has an easy arm action. He dominated in Hawaii Winter Baseball, striking out 27 in 14 innings, though he was shut down in November with a sore elbow. He should be healthy by spring training and could claim a role in the Atlanta bullpen in 2008.

RANKED ATLANTA BRAVES NO. 9 PROSPECT AFTER THE 2008 SEASON

After dominating as a reliever and posting a 1.17 ERA in his first two years as a pro, Medlen faced adversity for the first time in the minors at Mississippi in the opening two months of the 2008 season. He moved into the rotation and proceeded to pitch as well as any Southern League starter, going 6-5, 3.11 in 17 starts. Medlen features a 92-94 mph fastball and a plus curveball in the upper 80s. He also has a solid changeup and a slider he'll throw to give hitters another pitch to think about. The additional innings as a starter allowed him to improve his command. A converted shortstop, he's athletic and helps his cause as a hitter and fielder. Medlen is undersized, which raises questions about his durability as a starter, though his stress-free delivery and ability to throw strikes works in his favor. His command isn't as sharp as his control, and the last step in his development will be to throw more quality strikes. He could get a long look in spring training. He has the versatility to fit in as a starter, swingman or reliever depending on Atlanta's needs.

TOMMY HANSON, RHP

Sadly, Tommy Hanson's career proved to be brief, although at his peak he was exceptional. Hanson's major league career began auspiciously as the Braves released Tom Glavine to bring Hanson up. Hanson's fastball/breaking ball combo was excellent, and he was third in NL Rookie of the Year voting in 2009 despite not debuting until June. But Hanson could not sustain that success, his arm quickly betrayed him, and he last pitched in the majors in 2013, just five seasons after he debuted. He passed away in 2015. He was only 29 years old.

RANKED ATLANTA BRAVES NO. 1 PROSPECT AFTER THE 2008 SEASON

One of the team's big finds in the now-extinct draft-and-follow process, Hanson signed with the Braves for $325,000 in 2006 while turning down an opportunity to pitch at Arizona State. He made tremendous strides transforming from a thrower to a pitcher in 2007 under the tutelage of the late Bruce Dal Canton, his pitching coach at high Class A Myrtle Beach. Hanson broke out as one of the baseball's top pitching prospects in 2008. He dominated in a return to Myrtle Beach to start the season and easily handled a promotion to Double-A Mississippi, where he tossed a no-hitter with a career-best 14 strikeouts on June 25. He concluded the regular season leading the minors in opponent average (.175) and ranking second in strikeouts per nine innings (10.6) and fourth in strikeouts (163). Hanson capped his year by winning the pitching triple crown in the Arizona Fall League, going 5-0, 0.63 with 49 strikeouts in 29 innings. He also limited hitters in the offensive-oriented loop to a .105 average. After displaying a tendency to rely on his fastball early in his minor league career, Hanson has developed four quality pitches. His moving fastball resides in the low to mid-90s and explodes in on the hands of righthanders. He added a hard slider in the upper 80s midway through last season, which brought about comparisons to John Smoltz's best offering while taking Hanson's considerable potential to a higher level. His overhand 12-to-6 curveball is a plus pitch that makes his slider even more difficult for hitters to diagnose. His changeup is at least major league average and has improved impressively over the past two years. Hanson mixes his pitches well, uses both sides of the plate and does an outstanding job of altering the eye level of hitters. He hides the ball well in his delivery, making him even tougher to hit. The key to Hanson's success is working ahead in the count. While his slider has become his best pitch, he must establish his fastball command and use all of his pitches. The Braves believe Hanson is a future ace, which GM Frank Wren made clear early in the offseason when he refused to include the righthander in any trade talks, even those involving Jake Peavy.

YUNEL ESCOBAR, SS

Because he was traded midway through his fourth season with Atlanta, Escobar is remembered as much for his time with Toronto, Tampa Bay and Los Angeles as his time with the Braves. But the rare Cuban draftee did make an impact in Atlanta, serving as the club's everyday shortstop in the early part of a career that saw him rack up 1,500 hits.

DRAFT REPORT, JUNE 2005

Escobar is one of five Cuban defectors who had sought entry into the 2005 draft, ostensibly to get around the visa restrictions that were expected to hamper players from foreign countries. While the visa problems have since been remedied, Escobar and his cohorts are still in the draft, and he was rumored to be one of the players the Red Sox could take among their six selections in the first 59 picks. Scouts said Escobar stood out from the group because of his defensive polish, stature and strength. They said he has the bat speed and the strength in his hands to drive the ball from gap to gap, and they expect him to have enough of an offensive upside to go in the first five rounds pick on the strength of his bat alone. He pushes himself higher with his defensive skills, including a strong arm and plenty of range. Scouts were judging Escobar off games he was playing at Braddock High against recently released players, junior college players and other semi-pros. Escobar also will have to overcome the language and cultural obstacles that have felled other Cuban defectors.

RANKED ATLANTA BRAVES NO. 3 PROSPECT AFTER THE 2005 SEASON

Escobar was the most coveted of five Cuban defectors who entered the 2005 draft, causing teams to scramble when he declared himself eligible in mid-May. Atlanta was able to gain additional insight on him because he was a childhood friend of Braves catcher Brayan Pena. After signing for $475,000 as a second-round pick, Escobar had no problems handling low Class A. Escobar has solid all-around tools, featuring a steady glove, strong arm and a potent bat with budding power. He also has a large athletic frame that allows him to play a physical brand of baseball. He possesses strong hands and wrists as well as above-average arm strength. He made just six errors in 48 games at low Class A Rome. Escobar's range isn't remarkable. He's not as fast as most shortstops, though he has average speed and fluid actions. He's still adjusting to living in the U.S. and away from his family. Es-

cobar could quickly develop into the Braves long-term answer at shortstop, though Elvis Andrus will have something to say about that.

RANKED ATLANTA BRAVES NO. 10 PROSPECT AFTER THE 2006 SEASON

A Cuban defector who was a childhood friend of Braves catcher Brayan Pena, Escobar went in the second round after becoming draft-eligible just a month before the 2005 draft. He spent his first full season in Double-A, shifting between second base, shortstop and third base as part of a three-man infield rotation with Luis Hernandez and Martin Prado. He represented Cuba in the Futures Game last summer. Escobar has solid tools across the board. His smooth swing produces line drives from gap to gap. Though aggressive at the plate, he has good plate discipline and pitch recognition. He has consistent hands and a strong arm that's a plus at any infield position. Escobar hasn't shown the ability to drive the ball that many scouts projected before the 2005 draft. His modest range could prevent him from playing shortstop in the majors. He has just average speed and is a tick below-average for a middle infielder. A year ago, Escobar figured to be in a tight battle with Elvis Andrus as the Braves' long-term answer at shortstop. Because second baseman Marcus Giles was non-tendered, Escobar's best shot will probably come at that position or as a utilityman. He's ready for Triple-A.

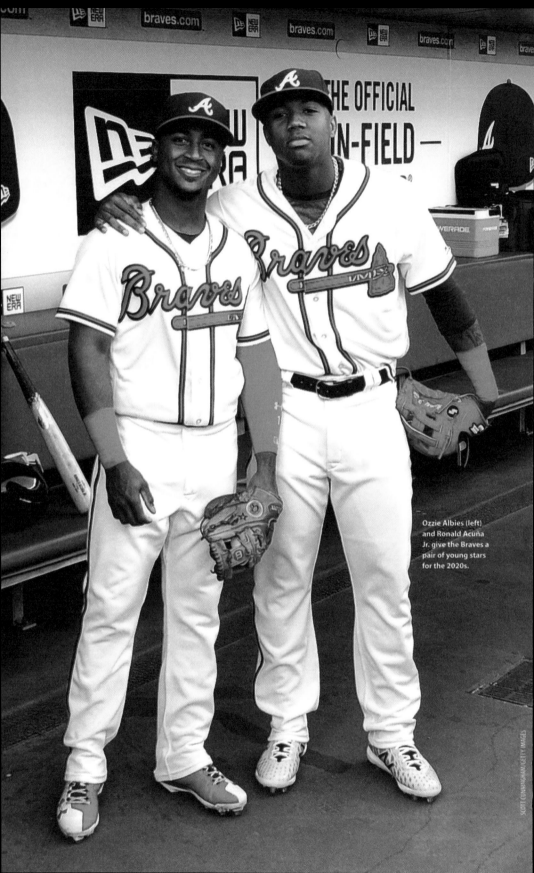

Ozzie Albies (left) and Ronald Acuña Jr. give the Braves a pair of young stars for the 2020s.

A new core to build around

L oyalty is a tricky subject in baseball.

It's a sport where players are traded, released or leave in free agency regularly. Managers and coaches are hired and fired quickly and everyone in baseball must always have an eye on their next landing spot, because few will stay in one organization for years.

Loyalty is often a fool's errand in a sport where everyone is being tested and evaluated every day.

But the Braves could say for a couple of decades that they were truly different. A whole lot of Braves stayed with the organization for decades.

The greatest player in franchise history, Hank Aaron, has been a part of the Braves organization (except as a player with the Brewers) since 1952. While many teams will keep Hall of Fame players on the staff in a minor consultant/team ambassador role, Aaron was a hands-on vice president and director of player development throughout the 1980s.

Bobby Cox was the Braves' manager from 1990 to 2011. John Schuerholz served as the team's general manager from late 1990 to 2007, and then served as the team president from 2007 to 2015.

Chipper Jones played in the Braves' organization from 1990 until he retired in 2012. Paul Snyder served in a variety of roles for the Braves for 50 years, beginning as a player in the Milwaukee Braves' system in 1957. He served two tours as scouting director and did a variety of other roles including manager, farm director and special assistant.

They weren't alone. Field staff like Rick Albert (who joined the Braves in 1972), Bobby Dews (1974), Brian Snitker (1977), Randy Ingle (1979), Bruce Dal Canton (1982) and Jim Beauchamp (1985) all logged more than 20 years with the Braves. The same could be said for scouts Stu Cann (1979), Joe Caputo (1981), Harold Cronin (1968), Ralph Garr (1986), Rod Gilbreath (1982) and Bob Wadsworth (1979).

There was a clear value placed on loyalty and retaining coaches and scouts who understood what the Braves wanted. Atlanta valued the wisdom that comes from experience.

And that makes the Braves' tumult of the 2010s somewhat surprising.

At the end of the decade, Snitker is now the Braves' big league manager. Schuerholz, Cox and Aaron are still on the masthead in consultant roles, so there are still some Braves

The Braves opened SunTrust Park in 2017, just in time for the rebuilding team to win the NL East in 2018 and 2019.

lifers with on-field and scouting experience who remain. But after having Schuerholz leading the team from 1990 to 2007, the Braves had three different regimes over the following 12 years—Frank Wren (2008-14), John Hart and John Coppolella (2015-17) and Alex Anthopoulos (2018-present).

Along the way, many of those Braves lifers either moved elsewhere, retired or were not retained.

On the field, the Braves earned wild card spots in 2010 (in Cox's final year as manager) and 2012 and won the National League East in 2013. But the farm system, long the strength of the team, thinned in the middle of the decade. In 2014 and 2015, the Braves ranked 26th and 29th on BA's farm system talent rankings. It was the first time the Braves had ranked outside of the top 15 since 1991.

The combination of a thin layer of prospect talent combined with the Braves' sub-.500 finish in 2014 cost Wren his job.

This is the Braves, so there still was some talent remaining in the farm system, but it was scattered, and the Braves draft approach had shifted.

The new regime of Hart and Coppolella intentionally made the big league club worse. The entire 2014 outfield of Justin Upton, B.J. Upton and Jason Heyward was traded away to bolster the farm system. Closer Craig Kimbrel, lefthander Alex Wood and shortstop Andrelton Simmons soon followed. The front office decided to jettison anyone who would have reached free agency before the club's next run of expected success. The goal was to build a winner by the time the Braves moved into new SunTrust Park in 2017.

Every move was done with the goal of adding significant young prospect talent that could help the team down the road. The team also adjusted its draft approach under new scouting director Brian Bridges, emphasizing upside and high school talent and increased its emphasis on the international amateur market as well.

Much like the Braves of the 1990s, the mid-2010s Braves focused on drafting and developing athletic, high-ceiling prep pitchers. While most teams have struggled to develop first-round high school pitchers, Atlanta has shown it can manage to keep young arms healthy and get them successfully to the majors.

Coppolella and Hart's approach worked.

The Braves went from 29th in the farm system rankings to No. 3 in just one year. They reached No. 1 in the farm system rankings in 2017 and 2018. Atlanta was innovative in its ways to acquire talent. The Braves effectively bought a first-round pick when the Diamondbacks traded 2015 first-rounder Touki Toussaint to the Braves because Atlanta was willing to take on the salary of injured righthander Bronson Arroyo.

Max Fried was one of a number of talented prospects the Braves acquired in trade during a mid-2010s rebuild.

At the same time, it also brought to Atlanta plenty of shame. Coppolella and Hart weren't around by the time the team started winning again because MLB found that the Braves had circumvented international signing and draft rules on multiple occasions. Coppolella was banned from baseball and multiple Braves international signees were declared free agents as punishment for the Braves' rules violations.

Anthopoulos, the club's third GM in just five seasons, inherited a team that was in many ways like the one Schuerholz took over before the 1991 season. There was significant young talent in the majors as well as a group of nearly-ready minor leaguers.

But much like Schuerholz, Anthopoulos added around the edges. Kevin Gausman and Darren O'Day were added in a low-cost deadline deal in 2018. Free agents Josh Donaldson and Dallas Keuchel were inked in 2019 and immediately became key contributors.

Anthopoulos enters the 2020s with some hurdles. Major League Baseball's penalties (including a complete ban on signing players for more than $10,000 in the 2019-20 signing period) have ensured that the Braves are lacking in young international talent at the lower levels of the farm system. That will make the Braves' attempts to bolster a playoff contender in 2020 and beyond more difficult.

But the club enters the 2020s with a young core headlined by outfielder Ronald Acuña Jr., second baseman Ozzie Albies and righthander Mike Soroka. It will be hard for Atlanta to ever match the success it had in the 1990s, but the future appears brighter than it has in years. And the approach remains the one that Schuerholz laid out years ago.

"Our farm system is the cornerstone and foundation of any success we have," Schuerholz told Baseball America in 1996. "It's absolutely essential. We have been able to utilize our developed players to help our club get better each and every year." ∎

BA Braves Top 10 Prospects year by year

2010

Player, Pos.	WAR	What happened
1. Jason Heyward, OF	36.9	Heyward had an amazing start to his career but has struggled to hit since. His defense remains excellent.
2. Freddie Freeman, 1B	37.4	The best first baseman in Atlanta Braves history, there's a solid case that he's the best in Braves all-time history.
3. Julio Teheran, RHP	20.2	Teheran has been a steady, reliable midrotation starter for a decade. He's a two-time all-star.
4. Mike Minor, LHP	17.8	The Braves' 2009 first-round pick had his best season of his career in 2019 with the Rangers.
5. Craig Kimbrel, RHP	19.6	The best reliever of the 2010s, Kimbrel had a 1.43 ERA in five seasons with Atlanta.
6. Christian Bethancourt, C	-1.1	Bethancourt had an amazing arm, but that wasn't enough to overcome his poor bat.
7. Randall Delgado, RHP	2.2	Traded away in the deal to acquire Justin Upton, Delgado had some success as a durable low-leverage reliever.
8. Zeke Spruill, RHP	-0.4	Spruill was sent to D-backs in the Upton trade. He reached Arizona briefly in 2013 and 2014.
9. Cody Johnson, OF	—	Johnson's power was legendary. So were his strikeouts. The strikeouts eventually won out.
10. Adam Milligan, OF	—	Milligan had a great 2009 season in Rome (.345/.393/.589) but wrecked his shoulder the next season.

2011

Player, Pos.	WAR	What happened
1. Julio Teheran, RHP	20.2	Teheran has been a steady, reliable midrotation starter for a decade. He's a two-time all-star.
2. Freddie Freeman, 1B	37.4	The best first baseman in Atlanta Braves history, there's a solid case that he's the best in Braves all-time history.
3. Randall Delgado, RHP	2.2	Traded away in the deal to acquire Justin Upton, Delgado had some success as a durable low-leverage reliever.
4. Mike Minor, LHP	17.8	The Braves' 2009 first-round pick had his best season of his career in 2019 with the Rangers.
5. Craig Kimbrel, RHP	19.6	The best reliever of the 2010s, Kimbrel had a 1.43 ERA in five seasons with Atlanta.
6. Matt Lipka, SS	—	Lipka was athletic and eventually had to move to the outfield. He ran well but never developed power.
7. Arodys Vizcaino, RHP	3.6	Vizcaino has always had great stuff, but going back to his minor league days, he's struggled to stay healthy.
8. Brandon Beachy, RHP	2.7	Beachy joined the Braves' rotation in 2011, but he had two Tommy John surgeries in three years after that.
9. Brett Oberholtzer, LHP	2.9	Oberholtzer never pitched for Atlanta. He did have a few good seasons with Houston and Philadelphia.
10. J.J. Hoover, RHP	1.0	Hoover had three impressive seasons as a reliever with the Reds, and a few seasons he'd like to forget.

2012

Player, Pos.	WAR	What happened
1. Julio Teheran, RHP	20.2	Teheran has been a steady, reliable mid-rotation starter for a decade. He's a two-time all-star.
2. Arodys Vizcaino, RHP	3.6	Vizcaino has always had great stuff, but going back to his minor league days, he's always struggled to stay healthy.
3. Randall Delgado, RHP	2.2	Traded away in the deal to acquire Justin Upton, Delgado had some success as a durable low-leverage reliever.
4. Andrelton Simmons, SS	36.9	A defensive whiz, Simmons won four Gold Gloves from 2013-18 and he's developed into an adequate hitter.
5. Sean Gilmartin, LHP	1.3	Control specialist was traded to Twins for catcher Ryan Doumit. His MLB career began after he was a Rule 5 pick.
6. Edward Salcedo, 3B/SS	—	Salcedo was a big-money international signing, but he struggled to hit and eventually moved to the outfield.
7. Tyler Pastornicky, SS	-1.9	Pastornicky was given the Braves backup infielder job in 2012, but he didn't hit or field all that well.
8. Christian Bethancourt, C	-1.1	Bethancourt had an amazing arm, but that wasn't enough to overcome his poor bat.
9. Zeke Spruill, RHP	-0.4	Spruill was sent to D-backs in the Upton trade. He reached Arizona briefly in 2013 and 2014.
10. Brandon Drury, 3B	0.7	Versatile infielder was traded in Upton deal. He has three different seasons with 400 or more plate appearances.

2013

Player, Pos.	WAR	What happened
1. Julio Teheran, RHP	20.2	Teheran has been a steady, reliable midrotation starter for a decade. He's a two-time all-star.
2. J.R. Graham, RHP	-0.5	Lost to the Twins in the Rule 5 draft, Graham wasn't all that effective in his 65 innings as a big league reliever.
3. Christian Bethancourt, C	-1.1	Bethancourt had an amazing arm, but that wasn't enough to overcome his poor bat.
4. Sean Gilmartin, LHP	1.3	Control specialist was traded to Twins for catcher Ryan Doumit. His MLB career began after he was a Rule 5 pick.
5. Lucas Sims, RHP	-0.1	The Braves eventually tired of waiting for Sims to develop and sent him to the Reds in 2018 Adam Duvall deal.
6. Mauricio Cabrera, RHP	0.8	Cabrera can match Aroldis Chapman for pure velocity, but control troubles have tripped him up.
7. Alex Wood, LHP	11.4	Wood's funky delivery seemed to help him baffle hitters, and despite concerns he's proven reasonably durable.
8. Evan Gattis, OF/C	8.3	Gattis was an outstanding $1,000 23rd-round signing. He has massive power.
9. Zeke Spruill, RHP	-0.4	Spruill was sent to D-backs in the Upton trade. He reached Arizona briefly in 2013 and 2014.
10. Jose Peraza, SS	0.5	Peraza was involved in two massive trades in six months before finding a spot in Cincinnati.

2014

Player, Pos.	WAR	What happened
1. Lucas Sims, RHP	-0.1	The Braves eventually tired of waiting for Sims to develop and sent him to the Reds in 2018 Adam Duvall deal.
2. Christian Bethancourt, C	-1.1	Bethancourt had an amazing arm, but that wasn't enough to overcome his poor bat.
3. J.R. Graham, RHP	-0.5	Lost to the Twins in the Rule 5 draft, Graham wasn't all that effective in his 65 innings as a big league reliever.
4. Jason Hursh, RHP	-0.2	The Braves' 2013 first-round pick has ended up being as solid org player for the Braves.
5. Mauricio Cabrera, RHP	0.8	Cabrera can match Aroldis Chapman for pure velocity, but control troubles have tripped him up.
6. Jose Peraza, SS	0.5	Peraza was involved in two massive trades in six months before finding a spot in Cincinnati.
7. David Hale, RHP	1.4	Hale has had two effective seasons in the majors so far—2014 and 2019.
8. Victor Caratini, 3B/C	0.9	Traded to the Cubs, Caratini has developed into a useful backup catcher who can also play first and third.
9. Tommy La Stella, 2B	2.6	La Stella morphed from a high-average, low-power backup into an all-star with some pop in 2019.
10. Sean Gilmartin, LHP	1.3	Control specialist was traded to Twins for catcher Ryan Doumit. His MLB career began after he was a Rule 5 pick.

2015

Player, Pos.	WAR	What happened
1. Jose Peraza, 2B	0.5	Peraza was involved in two massive trades in six months before finding a spot in Cincinnati.
2. Lucas Sims, RHP	-0.1	The Braves eventually tired of waiting for Sims to develop and sent him to the Reds in 2018 Adam Duvall deal.
3. Christian Bethancourt, C	-1.1	Bethancourt had an amazing arm, but that wasn't enough to overcome his poor bat.
4. Jason Hursh, RHP	-0.2	The Braves' 2013 first-round pick has ended up being as solid org player for the Braves.
5. Ozzie Albies, SS	9.9	Short but strong, the switch-hitting Albies has been a key part of two National League East titles so far.
6. Braxton Davidson, OF	—	Davidson could draw a walk and he had solid power potential, but he also hit .213 for his career.
7. Tyrell Jenkins, RHP	-0.4	Acquired in Jason Heyward trade, Jenkins pitched in majors in 2016 and was out of baseball in 2018.
8. Johan Camargo, SS	4	Camargo has carved a role on Braves' roster thanks to defensive versatility and solid bat.
9. Garrett Fulenchek, RHP	—	Braves' 2014 second-round pick was a bust. Traded a year later, he never played full-season ball.
10. Kyle Kubitza, 3B	-0.3	Kubitza had a shot at Angels' third base job in 2015. He hit .194/.256/.194 and was out of baseball soon after.

2016

Player, Pos.	WAR	What happened
1. Sean Newcomb, LHP	3.6	Acquired in trade that sent Andrelton Simmons to Anaheim, Newcomb has been erratic but has had moments.
2. Hector Olivera, 3B/OF	-0.2	A big-money bust signed by the Dodgers out of Cuba, Olivera was quickly traded and released after 77 pro games.
3. Kolby Allard, LHP	0.6	Allard has long shown he can set up hitters, but improved velocity helped him earn rotation spot with Texas.
4. Ozzie Albies, SS	9.9	Short but strong, the switch-hitting Albies has been a key part of two NL East titles so far.
5. Touki Toussaint, RHP	-0.2	Toussaint has a great arm, but has yet to find the consistency to make big league hitters pay.
6. Austin Riley, 3B	0.1	Riley hit 18 home runs in just 80 games with Atlanta in 2019. Improved selectivity is key to him improving.
7. Max Fried, LHP	3.8	Lefty with a very good fastball and even better curveball had a breakout season in 2019.
8. Mallex Smith, OF	6	Speedy outfielder was traded four times in four years but has gotten regular work and lead AL in steals in 2019.
9. Mike Soroka, RHP	5.5	Mature, heady Soroka went 13-4, 2.68 in 2019 his first full season in Atlanta. He also was an all-star.
10. Braxton Davidson, OF	—	Davidson could draw a walk and he had solid power potential, but he also hit .213 for his career.

2017

Player, Pos.	WAR	What happened
1. Dansby Swanson, SS	3.7	D-Backs 2016 No. 1 pick was acquired in a heist of a trade—him and Ender Inciarte for Shelby Miller.
2. Ozzie Albies, 2B/SS	9.9	Short but strong, the switch-hitting Albies has been a key part of two NL East titles so far.
3. Kolby Allard, LHP	0.6	Allard has long shown he can set up hitters, but improved velocity helped him earn rotation spot with Texas.
4. Mike Soroka, RHP	5.5	Mature, heady Soroka went 13-4, 2.68 in 2019 his first full season in Atlanta. He also was an all-star.
5. Ian Anderson, RHP	—	The third pick in the 2016 draft has lived up to every expectation so far.
6. Ronald Acuña Jr., OF	9.6	The 2017 Minor League Player of the Year has been one of best players in NL in his first two MLB seasons.
7. Kevin Maitan, SS	—	Maitan was a top international prospect, but he quickly outgrew short and was declared a free agent.
8. Sean Newcomb, LHP	3.6	Acquired in trade that sent Andrelton Simmons to Anaheim, Newcomb has been erratic but has had moments.
9. Patrick Weigel, RHP	—	Tommy John surgery has slowed his ascent but still has a chance to be a useful pitcher for Braves in the 2020s.
10. Max Fried, LHP	3.8	Lefty with a very good fastball and even better curveball had a breakout season in 2019.

2018

Player, Pos.	WAR	What happened
1. Ronald Acuña Jr., OF	9.6	The 2017 Minor League Player of the Year has been one of best players in NL in his first two MLB seasons.
2. Luiz Gohara, LHP	-0.3	Gohara had an exceptional fastball/slider combination, but shoulder injuries have dimmed his prospects.
3. Mike Soroka, RHP	5.5	Mature, heady Soroka went 13-4, 2.68 in 2019 his first full season in Atlanta. He also was an all-star.
4. Kyle Wright, RHP	-0.6	Wright has yet to have MLB success, but the Vanderbilt star has the arsenal to be a solid starter.
5. Ian Anderson, RHP	—	The third pick in the 2016 draft has lived up to every expectation so far.
6. Austin Riley, 3B	0.1	Riley hit 18 home runs in just 80 games with Atlanta in 2019. Improved selectivity is key to him improving.
7. Kolby Allard, LHP	0.6	Allard has long shown he can set up hitters, but improved velocity helped him earn rotation spot in Texas.
8. Max Fried, LHP	3.8	Lefty with a very good fastball and even better curveball had a breakout season in 2019.
9. Cristian Pache, OF	—	Pache may end up being the best defensive center fielder in the majors in the 2020s, while hitting for power.
10. Alex Jackson, C	—	Acquired in a low-cost deal, former top prospect has rebuilt his career after moving to catcher.

2019

Player, Pos.	WAR	What happened
1. Austin Riley, 3B	0.1	Riley hit 18 home runs in just 80 games with Atlanta in 2019. Improved selectivity is key to him improving.
2. Ian Anderson, RHP	—	The third pick in the 2016 draft has lived up to every expectation so far.
3. Mike Soroka, RHP	5.5	Mature, heady Soroka went 13-4, 2.68 in 2019 his first full season in Atlanta. He also was an all-star.
4. Kyle Wright, RHP	-0.6	Wright has yet to have MLB success, but the Vanderbilt star has the arsenal to be a solid starter.
5. Touki Toussaint, RHP	-0.2	Toussaint has a great arm, but has yet to find the consistency to make big league hitters pay.
6. Bryse Wilson, RHP	-0.6	A multi-sport high school star, Wilson has been a fast mover who will play entire 2020 season as a 22-year-old.
7. Drew Waters, OF	—	Waters pairs with Pache to give the Braves two of the better outfield prospects in the game heading into 2020.
8. Cristian Pache, OF	—	Pache may end up being the best defensive center fielder in the majors in the 2020s, while hitting for power.
9. William Contreras, C	—	Younger brother of Cubs catcher Willson has solid bat and athleticism behind the plate.
10. Luiz Gohara, LHP	-0.3	Gohara had an exceptional fastball/slider combination, but shoulder injuries have dimmed his prospects.

Andrelton Simmons is the only Atlanta Braves short-stop to win a Gold Glove.

ANDRELTON SIMMONS, SS

BIOGRAPHY

PROPER NAME: Andrelton Simmons. **BORN:** Sept. 4, 1989 in Mundo-Novo, Curacao.
HT.: 6-2. **WT.:** 195. **BATS:** R. **THROWS:** R. **SCHOOL:** Western Oklahoma State JC.
FIRST PRO CONTRACT: Selected by Braves in second round of 2010 draft; signed June 9, 2010.

Watch Andrelton Simmons scoop up a ball, set and throw and you can understand why scouts long dreamed of getting him onto the mound. His is one of the best arms to ever play shortstop, and it's easy to imagine a different career where he turned into a dominating closer. But Simmons was wise to rebuff all pleas to pitch because such a move would have taken from baseball one of the best defensive shortstops of the 21st century. Simmons is a remarkable defender thanks to his arm, hands and range. Much like Rafael Furcal (another Braves shortstop with a remarkable arm) the Braves decided to speed his development to fill a need at the major league level. Simmons was called up to Atlanta after just 44 games above Class A. A finger injury sent him to the injured list a little over a month later, but by then he'd already shown he was a major asset thanks to his exceptional glove. The Braves ended up trading him to the Angels after four seasons as they commenced a complete tear-down, but by then, Simmons had already made his mark as one of the best shortstops in Braves history.

CAREER STATISTICS

Year	Club (League)	Class	AVG	G	AB	R	H	2B	3B	HR	RBI	BB	SO	SB	OBP	SLG
2010	Danville (APP)	R	.276	62	239	36	66	11	1	2	26	16	14	18	.340	.356
2011	Lynchburg (CAR)	HiA	.311	131	517	69	161	35	6	1	52	29	43	26	.351	.408
2012	Mississippi (SL)	AA	.293	44	174	29	51	9	2	3	21	20	20	10	.372	.420
	Atlanta (NL)	MAJ	.289	49	166	17	48	8	2	3	19	12	21	1	.335	.416
2013	-- (WBC)	INT	.370	7	27	9	10	3	0	2	6	1	1	0	.400	.704
	Atlanta (NL)	MAJ	.248	157	606	76	150	27	6	17	59	40	55	6	.296	.396
2014	Atlanta (NL)	MAJ	.244	146	540	44	132	18	4	7	46	32	60	4	.286	.331
2015	Atlanta (NL)	MAJ	.265	147	535	60	142	23	2	4	44	39	48	5	.321	.338
2016	Inland Empire (CAL)	HiA	.333	2	6	2	2	1	0	0	0	0	0	0	.333	.500
	Salt Lake (PCL)	AAA	.333	4	18	0	6	1	0	0	5	0	2	1	.333	.389
	Los Angeles (AL)	MAJ	.281	124	448	48	126	22	2	4	44	28	38	10	.324	.366
2017	Los Angeles (AL)	MAJ	.278	158	589	77	164	38	2	14	69	47	67	19	.331	.421
2018	Los Angeles (AL)	MAJ	.292	146	554	68	162	26	5	11	75	35	44	10	.337	.417
2019	Orem (PIO)	R	.500	2	6	1	3	0	0	0	0	0	0	1	.500	.500
	Inland Empire (CAL)	HiA	.333	1	3	0	1	0	0	0	0	1	0	0	.500	.333
	Los Angeles (AL)	MAJ	.267	101	390	46	104	19	0	7	40	24	37	10	.313	.369
Major League Totals			**.269**	**1028**	**3828**	**436**	**1028**	**181**	**23**	**67**	**396**	**257**	**370**	**65**	**.316**	**.380**
Minor League Totals			**.301**	**246**	**963**	**137**	**290**	**57**	**9**	**6**	**104**	**66**	**79**	**56**	**.353**	**.398**

The Braves' wizard of ahh's

NOVEMBER 2013

FOR SIMMONS, GLOVE IS ALL YOU NEED

by DAVID O'BRIEN

On the outside of Braves shortstop Andrelton Simmons' glove are two words stitched into the leather: "God Given."

You would be hard-pressed to find anyone to dispute that notion after they've seen Simmons play a while. He does things defensively that few who've played the game have done as well.

"He's a born shortstop," said Braves first base coach Terry Pendleton, a former third baseman who compares Simmons to Ozzie Smith, the great Cardinals shortstop Pendleton played next to at the beginning of his career.

Braves teammates don't need statistics, advanced or otherwise, to inform them or help them describe the level of defense they witness nightly from Simmons.

"When you're on another team, you hear rumors about, 'Oh, this guy is really good,' " said Atlanta third baseman Chris Johnson, who played for the Astros and Diamondbacks in 2012, Simmons' rookie season. "So I was excited to see him. And he's that and more. I mean, he's the best defensive player I've ever seen. Ever. By far."

Catcher Gerald Laird, who just completed is first season with the Braves after 10 with the Rangers, Tigers and Cardinals, said of Simmons: "He is the best (shortstop) I've played with. The good ones have great body control. It's almost art, watching it. The things Simmons can do, it's special."

And Braves pitcher Kris Medlen: "Alex Gonzalez was the greatest shortstop I ever played with, and (Simmons) trumps him. It's unbelievable. I think taking away runs is just as valuable as driving them in. That's a statistical thing they're trying to (quantify) now, right?"

Even if teammates don't need anything more to convince them of Simmons' supremacy, there is data to suggest the cannon-armed Curacao native, who turned 24 in September, was indeed the best defensive player in baseball in 2013, his first full season in the majors.

Based on measuring defensive runs saved, no player has equaled Simmons since the statistic came into use in 2003. He had an estimated 41 defensive runs saved this season, six above the previous record by Yankees outfielder Brett Gardner in 2010. Simmons' 5.4 defensive win above replacement matched infielder Terry Turner's score with the 1906 Cleveland

Naps as the highest ever calculated, according to Baseball-Reference.com.

"It's definitely nice to hear," Simmons said. "And every time you hear something good—you have your own standards and then you hear people say, 'OK, you're here,' it makes you want to stay here and go higher. So that's pretty cool."

Simmons' swing and hitting approach are still works in progress, and he hit just .256/.304/.400 in 772 at-bats over two major league seasons. But his 17 homers in 2013 ranked fourth among National League shortstops, and he had a few torrid stretches in which he showed what he can do when he utilizes the swing adjustments he has worked on since spring training.

He had his best month in July, batting .289 with three triples, five homers, 17 RBIs and two strikeouts in 108 at-bats.

"He's trying to get better all the time," Braves assistant hitting coach Scott Fletcher said. "Sometimes it just takes time. But his eye-hand coordination is so good that he hits what he swings at so much and can still do a lot of things (on offense). And as he continues, you're going to see better and better things from him."

Simmons intends to add 15 pounds of muscle this winter, which he thinks will help him stay strong through the long season. He also believes he can get even better on defense.

"You can always get better at making decisions," he said. "Like when not to throw a ball, when to throw or go for a double play when the ball's not really in a place for a double play. Sometimes I'm too aggressive. I'm still trying to find that spot where if I'm risking something, the reward is worth it."

He has the physical tools of an elite infielder—great range and hand-eye coordination, fluid footwork and an arm that might be the strongest of any major league position player. So strong, it allows Simmons to position himself deeper than most shortstops.

"I tell people, 'If Ozzie Smith had his arm, oh my God,' " Pendleton said. "Ozzie played years with a torn rotator cuff. He never had that type of arm on him. It makes a difference."

Dodgers manager Don Mattingly was asked about the Braves shortstop during this year's NL Division Series against Atlanta.

Draft Report

June 2010

Like Connors State outfielder Marcus Knecht, Simmons is an Oklahoma junior college player who went from obscurity to scouts' must-see lists. Simmons turned down small bonus offers to sign out of Curacao at age 16, and that would have spelled the end of any professional baseball hopes if Western Oklahoma State coach Kurt Russell hadn't seen him on a Caribbean scouting trip. Simmons is the best defensive shortstop in the draft, an athletic 6-foot-1, 180-pounder with a cannon for an arm and plus actions and instincts. In fact, some teams might be more tempted to draft him as a pitcher, because he has run his fastball up to 95 mph and flashed a mid-80s slider in limited action. That decision became even more difficult when he missed a month with a broken toe, though he returned to help the Pioneers finish third at the Division II Junior College World Series. Simmons' righthanded swing is long, but he makes enough contact and has pop to go with his average speed. He might not provide a huge impact with his bat, but he should hit more than enough to make keeping his glove in the lineup worthwhile. Simmons is only a freshman, but he'll turn 21 in September and needs to start his pro career.

"(Simmons) is young, tremendous—some of the plays (he) makes are off the charts," Mattingly said.

There's an intangible that separates most great defenders from the rest: instincts. Marvelous instincts.

Like the last Braves defender of his ilk, center fielder Andruw Jones, Simmons has an uncanny ability to sense where a ball will be before it's hit there.

His talent may be "God given," as it says on his glove, but Simmons also is a notoriously hard worker. So much that Pendleton and other coaches sometimes shut him down, tell him to leave the batting cage or stop hitting him ground balls before games. Pendleton said if they don't, Simmons will keep working past the point of diminishing return, until he's exhausted.

Simmons has churned out a lengthy catalog of mind-blowing plays, making him a fixture on highlight segments. But big leaguers will tell you the foundation for an elite defensive player is first making the routine plays. Simmons does.

"You know he's going to make good throws; you know he's going to make good decisions," Braves second baseman Dan Uggla said. "And he's very accurate as well. He's a fun, fun person to play next to . . .

"The thing about Andrelton, he's not a flashy shortstop. You don't see the wristbands, you don't see any kind of flair or anything like that. He's just, like, 'Give me the glove and I'll make every play.' "

He makes the routine plays, and as Medlen said, "He makes the spectacular plays look routine. It's like, 'Did you just see that play?' He made that look really easy when it shouldn't have been that easy. I think people are starting to take notice. You can see in other dugouts, when he makes a play it's like, 'Whew, (expletive).' It makes you excited. It makes you go, 'Hit it to him.' "

Medlen said the ball makes a different sound when Simmons throws it, and Johnson agreed.

"Oh, yeah, you can hear it when he releases it," Johnson said. "It's kind of got that (pfft sound). It just, like, flicks out of his hand.

"It's pretty cool because usually when people hit a ball in that hole (between third and short) they're like, 'I'm going to beat this one out.' But we know you're not. You may think you are, but we know you're not."

Although the accuracy of fielding statistics frequently is disputed, in the case of Simmons, the defensive runs saved ranking matches the opinion of those who watch him play daily and compare him with the best they've seen. Pendleton came up in the Cardinals system and played from 1984-90 alongside Smith, a.k.a. "The Wizard of Oz."

He sees a lot of Smith in Simmons.

"They can change a game with their glove," Pendleton said. "There are other shortstops who can do that, but their instincts, and the way (Smith and Simmons) go about doing things and the way they think the game—they'll do things instinctively that others won't. But I keep reiterating to everybody, this kid has a year in the big leagues, and Ozzie did it for 20."

Pendleton is old-school that way, careful not to go overboard with praise for such a young player. But when it comes to Simmons, Pendleton goes as far as he'll ever go in lauding such a young player.

"Just the little things he does," Pendleton said. "And some of the big things that look so little to him, but to us who've played defense out there and know how tough a ball can be, we'll stop and look at each other because it's like, 'No way he just did that and made it look that easy.' But he does things like that.

"That's the kind of things Ozzie did. Made 'em look easy." ■

Andrelton Simmons scouting reports

ATLANTA BRAVES
NO. 15 PROSPECT AFTER 2010 SEASON

Simmons turned down several small offers from pro teams when he was 16 and growing up in Curacao, and it appeared his days on the diamond were numbered until Western Oklahoma State JC head coach Kurt Russell saw him during a Caribbean scouting trip. As a 20-year-old freshman in 2010, Simmons generated immediate scouting buzz despite missing a month with a broken toe. In 38 games, he hit a team-high .472 with seven homers, 40 RBIs and 15 stolen bases, and he also pitched 20 innings to help the Pioneers to third place in the Division II Junior College World Series. The best defensive player available in the 2010 draft, Simmons went in the second round and signed for $522,000. He has athletic actions, excellent range, soft and quick hands and an incredible feel for the position. His best tool is his arm, which has delivered fastballs clocked as high as 98 mph. While the Braves considered putting him on the mound, he wants to play shortstop and they fell in love with his defense after watching him in his pro debut. The question mark is Simmons' bat. He has some pop and is able to drive the ball, but his swing is long and he'll have to work on his approach to succeed against more advanced pitching. He runs well and has good instincts on the basepaths. Simmons will remain an everyday player for the time being. Given his age and experience, he could open 2011 with Atlanta's new high Class A Lynchburg affiliate.

ATLANTA BRAVES
NO. 4 PROSPECT AFTER 2011 SEASON

Western Oklahoma State JC head coach Kurt Russell discovered Simmons in Curacao, and several clubs were interested in him as a pitcher after seeing his fastball hit 98 mph in his lone junior college season. Atlanta granted his wish to play shortstop, and he responded by winning the Carolina League batting title (.311) in 2011. Managers rated him as the circuit's top defensive shortstop, best infield arm and most exciting player. Simmons is a premier defender with a cannon for an arm and soft, quick hands. He covers lots of real estate with his quickness, ability to charge the ball and feel for the position. He committed careless errors by trying to make every play early in 2011 but improved in that regard. An aggressive hitter, Simmons knows the strike zone but doesn't walk much. He has bat speed and can turn on fastballs, but he won't have more than gap power. An average runner, he needs to improve his reads and jumps after getting thrown out 18 times in 44 steal attempts. Simmons will open 2012 in Double-A Mississippi, and more than few observers believe he already can play defense at a major league level. Tyler Pastornicky may get the first crack at the Braves' shortstop job, but Simmons is their shortstop of the future.

Julio Teheran ranks eighth in career innings for Atlanta Braves pitchers.

TOM PRIDDY

JULIO TEHERAN, RHP

BIOGRAPHY

PROPER NAME: Julio Alberto Teheran. **BORN:** Jan. 27, 1991 in Cartagena, Colombia.
HT.: 6-2. **WT.:** 205. **BATS:** R. **THROWS:** R.
FIRST PRO CONTRACT: Signed as international free agent by Braves, July 2, 2007..

Because he's been more dependable than dominating and because he is pitching for an organization that boasted three Hall of Famers in its rotation for years, it's easy to fail to fully appreciate what Teheran has meant to the Braves in the 2010s. Since he settled into Atlanta's rotation in 2013, Teheran has been the pitcher the Braves could depend on most every fifth day, year in and year out. He made 30 or more starts in seven straight seasons to finish off the decade. At his best, he was a two-time all-star and finished fifth in the 2013 NL Rookie of the Year race. He hasn't always been at his best, and he's had to figure out how to succeed with significantly less velocity than he had when he first reached the majors. Others may have briefly been more dominating, but Teheran enters the 2020s as one of the two best starting pitchers Atlanta has had in the post-Glavine-Smoltz-Maddux era.

CAREER STATISTICS

Year	Club (League)	Class	W	L	ERA	G	GS	CG	SV	IP	H	R	ER	HR	BB	SO	AVG
2008	Danville (APP)	R	1	2	6.60	6	6	0	0	15	18	12	11	2	4	17	.305
2009	Danville (APP)	R	2	1	2.68	7	7	0	0	44	36	17	13	2	7	39	.229
	Rome (SAL)	LoA	1	3	4.78	7	7	0	0	38	42	20	20	2	11	28	.288
2010	Rome (SAL)	LoA	2	2	1.14	7	7	0	0	39	23	8	5	1	10	45	.168
	Myrtle Beach (CAR)	HiA	4	4	2.98	10	10	0	0	63	56	22	21	6	13	76	.233
	Mississippi (SL)	AA	3	2	3.38	7	7	0	0	40	29	15	15	2	17	38	.204
2011	Gwinnett (IL)	AAA	15	3	2.55	25	24	0	0	145	123	46	41	5	48	122	.232
	Atlanta (NL)	MAJ	1	1	5.03	5	3	0	0	20	21	11	11	4	8	10	.276
2012	Gwinnett (IL)	AAA	7	9	5.08	26	26	1	0	131	146	81	74	18	43	97	.289
	Atlanta (NL)	MAJ	0	0	5.68	2	1	0	0	6	5	4	4	0	1	5	.217
	Licey (DL)	WIN	2	1	3.23	7	7	0	0	31	24	12	11	2	9	24	--
2013	Atlanta (NL)	MAJ	14	8	3.20	30	30	0	0	186	173	69	66	22	45	170	.246
2014	Atlanta (NL)	MAJ	14	13	2.89	33	33	4	0	221	188	82	71	22	51	186	.232
2015	Atlanta (NL)	MAJ	11	8	4.04	33	33	0	0	201	189	99	90	27	73	171	.253
2016	Gwinnett (IL)	AAA	0	1	1.80	1	1	0	0	5	3	2	1	0	0	5	.167
	Atlanta (NL)	MAJ	7	10	3.21	30	30	1	0	188	157	70	67	22	41	167	.223
2017	Atlanta (NL)	MAJ	11	13	4.49	32	32	0	0	188	186	103	94	31	72	151	.257
2018	Atlanta (NL)	MAJ	9	9	3.94	31	31	0	0	176	122	80	77	26	84	162	.196
2019	Atlanta (NL)	MAJ	10	10	3.77	32	32	0	0	170	145	77	71	20	81	156	--
Major League Totals			77	72	3.66	228	225	5	0	1355	1186	595	551	174	456	1178	.236
Minor League Totals			35	27	3.48	96	95	1	0	520	476	223	201	38	153	467	.246

From a fireballer to a crafty veteran

AUGUST 2009

TEHERAN SHOWS OFF ELECTRIC STUFF

by BEN BADLER

With Tommy Hanson in the big leagues, the Braves' best pitching prospect on a pure stuff level might be Rookie-level Danville righthander Julio Teheran.

Teheran, who signed out of Colombia in 2007, made a compelling case for that claim in an Appalachian League game at the Burlington Royals.

Teheran pitched the best game of his career on July 13, carrying a perfect game into the sixth inning and finishing after striking out 11 batters in eight innings, allowing just one run, two hits and one walk while working efficiently with his pitches.

"He was plus across the board with all his pitches and his command," Danville manager Paul Runge said. "He was in complete control."

Just 18 years old, Teheran's repertoire rivals that of the top high school first-round draft picks.

Teheran threw a lively fastball with plus-plus velocity, sitting at 94-95 mph deep into the game, ranging from 92-95 mph and touching 96 once. Teheran was able to overpower several Royals hitters with his fastball, which batters were unable to cheat on because of Teheran's secondary pitches.

Despite his youth, Teheran already came into the season with a plus changeup that some scouts have labeled a 70 pitch on the 20-80 scouting scale. Teheran showed an outstanding 79-82 mph changeup with late tail and fade, giving him nearly 15 mph of separation between his fastball and his changeup.

Teheran also threw a curveball with good depth that he was able to command for most of the game at 75-77 mph. Through the first seven innings, Teheran threw nine of his 11 curveballs for strikes (all called). Of Teheran's 11 strikeouts, six of them were on curveballs that hitters watched go by for strike three, either back-dooring lefthanded batters or often buckling the knees of righties. His mechanics weren't effortless, but they did provide some deception.

"He's got a plus fastball and then when he throws his changeup, obviously it makes his fastball look that much better," Runge said. "But the thing that was impressive tonight was that he had plus command of his breaking ball and he had plus control of his curveball. That may have been the best curveball we've seen him throw in his young career. When you see pitchers develop like that, you know they've got a chance to move really fast."

After Thursday's start, Teheran lowered his ERA to 2.68 through 43.2 innings, giving him 39 strikeouts (8.0 per nine innings) and seven walks (1.4 per nine) on the season. Teheran is in his second season at Danville, though a sore shoulder limited him to just 15 innings in 2008.

"He's just matured so much on the mound," said Runge, who also managed Teheran last year. "His mound presence is beyond his years. When you look at him out there, he looks like a major leaguer. So we're very pleased with his progress." ■

Julio Teheran scouting reports

ATLANTA BRAVES
NO. 10 PROSPECT AFTER 2007 SEASON

The Braves believe they signed the top amateur pitcher in Latin America when they inked Teheran for $850,000. His cousin Miguel is one of the scouts who signed him for the Braves, and he reportedly turned down a higher offer from the Yankees. He showed every indication during instructional league that he'll be as good as advertised. Teheran is a mature teenager with a vast repertoire, great makeup and tremendous upside. Scouts love how easily the ball comes out of his hand and how loose his arm works. His fastball sat at 94-95 during instructional league. He throws an advanced changeup at 81-82 with good sinking action. His 78-79 mph curveball has late, hard bite. Teheran has a pump delivery and struggles at times with his command. His arm action is a little short in the backside and he needs to get stronger, which should occur naturally as he matures physically. Teheran has a chance to move rapidly through the system and become a standout at the major league level. The Braves have no plans to rush him, and likely will send him to the Gulf Coast League in 2008 in order to help him adapt to pro ball and a new culture.

ATLANTA BRAVES
NO. 8 PROSPECT AFTER 2008 SEASON

The top amateur pitcher on the international market in 2007, Teheran signed for $850,000, thanks in part to his cousin Miguel, a Braves scout. Impressed by his maturity in spring training, Atlanta sent him to the Appalachian League, where he was the youngest pitcher at age 17. He developed a sore shoulder after two starts, and was used sparingly afterward. Teheran throws easy gas, displaying a 90-93 mph fastball with above-average life in instructional league. His changeup is also a plus pitch and he'll throw it any time in the count. His poise is remarkable, and he has a strong idea of what he needs to accomplish by working both sides of the plate as well as the top and bottom of the zone. Teheran needs to tighten the spin on his rolling curveball. He also must do a better job commanding his pitches in the zone. Though doctors found nothing wrong with his shoulder, he'll have to get stronger. He's still learning that he can't just overpower every hitter he faces. The Braves feel no need to rush Teheran and may keep him in extended spring before sending him back to Danville. He has top-of-the-rotation ability and will get all the time he needs to develop.

ATLANTA BRAVES
NO. 3 PROSPECT AFTER 2009 SEASON

The Braves signed Teheran for $850,000, the largest bonus given to a pitcher on the international market in 2007. After pitching sparingly in 2008 because of shoulder tendinitis, Teheran returned to the Rookie-level Appalachian League last summer and ranked as the loop's top prospect. Teheran throws easy heat with plus command and mound presence beyond his years. His fastball resides at 92-96 mph and holds its velocity throughout the game. His sharp, mid-70s curveball has good depth and can be a plus pitch, particularly after he tightened its spin. His 79-82 mph changeup is also an above-average pitch at times, with depth, fade and screwball-like movement. He has impressive poise that some scouts believe borders on cockiness. Teheran is still learning how to pitch. His physical stamina needs some work, and scouts have some concerns about his mechanics, which aren't effortless. He has a long arm rotation in the back of his herky-jerky delivery that creates deception but attracts questions about his durability. Teheran has all the ingredients to develop into a frontline starter. He's expected to return to low Class A Rome to open the 2010 slate. While the Braves will be cautious due to his youth and lack of physical maturity, Teheran could accelerate his timetable.

ATLANTA BRAVES
NO. 1 PROSPECT AFTER 2010 SEASON

The Braves signed Teheran out of Colombia in 2007 for $850,000, the largest bonus for a pitcher on the international market that year. His cousin Miguel was one of the scouts who signed him, and that relationship contributed to Julio's decision to turn down a higher offer from the Yankees. It took some time to start living up to his projections, as his 2008 pro debut lasted just 15 innings due to shoulder tendinitis. He returned to Rookie-level Danville in 2009 and ranked as the Appalachian League's top prospect before earning a late-season promotion to low Class A Rome. Atlanta turned Teheran loose last season, when he advanced three levels while ranking second in the system in ERA (2.59) and strikeouts (159 in 142 innings). He overpowered the low Class A South Atlantic League in April and May before jumping to high Class A Myrtle Beach, where he ranked as the No. 1 prospect in the Carolina League, then earned a promotion to Double-A Mississippi in late July. Teheran also stood out at the Futures Game, where he didn't throw a fastball under 95 mph. Teheran has an electric arm, the ability to throw all of his pitches for strikes and the knowledge of how to exploit batters' weaknesses. His fastball clocks consistently in the 94-96 mph range, and he maintains his velocity throughout a game. He has a pair of above average secondary pitches, with his changeup grading slightly better than his curveball. His changeup shows nice fade and he's willing to throw it in any count. His curve resides in the low 80s with hard bite and depth. Teheran's command is impressive, though he struggled a little with his precision shortly after being promoted to Double-A. He works both sides of the plate, usually keeping all of his offerings at the knees and below. Teheran needs to get stronger, but that will come naturally as his body matures. Some scouts say his delivery has a little bit of violence and worry about the long-term wear and tear on the elbow and shoulder, while others believe he throws easy gas and aren't worried about his mechanics. Comparisons to a young Pedro Martinez are commonplace, and Teheran's biggest backers think he's more advanced at the same stage of his career. The Braves thought Teheran could jump on the fast track, and he exceeded their expectations, advancing to Double-A as a teenager. He may split 2011 between Mississippi and Triple-A Gwinnett, with a late season cup of coffee in Atlanta a possibility. Chances are his first opportunity for a job in the big league rotation won't come until 2012. He has front-of-the-rotation talent and will challenge Tommy Hanson for the role as the Braves' No. 1 starter by the middle of the decade.

ATLANTA BRAVES
NO. 1 PROSPECT AFTER 2011 SEASON

No teenage pitcher over the past two decades has sped through the Braves system faster than Teheran. He signed as a 16-year-old out of Colombia in 2007 for $850,000, the largest bonus for an international amateur pitcher that year. The Yankees actually offered him more money, but Atlanta had an edge in that his cousin Miguel was one of the scouts who signed him. Teheran battled shoulder tendinitis during his 2008 pro debut but hasn't slowed down since. He ranked as the No. 1 prospect in the Rookie-level Appalachian League in 2009 and again in the high Class A Carolina League the following year. That success notwithstanding, Teheran put together his best pro season in 2011. He made a pair of emergency starts in Atlanta in mid-May before returning for three appearances in September. In between, he led the Triple-A International League with 15 wins while ranking second in ERA (2.55) and opponent average (.232). With an electric arm, excellent instincts and maturity beyond his years, Teheran makes pitching look easy. He mixes four pitches to keep hitters off balance and does a good job of getting ahead in the count. A lanky hurler who throws on an impressive downward plane, Teheran works low in the zone and also is capable of getting batters to chase high fastballs. His heater sits at 93-95 mph and touches 97. He commands the pitch to both sides of the plate and isn't afraid to pitch inside. His changeup is nearly as good as his fastball, featuring outstanding depth and fade. He seems to know to throw his changeup when the batter least expects it. Teheran throws two breaking balls--a curveball in the low 80s with late bite, and a slider he uses less frequently--and developing a consistently reliable one is his main need at this point. Otherwise, he just needs to refine a few things, such as his fastball command and his pickoff move. The Braves have ironed out his delivery and will continue to monitor his mechanics in order to minimize the violence associated with generating such tremendous power. His pitching coaches rave about Teheran's work ethic, desire to improve and willingness to accept constructive criticism. Teheran has the ability to become a No. 1 starter. He'll need to add some strength and become a little sharper with all of his pitches in order to attain that status--which is why he may start 2012 back in Triple-A--but the goal is well within reach.

ATLANTA BRAVES
NO. 1 PROSPECT AFTER
THE 2012 SEASON

Expectations never have been a problem for Teheran. Signed as a 16-year-old out of Colombia in 2007 for $850,000, the largest bonus given to any international pitcher that year, he overcame a bout of shoulder tendinitis in the Rookie-level Appalachian League in 2008 to rank as that circuit's top prospect a year later. He also made his major league debut in 2011 and entered last spring as a leading candidate to break camp in the Atlanta rotation. Instead, Teheran struggled with leaving pitches up in the strike zone and allowed nine homers while in big league camp. He performed well in the first two months at Triple-A Gwinnett and tossed the first nine-inning complete game of his career on June 3 before making an emergency start for the Braves. He wasn't the same pitcher after returning to the IL, going 2-7, 6.46 in his final 15 starts. Though Teheran was just 21 and trying to incorporate some mechanical adjustments, his downturn still was stunning. Teheran has an electric arm, but his delivery had some violence that the Braves wanted to iron out in order to reduce his risk of injury. In 2012, they decided to reduce the bend on his back leg during his windup. He had been turning and coiling his body to generate more momentum toward the plate, placing additional strain on his right knee and elbow. Atlanta worked with Teheran on keeping his back leg straighter in order to create a better center of balance, particularly in his core. The alterations not only led to less initial success, but also to a reduction in fastball velocity. After sitting at 93-95 mph and reaching 97 in 2011, Teheran operated mostly at 90-93 last season. To his credit, he stuck with the changes and showed signs of regaining his previous velocity. He still has above-average fastball command and the ability to work both sides of the plate. His changeup remains the best in the system, a 79-81 mph offering with outstanding depth and fade. Teheran continues to search for a consistently reliable breaking ball. His curveball has good rotation but he hangs it too often, and he trusts his slider even less than his curve. He has an impressive knowledge of how to set up hitters, along with impeccable work ethic and determination. Though Teheran couldn't crack the Braves rotation in 2012, he remains firmly in their long-term plans and has as much upside as any starter in the organization--including the big league club. He won't be a No. 1 starter without a better breaking ball, but he definitely has the package to become a No. 2 or 3. He'll compete for a starting job again this spring, and Atlanta won't be concerned if he winds up back at Gwinnett to open the season.

Mike Soroka threw 143 innings in his first full pro season, demonstrating his durability at a very young age.

MIKE SOROKA, RHP

BIOGRAPHY

PROPER NAME: Michael John Graydon Soroka. **BORN:** Aug. 4, 1997 in Calgary, Alberta.
HT.: 6-5. **WT.:** 225. **BATS:** R. **THROWS:** R. **SCHOOL:** Bishop Carroll HS, Calgary.
FIRST PRO CONTRACT: Selected by Braves in first round (28th overall) of 2015 draft; signed
June 26, 2015.

Mike Soroka has always been more advanced than his peers. He was young for his draft class,
but he quickly showed advanced maturity. Before he turned 20, he already analyzed his own
strengths and weaknesses like a 10-year vet. The Braves have a leadership development program that they pick out minor leaguers to attend. After attending the camp in its first year,
Soroka returned for the second year as a counselor to help execute the program. His excellent
rookie season in 2019 is a harbinger of a solid career to come.

CAREER STATISTICS

Year	Club (League)	Class	W	L	ERA	G	GS	CG	SV	IP	H	R	ER	HR	BB	SO	AVG
2015	Braves (GCL)	R	0	0	1.80	4	3	0	0	10	5	2	2	0	1	11	.143
	Danville (APP)	R	0	2	3.75	6	6	0	0	24	28	12	10	0	4	26	.283
2016	Rome (SAL)	LoA	9	9	3.02	25	24	1	0	143	130	58	48	3	32	125	.244
2017	Mississippi (SL)	AA	11	8	2.75	26	26	0	0	154	133	58	47	10	34	125	.233
2018	Rome (SAL)	LoA	0	0	0.00	1	1	0	0	4	0	0	0	0	0	3	.000
	Gwinnett (IL)	AAA	2	1	2.00	5	5	1	0	27	20	6	6	0	6	31	.204
	Atlanta (NL)	MAJ	2	1	3.51	5	5	0	0	26	30	14	10	1	7	21	.288
2019	Gwinnett (IL)	AAA	1	0	3.86	2	2	0	0	9	5	4	4	1	1	10	--
	Atlanta (NL)	MAJ	13	3	2.56	28	28	0	0	169	144	52	48	13	39	138	--
Major League Totals			**15**		**42.69**		**33**	**33**	**0**	**0**	**194**	**174**	**66**	**58**	**14**	**46**	**159**	**.288**
Minor League Totals			**23**		**202.84**		**69**	**67**	**2**	**0**	**371**	**321**	**140**	**117**	**14**	**78**	**331**	**.235**

An advanced feel for the craft of pitching

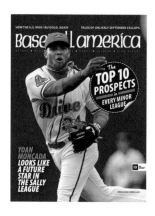

APRIL 2016

ALIGNMENT TWEAK HAS SOROKA ON RIGHT TRACK

by J.J. COOPER

Looking at the final numbers from Braves right-hander Mike Soroka's debut would lead one to believe that he's still waiting for his first big challenge in pro ball. After all, the Calgary native went 0-2, 3.18 with 37 strikeouts and only five walks in 34 innings last year in his pro debut at two Rookie-level stops.

But when the first-round pick arrived in low Class A Rome as one of the youngest players in the South Atlantic League, the 18-year-old showed up with a significant tweak. It's an adjustment he believes is the proper response to his first taste of pro adversity.

Last year whenever a righthander stepped into the batter's box, Soroka was in control. He'd pound them inside with his two-seam sinker, setting up his slurvy breaking ball or his changeup to finish them off. It worked extremely well. Righthanders were held to a .119/.169/.134 batting line. Only one of the 71 righthanded hitters had an extra-base hit against him—a double.

But when Soroka faced a lefthander, the balance of power swung sharply. As devastating as Soroka was against righties, he was powerless against lefties. They hit .373/.417/.448 against him. While Soroka struck out 36 of the righthanded hitters he faced, he whiffed just 15 percent of the lefties.

"A lot of lefties were getting too comfortable," Soroka said. "Lefties weren't having much trouble because everything to them was away, away, away. My fastball would run back away. Even if I threw a changeup, they just had to get their hands out and punch the ball."

In the past, Soroka set up on the third-base side of the rubber. It fit well with his sinker/slider combination, but the closed-off finish to his delivery made it hard to locate well to his glove side. So while everything was in on righthanders, a lefty could get a very comfortable at-bat, knowing that Soroka had nothing that could run in on their hands.

In the offseason, Soroka slid to the middle of the pitching rubber. It's a compromise of sorts because he's still far enough over on the rubber to get in on righthanded hitters, but now he can also locate to his glove side (in on the hands of lefthanded hitters). And the move has also allowed him to be more direct to home plate, taking away some of the cross-body delivery that concerned scouts in the past.

"This year I'm almost perfectly online," he said. "It's been a slow migration (back and forth on the rubber). It started when my sinker started coming along. I moved to the third-base side. I had that slider and that two-seamer. But I was also landing much more closed.

"To get to the other side I had to really fly open. We started working before the draft. I was then landing a couple inches closed, but still from the third base side it was hard to get in. I moved closer to the middle (of the rubber). Now that I'm right online, getting in on lefties is no problem. And now that I'm farther this way, I don't have to hook my slider so much. I can start it top corner of the zone (instead of out of the zone). That's a lot easier on the sight points."

A couple of weeks into the 2016 season, the difference has been noticeable. In his second start of the year, Columbia loaded the lineup with five lefthanded hitters. But where 2015 Soroka would have been helpless, the new-and-improved Soroka dominated. He held Columbia to one hit and one walk in six scoreless innings while striking out five. Soroka's other 13 outs all came on the ground—12 ground outs, one of which was a double play.

Consistently he was able to get in on lefthanders after setting them up by pitching away.

Three starts into the season, no one was hitting Soroka too much. He went 0-1, 2.40 with 12 hits allowed, three walks and 18 strikeouts in 15 innings. But his .238/.261/.381 line against lefthanded hitters was especially notable.

In April, Soroka has been just as comfortable locating to his glove side, in on lefties, as he was locating to his arm side. If he can keep that up, one of the youngest pitchers in the South Atlantic League will also be one of the best. ∎

Draft Report

June 2015

There hasn't been a player out of Alberta selected in the top 100 picks since the Red Sox picked Chris Reitsma 34th overall in 1996, and while Soroka probably won't go that high, he should end up off the board in the first few rounds in June. Armed with three pitches, Soroka attacks hitters with a low 90s fastball that he can spot down and to both sides of the plate. His best pitch is his above-average curveball, which projects as a plus pitch. In a spring start against the Toronto Blue Jays, Soroka's breaking ball froze righthanded hitters, including star catcher Russell Martin. The pitch is as tight as any breaking ball in this class, and breaks very late as it drops into the bottom of the strike zone with 12-to-6 or 11-to-5 shape. Soroka also has feel for a changeup, which scouts see as a potential average pitch. There's some concern about the across-body finish to his arm action, but he has no history of arm trouble and has a physical, 6-foot-5 body. Soroka projects as a middle of the rotation starter, though he is a strong student and may be tough to sign away from his commitment to California.

Mike Soroka
scouting reports

APPALACHIAN LEAGUE
NO. 8 PROSPECT IN 2015

Soroka showed off an upper-80s fastball and tight breaking ball in the 2013 Perfect Game showcase. Over the next 18 months, the Calgary-born righthander gained significant strength, saw his fastball increase in velocity and signed with the Braves for $1,974,700 as the 28th overall pick in the 2015 draft. Soroka projects as a three-pitch horse. His fastball operated in the low 90s at Danville, and he flashed feel for his changeup and sharp breaking ball. He pounded the strike zone with all three pitches, surrendering just four walks. None of Soroka's individual pitches is overwhelming, but he can compete in the strike zone with each pitch, and he has the athleticism and balance to consistently throw strikes. Soroka's control is above-average at present, and he could develop plus command as he continues to build innings.

RANKED ATLANTA BRAVES
NO. 9 PROSPECT AFTER 2015 SEASON

The Braves nabbed Soroka with the 28th overall selection in 2015 as compensation for the Twins signing Ervin Santana. Soroka helped the Canadian Junior National team finish third in the 2014 COPABE 18U Pan American Games. He also tossed 13 scoreless innings during the team's trip through the Dominican Summer League in May prior to becoming the highest-drafted player ever out of Alberta. Soroka pounds the strike zone aggressively with three pitches and works off his consistent low-90s fastball with solid movement. The solidly built hurler has excellent athleticism, commands his stuff to both sides of the plate and does an excellent job of living in the lower part of the strike zone. Soroka's above-average curveball shows tight spin and a late, sharp downward break. He has shown a good feel for an early-stages changeup. Soroka's cross-body finish created some concerns among scouts, even though he has not had any injury problems. Soroka was limited to 34 innings in his first taste of pro ball. The Braves will be patient with the Canadian's development--he's one of the youngest players in his draft class--though he could open the 2016 season at low Class A Rome.

RANKED ATLANTA BRAVES
NO. 4 PROSPECT AFTER 2016 SEASON

The Braves loved what they saw in Soroka when he pitched on the Canadian Junior National Team and they took the righthander with the 28th overall pick in the 2015 draft. Efficient due to his advanced feel for pitching, Soroka wound up working more innings (143) than any prep first-rounder in his first full season in at least a decade. He served as No. 1 starter in both rounds of the South Atlantic League playoffs for low Class A Rome. Soroka's intelligence is readily apparent on the mound and helped him adjust after lefthanded hitters pounded him in his pro debut. He switched sides of the pitching rubber to locate better to his glove side and it worked. He limited lefthanders to a .648 OPS in 2016. Soroka mixes three above-average pitches with aplomb and generates lots of groundouts due to his plus control and ability to pound the lower half of the strike zone. His 90-92 mph fastball has excellent sinking action and touches 95 when he guns for a strikeout. His curveball has tight spin, his changeup has solid movement and he reads hitters' swings to attack their weakness. Strong with a solid presence on the bump, Soroka is a former hockey player and a solid all-around athlete who fields his position well. Soroka was one of the youngest players in his draft class and among the youngest pitchers in the SAL in 2016. While his next step will be high Class A, he projects as a mid-rotation starter in the big leagues.

RANKED ATLANTA BRAVES
NO. 3 PROSPECT AFTER 2017 SEASON

The Braves skipped Soroka over high Class A in 2017 and made him the second-youngest player in Double-A on Opening Day. He responded by finishing second in the Southern League in ERA (2.75). Soroka is a sinker/slider pitcher who touches 95 mph but lives at 90-93 mph with his two-seamer. His delivery has a little crossfire action that adds deception and has not affected his plus control. He started to throw his four-seamer more to alter hitters' eye levels. Soroka's plus breaking ball is hard to classify. At it's best it's an above-average 84-86 mph curveball because of 1-to-7 shape, but it's tighter and has a sharper break than normal. When his adrenaline is flowing, it morphs into a high-80s pitch with slider tilt. His changeup flashes above-average with some late run but could use more consistency. It's vital for Soroka to handle lefties. His sinker and breaking ball eat up righthanders, but those same offerings end up down and in where lefties can feast, so his changeup must show run away from lefties. Soroka's pure stuff doesn't match Kyle Wright, Luiz Gohara or Ian Anderson, but his exceptional makeup, pitchability and athleticism make him a safe bet to be a mid-rotation starter.

RANKED ATLANTA BRAVES
NO. 3 PROSPECT AFTER 2018 SEASON

Wherever he has gone, Soroka has been the youngest player on the field. And when he made his MLB debut in early May he was the youngest player in the majors. Less than three years after he was drafted, Soroka was in the big leagues holding the Mets to one run over six innings. He made four more starts for the Braves before being shut down with shoulder soreness. He didn't return until a brief instructional league outing.

Soroka attacks hitters with a sinker/slider combination that generates more weak contact than strikeouts. He mixes a plus 92-94 mph two-seamer that he works down and in to right-handed hitters (and down and away from lefthanders) with a 92-94 mph four-seamer that he elevates. He is at his best when he's keeping the ball down, which sets up his above-average 85-87 mph slider that he turned into a harder, sharper pitch in 2018. Soroka mixes in an average changeup sporadically against lefthanded hitters. What makes it all work is Soroka's plus control and above-average command. He has a clean delivery and has long impressed with his competitive, mature makeup.

Soroka showed his normal velocity at instructs, and the Braves expect he will be at full strength for spring training. But Soroka's shoulder injury was a first hiccup for a pitcher who had never suffered a setback as a pro. He should pitch in the Braves rotation in 2019. His command, stuff and outstanding makeup fit the mold of a mid-rotation starter.

None of Soroka's individual pitches is overwhelming, but he can compete in the strike zone with each pitch, and he has the athleticism and balance to consistently throw strikes. Soroka's control is above-average at present, and he could develop plus command as he continues to build innings.

Ozzie Albies skipped over high Class A and made it to the majors after just three pro seasons.

OZZIE ALBIES, 2B

BIOGRAPHY

PROPER NAME: Ozhaino Jurdy Jiandro Albies. **BORN:** Jan. 7, 1997 in Willemstad, Curacao.
HT.: 5-8. **WT.:** 165. **BATS:** B. **THROWS:** R.
FIRST PRO CONTRACT: Signed as international free agent by Braves, July 2, 2013.

After the Braves acquired Dansby Swanson from the D-backs, they faced a fascinating decision. Swanson was the first pick in the draft in 2015 and was viewed as a prototypical shortstop. But the Braves already had Ozzie Albies. Albies didn't have Swanson's shortstop frame, but he was faster, more explosive and potentially rangier. Eventually the Braves decided to keep Swanson at shortstop and move Albies to second base, but in their first two major league seasons together, it's been Albies who looks like a budding star.

CAREER STATISTICS

Year	Club (League)	Class	AVG	G	AB	R	H	2B	3B	HR	RBI	BB	SO	SB	OBP	SLG
2014	Braves (GCL)	R	.381	19	63	16	24	3	0	0	5	11	6	7	.481	.429
	Danville (APP)	R	.356	38	135	25	48	4	3	1	14	17	17	15	.429	.452
2015	Rome (SAL)	LoA	.310	98	394	64	122	21	8	0	37	36	56	29	.368	.404
2016	Gwinnett (IL)	AAA	.248	56	222	27	55	11	3	2	20	19	39	9	.307	.351
	Mississippi (SL)	AA	.321	82	330	56	106	22	7	4	33	33	57	21	.391	.467
2017	Gwinnett (IL)	AAA	.285	97	411	67	117	21	8	9	41	28	90	21	.330	.440
	Atlanta (NL)	MAJ	.286	57	217	34	62	9	5	6	28	21	36	8	.354	.456
2018	Atlanta (NL)	MAJ	.261	158	639	105	167	40	5	24	72	36	116	14	.305	.452
2019	Atlanta (NL)	MAJ	.297	157	630	99	187	43	8	24	84	51	111	14	.352	.505
Major League Totals			**.280**	**372**	**1486**	**238**	**416**	**92**	**18**	**54**	**184**	**108**	**263**	**36**	**.332**	**.475**
Minor League Totals			**.304**	**390**	**1555**	**255**	**472**	**82**	**29**	**16**	**150**	**144**	**265**	**102**	**.365**	**.424**

Big tools in a small package

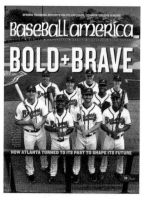

APRIL 2016

BRAVES HAVE GOOD PROBLEM AT SHORTSTOP

by J.J. COOPER

When the Braves front office came to take shortstops Dansby Swanson and Ozzie Albies away from big league manager Fredi Gonzalez in spring training, he begged for more time.

The Braves hadn't started to play games on the minor league side yet when Gonzalez made his pitch. He promised that he could give the dynamic duo at-bats they couldn't get yet in minor league camp. He wanted to give them a greater taste of big league camp.

Really, he just was having too much fun watching them play.

"They let me have them a week later than they wanted to," Gonzalez said. "I joke all the time: There are times I can't wait to get the veteran guys out (of the game) to watch those guys play. They energize the coaching staff. We want to teach these guys.

"You wouldn't believe how many conversations we had. 'Gun to your head, who plays short? Who plays second?' "

Eventually, Swanson and Albies were shipped out to minor league camp, where the debate about which will play shortstop continued. Atlanta's rebuilding effort largely has focused on pitchers. The position-player talent does not match the arms overall, but Swanson and Albies will be two of the cornerstone pieces in the rebuilding project.

Swanson, the No. 1 overall pick in the 2015 draft who was acquired from the Diamondbacks in December in the Shelby Miller trade, has the more prototypical shortstop body. Albies reminds longtime Braves coaches of Rafael Furcal, though he doesn't have Furcal's cannon arm.

The Braves are confident that either could capably play shortstop in the major leagues. But they have yet to figure out which would do a better job at shortstop.

In most cases a team would try to separate two premium shortstop prospects so that both can both play the position, but the Braves toyed with the idea of keeping them together this season and having them alternate between second base and shortstop week by week. On the back fields in spring training, they played on the same team, swapping back and forth from shortstop to second base.

Eventually the Braves decided to let them both play shortstop full time. Albies will be the shortstop at Double-A Mississippi. Swanson will start his Braves career as the high Class A Carolina shortstop. The decision has been put off, at least for a little while.

Both will play key roles in the Braves' future. It's just that no one knows exactly which one will be the shortstop yet. ∎

JUNE 2016

UBER-CONFIDENT ALBIES DIDN'T EXPECT TO MOVE THIS QUICKLY

by JOSH NORRIS

In one game against Durham, Triple-A Gwinnett shortstop Ozzie Albies made it from home to first in 3.97 seconds—and he didn't even get a strong first step out of the lefthanded batter's box. That's 80-grade speed on the 20-80 scouting scale. Point is, the man can fly.

But even he didn't expect to move this quickly.

A year ago at this time, Albies was the shortstop for low Class A Rome and in just his 55th game in full-season ball. Now, he's playing every day in Triple-A, where he's far and away the youngest player in the International League. This, after starting the year as far and away the youngest player in the Double-A Southern League.

Throw a new position into the mix—Albies on Sunday started at second base for just the second time in his pro career—and it'd be understandable if Albies felt a little bit over-whelmed by his quick ascension. Instead, the 19-year-old is taking it in stride.

"It's just something I have to go with and play the game. It's the same game, but just the level changed. That's all," he said.

After acquiring Dansby Swanson, the former Vanderbilt shortstop and last year's No. 1 overall pick, in an offseason trade that sent righthander Shelby Miller to the Diamondbacks, the Braves suddenly had a glut of talented shortstop prospects. So, to make sure each player got everyday reps at the position, Albies was vaulted over high Class A Carolina and sent straight to Double-A Mississippi to open the year.

That, Albies said, was always part of his plan.

"My goal was to start this year at Mississippi," he said, "and it happened. So I was ready for it. When I got sent down from (big league) spring training camp, I was doing really well . . . I expected and was thinking they were going to send me there, and it happened."

On a stacked team that included righthander Chris Ellis and lefty Sean Newcomb—both of whom came over in the trade that sent shortstop Andrelton Simmons to the Angels—Albies shined. Before moving to Gwinnett on April 29, he was hitting .369/.442/.512—his average and on-base percentage placed him in the among the top two in the league, and his slugging percentage ranked seventh—with a home run and seven RBIs.

Over the last five weeks, Albies is finding out quickly that Triple-A is a much different animal. The pitchers, he said, are far less predictable. With Mississippi, he knew he could expect a fastball if he got to a 2-0 count. Not so in the International League, which is full of veterans with major league experience. In the same count, a veteran might still go with offspeed to see if a hitter—particularly one as inexperienced as Albies—will get himself out.

"The pitchers here are more consistent. They throw everything for a strike. No matter the count, you can expect a different pitch," he said. "They're more veteran and they know

Ozzie Albies learned from a pair of veteran infielders in his final tune-up for the majors with Triple-A Gwinnett.

how to locate pitches."

Fortunately for Albies, he's also got a couple of veterans on his team who can provide advice and help him develop into the player the Braves believe he can become. Particularly helpful are shortstops Erick Aybar and Reid Brignac—a pair with nearly 6,000 combined major league plate appearances. Their experience came in handy at a crucial juncture during Saturday night's game.

With one out and Gwinnett down a run and the tying run on third, Durham had a meeting at the mound. While that was going on, Aybar, who was in the on-deck, came up behind Albies, who was getting set to hit, placed his hands on Albies' shoulders and began offering some advice for the situation.

"He was telling me to stay through the ball," Albies said. "He told me, 'He's not going to throw you anything close to the strike zone, so just be ready for a fastball in case he opens with a fastball, but he's going to throw a lot of stuff,' and he opened with a fastball."

Albies jumped on the first pitch he saw and shot a hard grounder toward second baseman Nick Franklin, who bobbled the ball long enough to allow the tying run to score. And although Gwinnett fell in extra innings, Albies took small, unseen step forward.

Brignac, himself a former highly touted prospect—he ranked among Tampa Bay's Top 10 prospects six times, placed in six league Top 20s and ranked as high as No. 17 on the BA Top 100 Prospects—is happy to offer guidance to the next wave, just as veterans did for him when he was coming through the ranks.

"Nineteen is young, but he's a very mature kid. He's a hard-worker, and he's just going to continue to get better, and I think that's why the Braves pushed him to be up here around a lot of veteran guys playing for a long time," Brignac said. "We don't cut him much slack, and that's kind of our job as veteran players to stay on him and keep his mind right when he's scuffling a little bit and say, 'We've all been through this. You're not going through anything that we haven't gone through already. It's going to come and it's going to go, so just keep a good mind set and you'll be fine.' "

Albies is well aware that this is the last year for Turner Field in Atlanta, and he would very much like to be in the majors next year when the Braves open SunTrust Park. Truly, he'd like to be there even sooner than that. It doesn't matter whether he's at second base or shortstop, he just wants to be in the majors as quickly as possible.

"My goal is to reach there this year," he said," but to open the season up there next year, that would be awesome." ■

Ozzie Albies scouting reports

ATLANTA BRAVES
NO. 5 PROSPECT AFTER 2014 SEASON

Unlike several other suitors, the Braves ignored Albies' small stature and signed him for $350,000 out of Curacao. In addition to making his professional debut in the U.S. in 2014 as a 17-year-old, he excelled while being named the top prospect in the Rookie-level Appalachian League, which he led in batting (.356) and on-base percentage (.429). Scouts and opponents alike rave about Albies' energy and ability. One of the youngest players in pro ball in 2014, he demonstrated an uncannily advanced feel for the game despite playing it at top speed. A natural top-of-the-lineup batter who should hit for a high average, Albies has a quick swing with plus bat speed from both sides of the plate. He stays inside the ball and makes consistent contact with his superior hand-eye coordination, yet he's strong enough to drive the ball from gap to gap. His strike-zone judgment is far beyond his years, and he keeps the ball out of the air in order to take advantage of his plus speed. Defensively, Albies has soft hands with above-average range at shortstop, which he pairs with a strong, accurate arm with a quick release. Albies has already progressed quickly and could continue to move at a rapid rate as he enters the full-season ranks. He will open 2015 at low Class A Rome.

ATLANTA BRAVES
NO. 4 PROSPECT AFTER 2015 SEASON

Albies' development led the Braves to trade second baseman Jose Peraza to the Dodgers in the July 30 deal that netted Hector Olivera. The Rookie-level Appalachian League's top prospect in 2014, Albies enjoyed a strong first full season at low Class A Rome in 2015 before a fractured right thumb cost him the final month of the season. He ranked fourth in the South Atlantic League with a .310 batting average. Albies combines quick-twitch athleticism, plus speed and an unbridled exuberance that makes him an ideal table-setter at the top of the lineup. His superior hand-eye coordination and quick swing generate solid bat speed and consistent contact from both sides of the plate. He sprays hits to all fields and does a good job of keeping the ball out of the air. His strike-zone judgment is advanced, but his aggressiveness cuts into his on-base percentage. Defensively, Albies has soft, steady hands with quick feet and above-average arm strength with a quick release and good accuracy.

ATLANTA BRAVES
NO. 2 PROSPECT AFTER 2016 SEASON

Albies continued his rapid ascent through the organization in 2016. At age 19, he skipped high Class A and led the Double-A Southern League in average (.321) and on-base percentage (.391). Despite struggling during a two-month stint in Triple-A at midseason, he thrived in a return to Mississippi before breaking the tip of a bone in his right elbow on Sept. 9, keeping him out of the SL playoffs. Albies shifted to second base when he teamed with Dansby Swanson at Mississippi. The definition of a quick-twitch athlete, Albies' first-step quickness, soft hands, above-average arm strength and baseball instincts make him a plus defender at both middle-infield spots. He has work to do making the pivot on double plays, which should come with experience. His offensive strength is his ability to make hard and consistent contact from both sides of the plate, thanks to his plus bat speed and superior hand-eye coordination. He draws walks and uses his plus speed to beat out grounders and steal bases, making him an ideal top-of-the-lineup hitter.

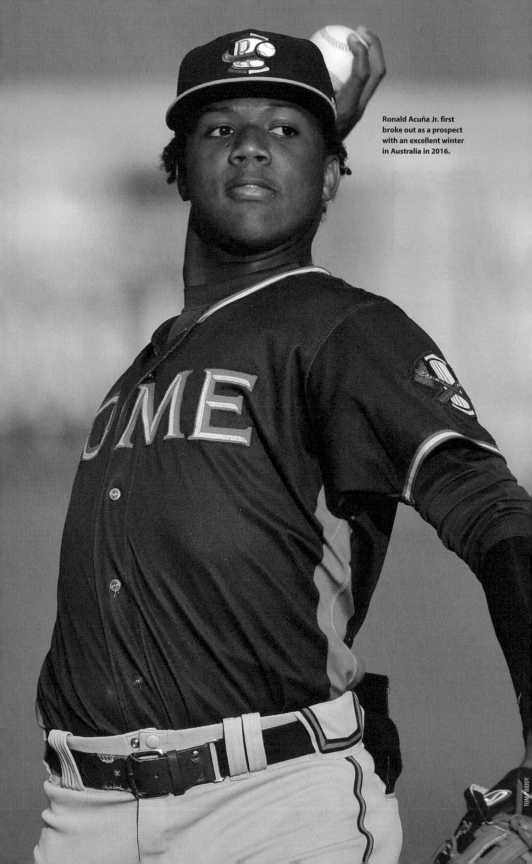

Ronald Acuña Jr. first broke out as a prospect with an excellent winter in Australia in 2016.

TONY FARLOW

RONALD ACUÑA JR., OF

PROPER NAME: Ronald Jose Acuña Jr. **BORN:** Dec. 18, 1997 in La Guaira, Venezuela.
HT.: 6-0. **WT.:** 180. **BATS:** R. **THROWS:** R.
FIRST PRO CONTRACT: Signed as international free agent by Braves, July 2, 2014.

In the 1980s, the Braves' farm system produced Tom Glavine and John Smoltz. In the 1990s, it produced Chipper and Andruw Jones. The 2000s were a slightly more fallow period, but Freddie Freeman and Jason Heyward were finishing their minor league careers at the end of the decade. The 2010s will likely be remembered as the decade that saw the Braves graduate Ronald Acuña Jr. to the majors along with Ozzie Albies. Acuña won Baseball America's Minor League Player of the Year in 2017. He was the NL Rookie of the Year in 2018. It will be a surprise if he doesn't add a MVP award to that trophy shelf at some point in the 2020s.

CAREER STATISTICS

Year	Club (League)	Class	AVG	G	AB	R	H	2B	3B	HR	RBI	BB	SO	SB	OBP	SLG
2015	Braves (GCL)	R	.258	37	132	31	34	9	2	3	11	18	23	11	.376	.424
	Danville (APP)	R	.290	18	69	10	20	5	2	1	7	10	19	5	.388	.464
2016	Braves (GCL)	R	.333	2	6	1	2	0	0	0	1	1	1	0	.500	.333
	Rome (SAL)	LoA	.311	40	148	27	46	2	2	4	18	18	28	14	.387	.432
	Melbourne (ABL)	WIN	.375	20	72	15	27	5	1	2	13	10	13	13	.446	.556
2017	Florida (FSL)	HiA	.287	28	115	21	33	3	5	3	19	8	40	14	.336	.478
	Mississippi (SL)	AA	.326	57	221	29	72	14	1	9	30	18	56	19	.374	.520
	Gwinnett (IL)	AAA	.344	54	221	38	76	14	2	9	33	17	48	11	.393	.548
	Peoria (AFL)	WIN	.325	23	83	22	27	5	0	7	16	12	22	2	.414	.639
2018	Gwinnett (IL)	AAA	.211	23	90	9	19	2	0	1	3	11	25	5	.297	.267
	Atlanta (NL)	MAJ	.293	111	433	78	127	26	4	26	64	45	123	16	.366	.552
2019	Atlanta (NL)	MAJ	.277	154	618	126	171	22	2	41	101	75	186	35	.363	.518
Major League Totals			**.284**	**265**	**1051**	**204**	**298**	**48**	**6**	**67**	**165**	**120**	**309**	**51**	**.364**	**.532**
Minor League Totals			**.301**	**259**	**1002**	**166**	**302**	**49**	**14**	**30**	**122**	**101**	**240**	**79**	**.371**	**.468**

Atlanta's star of the decade to come

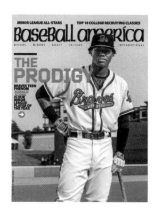

SEPTEMBER 2017

2017 MINOR LEAGUE PLAYER OF THE YEAR: RONALD ACUÑA

by KYLE GLASER

It took Damon Berryhill just two at-bats to realize Ronald Acuña Jr. was special.

It was July 13. Berryhill, the manager of the Braves' Triple-A Gwinnett affiliate, had just received the touted Acuña after his promotion from Double-A Mississippi. Berryhill placed Acuña in Gwinnett's leadoff spot immediately, eager to see how the precocious Venezuelan would fare.

"His first game, we're facing Charlotte and he swung at (consecutive) sliders to strike out his first at-bat," Berryhill said. "He was probably excited; it was the one time I did see him chase out of the zone.

"But his next at-bat, he walked up and first slider (in the zone) he saw, he hit it over the right-field wall for a home run. Right then, I knew, this is what they've been telling me."

Acuña delivered a minor league season for the record books in 2017. At the tender age of 19, he shot from high Class A to Double-A to Triple-A, and managed to perform better at every level. Overall he hit .325 with 21 home runs, 82 RBIs and 44 stolen bases. He did it all while showcasing top-flight speed, strong defense in center field and a big arm.

For a historic season not even he saw coming, Acuña is Baseball America's 2017 Minor League Player of the Year.

"Before the season started my goal this year was 45 stolen bases and 15 home runs, but I got 20 home runs already, so that was cool," Acuña said through a translator. "I didn't expect it to be in Triple-A. When I got called up from high A to Double-A I wasn't surprised because they told me it was going to be one month in high A. When I got called up from Double-A to Triple-A, that was a surprise. I did not expect that at all."

The Braves front office didn't either.

Acuña was limited to just 40 games last season at low Class A Rome because of a broken thumb, and his numbers at high Class A Florida to start this season—.287 with an

.814 OPS—were solid but not jaw-dropping.

But Braves player development personnel saw something beyond the stat line, something they felt would allow Acuña to do the improbable and actually perform better as the competition level improved.

"It was the approach," Braves assistant farm director Jonathan Schuerholz said. "You see him laying off breaking balls out of the zone, he's swinging at fastballs, he's hitting balls hard when he is getting pitches to hit. He's playing plus defense. He's doing everything we look at that aren't necessarily stat-driven markers . . .

"His approach was advanced for that level."

Advanced for the level is a common theme with Acuña. Even before this season, he made a habit of rising quicker and performing better than his similar-aged peers. He skipped the Dominican Summer League entirely after signing as an international free agent in 2014 and came straight to the U.S., where he delivered an .818 OPS over two Rookie-level stops in 2015, his first professional season. After missing most of last season with his broken thumb, Acuña was sent to play in the offseason Australian Baseball League, where he hit .375 with a 1.001 OPS despite being almost six years younger than the league's average player.

One reason Acuña has been able to handle everything thrown at him is he knew what to expect. His father Ron was a Mets outfield prospect in the late 1990s and early 2000s and played eight seasons in the minors, topping out at Double-A. Growing up in Venezuela, Acuña got a crash course from his father on what was truly needed to be a successful ballplayer.

"It meant a lot having a dad who played the game, a lot of experience," Acuña said. "Every time I'm doing something wrong, I can relay it to my dad and he can tell me I need to do things this way or that way."

In a roundabout way, his father's playing career is what led Acuña to becoming a Brave.

Rolando Petit, the Braves' director of Cuban and Venezuelan scouting, tried to sign Acuña's father for the Braves when he was an amateur in Venezuela. While Ron Acuña took the Mets' offer instead, he and Petit stayed in contact throughout his career.

It was in that context, after his playing career was done, that the elder Acuña made sure Petit got an early look at his son on the youth fields of La Sabana in northern Venezuela.

Acuña's first international report

April 2015

Ronald Acuña, a 17-year-old who signed for $100,000 on July 2, is a projectable, athletic center fielder. With slightly above-average speed and a plus arm, he has a good chance to stay in center field and potentially be an above-average defender depending how much of his speed he's able to retain with his 6-foot, 180-pound frame. Acuña is toolsy, with average raw power that could increase with his strength projection. Being able to repeat his righthanded swing to make more frequent contact in games and tap into that power will be the key for Acuña. Even though Acuña wasn't signed for a big bonus, there's a chance he could start in the Rookie-level Gulf Coast League, although he could stay back in the DSL.

—BEN BADLER

In figuring out how to handle Ronald Acuña Jr., the Braves harkened back to Andruw Jones' development.

"You have to understand his dad was a professional player and he had really good tools," Petit said. "I liked his dad a lot. I've known his mom, his uncle. His godfather was the one who used to call me to go and see his dad. So I saw Ronald the first time when he was 14 years old. I talked to his dad and questioned his dad. I asked his dad who was going to be a better hitter and his dad didn't hesitate. He said, 'He is going to be a better hitter than me.' "

That was enough for Petit, who kept close watch on Ronald through the next year and a half and signed him for $100,000 on the first day of the 2014 international signing period.

It was not a large bonus. Nearly 200 other international players signed for more during that signing period. The Braves themselves signed six players for larger bonuses.

In fact, when Acuña woke up the morning of July 2, 2014, the first day of the signing period, he planned to sign with another team, for even less money.

"I was going to sign with the Royals," Acuña said. "But that same day, the Braves called and offered me more money. So, I decided to sign with the Braves."

It's surprising, in retrospect, that Acuña was not more highly sought as an amateur. But even Petit, who had a unique insight into Acuña's background and makeup, did not see this coming.

"I truly believed when we signed him he could hit, but to be honest with you I don't think any scout can tell you that any kid is going to run that fast through the system," Petit said. "It's him. He's made it. With his mind, his consistency, his desire, his natural tools."

That combination has turned Acuña into a force in the minors, and one the Braves front office had to dig into their past to learn how to handle best.

"Talking internally about how we were going to handle this season, it took us back to the days of Andruw Jones," Schuerholz said. "I'm not trying to make a comparison there at all, because I don't think it's fair to do that. But in terms of a very talented player and how he progresses through, we went back to (former scouting director) Paul Snyder and the days when they were bringing Andruw through and the common thread was, 'When he shows you he's ready at a level, move him up. Don't let him just sit at a level and get bored, because he's one of those special players who will rise to the challenge and will shine at every level if you let him.' And as you can tell, he did that."

Acuña did that to the point that tales of his feats began to take on almost a mythic quality. There was the time in Syracuse he hit a ball nearly 450 feet—against the wind. ("It was probably the farthest ball we've had hit this year and it was against the wind," Gwinnett hitting coach John Moses said. "Our jaws just dropped.") There was the time he raced home for the go-ahead run in the ninth inning on a chopper back to the pitcher. There was the time he went home to first on an infield single in 3.85 seconds—a Billy Hamilton-esque time out of the righthanded batter's box.

There were the four hitting streaks of at least 10 games, the highlight-reel catches, the runners gunned down on a line to the plate.

Really, there was everything.

"He's got the full package," Berryhill said. "It's really kind of a couple times in a lifetime you get the opportunity to see someone as advanced as he is at 19. He's one of those special kids." ■

Ronald Acuna was once projected as a table-setter. He does have plus speed, but he soon proved he could hit for power too.

Ronald Acuña scouting reports

ATLANTA BRAVES
NO. 26 PROSPECT AFTER 2015 SEASON

Signed out of Venezuela on July 2, 2014, for $100,000, Acuña opened eyes in his first taste of pro ball. The 17-year-old skipped the Dominican Summer League in 2015 and never looked overmatched in either the Rookie-level Gulf Coast or Appalachian leagues, where he ranked as the Nos. 11 and 14 prospect, respectively. Acuña impressed the Braves in minor league camp with his outstanding feel for the game, which convinced the organization to challenge him against older competition. He showed plus speed in center field and on the bases and should be a stolen-base threat at higher levels. He takes good routes to balls in the gaps and flashed well above-average arm strength with solid accuracy and carry on his throws. Acuña has quick hands and an aggressive swing but has advanced plate discipline. He barrels pitches consistently and showed excellent raw power that should generate solid extra-base production as his body matures. Acuña projects as more of a gap-to-gap hitter and profiles as a table-setter. He could push his way to low Class A Rome in 2016.

ATLANTA BRAVES
NO. 6 PROSPECT AFTER 2016 SEASON

The Braves have been aggressive in challenging Acuña since he signed for a modest $100,000 in 2014. He performed well in his U.S. debut after bypassing the Dominican Summer League in 2015 and proceeded to get off to a fast start at low Class A Rome in 2016 before a broken thumb sidelined him from mid-May to mid-August. Despite the injury, Acuña displayed his electric tools in all phases of the game. He uses his plus speed to cover center field from gap to gap and has the arm strength to play any position in the garden. He reads balls well, takes good angles and shows impressive anticipation along with excellent first-step quickness. Acuña is aggressive at the plate but has above-average discipline for a teenager. While his body is still developing, he has plus raw power and barrels pitches consistently with his above-average bat speed. Those traits should allow him to hit for average at higher levels. He needs work on stealing bases more consistently but has the speed to make an impact on the basepaths. His shortened season at Rome notwithstanding, Acuña should open the 2017 campaign at high Class A Florida after making up for lost time in the winter Australian Baseball League. Though risky, Acuña has as high a ceiling as any Braves position player.

ATLANTA BRAVES
NO. 1 PROSPECT AFTER 2017 SEASON

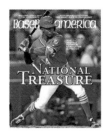

Acuña's father Ron was a long-time Mets minor leaguer. But from an early age, the elder Acuña knew that his son would likely end up the better player. Ronald signed for $100,000, choosing the Braves over the Royals, and was advanced enough to begin his pro career in the U.S. in 2015. Acuña missed much of 2016 with of a thumb injury and began 2017 at high Class A Florida. The Braves were confident he was ready for an in-season promotion--and they were right. Acuña blitzed through Double-A Mississippi in just two months and was even better for Triple-A Gwinnett, earning Minor League Player of the Year honors. The Braves' experience with Andruw Jones, who similarly jumped three minor league levels in a POY season in 1996, influenced their decision to move Acuña aggressively. They quickly realized he thrived when challenged. Acuña has a wide range of strengths and few glaring weaknesses. Multiple scouts predicted multiple all-star appearances in his future. He's the rare prospect who actually carries future 60 (or better) grades on the 20-80 scale for all five tools. Acuña is a 70 runner with 70 defense who has a 60 arm and 60 hit tool. Many scouts project him to future 70 power. He already uses the whole field, and he went deep six times in 2017 to right or right-center field. Acuña used the opposite field more often as the season progressed. Not coincidentally he became tougher to strike out. Scouts looking for flaws noted that his strong arm is sometimes inaccurate and he could sometimes be stymied by quality fastballs up and in. But he already shows an ability to lay off breaking balls and velocity out of the zone. When he gets a pitch to hit, Acuña has extremely fast hands with strong wrists that whip the bat through the zone with excellent bat speed. He already generates exceptional exit velocities, which should pay off with 25-30 home runs once he matures. Even though he has fewer than 1,000 minor league at-bats, Acuña is big league ready and will head to spring training expected to play a significant role in 2018. With Ender Inciarte in center field, his initial role will be left or right fielder. The track record for 20-year-old big leaguers is spotty, but Acuña's defense and plate discipline should help ease his transition.

MIKE MINOR, LHP

Minor was a change of pace for the Braves. The Braves' approach for years was to draft high school pitchers and develop them. Since Ken Daley was drafted in 1980, the Braves had drafted only two college pitchers (Derek Lilliquist and Joey Devine) in the first round in the previous 29 drafts. Over that span, the Braves had drafted nine prep pitchers in the first round. Minor lived up to expectations that he would be a fast mover. He joined the Braves' rotation just two years after he was drafted. He was a steady presence at the back of the rotation for the first half of the decade before Tommy John surgery forced him to miss the 2015 season. He left in free agency after that year.

RANKED ATLANTA BRAVES NO. 4 PROSPECT AFTER THE 2009 SEASON

Minor was the Southeastern Conference freshman of the year in 2007 and Baseball America's Summer Player of the Year in 2008. After a 6-6, 3.90 junior season, Minor signed for $2.42 million. Minor's repertoire consists of four pitches, with his plus changeup rating as his best offering. His fastball has excellent movement and sits in the upper 80s, and he is capable of increasing and reducing the velocity of the pitch to keep hitters off balance. Both his command and control are outstanding. His pickoff move is also a significant weapon. Minor still is trying to determine which breaking ball to work with. He threw an above-average slider with good depth during his first two years at Vanderbilt, but he had trouble snapping the pitch and locating it after adding a curveball last spring. He's not overpowering and his repertoire is similar to that of former Vanderbilt ace Jeremy Sowers. Minor could open his first full season in Double-A. His greatest attribute is his savvy.

RANKED ATLANTA BRAVES NO. 4 PROSPECT AFTER THE 2010 SEASON

Atlanta signed Minor to a $2.42 million bonus in 2009, the biggest in franchise history and the largest ever given to the seventh overall pick in the draft. His pure stuff was better than expected last year, when he reached the major leagues three days after his one-year anniversary of turning pro. He tied a Braves franchise rookie record with 12 strikeouts in a start against the Cubs. Minor mixes three pitches with impressive command and acumen. His best offering is his changeup, which could become a plus-plus pitch as he gains experience. After throwing his fastball in the upper 80s in late 2009, he added velocity and worked at 91-94 mph in the early innings of his starts last season. His heater has significant movement, as does his slurvy curveball, which dives with three-quarters tilt. Minor can add and subtract with his pitches to keep hitters off-balance. He has a great pickoff move and fields his position well. Minor should open 2011 as Atlanta's fifth starter. He has a ceiling as a No. 2 starter.

MAX FRIED, LHP

Fried had to have plenty of patience. A 2012 draftee, he missed almost two full seasons with an elbow injury early in his minor league career. When he returned in 2016, he headed back to low Class A, a level he had already handled in 2013. Fried finally arrived in Atlanta for good in 2018 and has impressed with one of the better curveballs in the National League.

RANKED SAN DIEGO PADRES NO. 2 PROSPECT AFTER THE 2012 SEASON

Fried transferred to the Harvard-Westlake School for his 2012 senior season when his previous high school eliminated its athletic program. There he teamed briefly with righty Lucas Giolito before a strained elbow ligament sidelined Giolito in March. Regardless, Fried (seventh overall) and Giolito (16th, Nationals) became the seventh pair of prep teammates selected in the first round of the same draft. Fried's arm action, projectable frame and steady 90-94 mph fastball from the left side would have made him a first-round pick. The quality of his breaking ball coupled with his athleticism and work ethic made him the top high school pitcher in his draft class, a Clayton Kershaw with less power or a Tyler Skaggs with firmer stuff. The Padres have clocked Fried as high as 96 mph, but they're equally impressed with his ability to two-seam his fastball at 90-91 and command it to his arm side. His curveball sits in the mid-70s now with top-to-bottom spin and plus depth, and scouts expect plus-plus grades and steady high-70s readings down the line.

RANKED ATLANTA BRAVES NO. 8 PROSPECT AFTER THE 2017 SEASON

The first high school pitcher drafted in 2012, Fried has endured Tommy John surgery, a trade and bouts of wildness. Fried's fastball and curveball combo can be devastating when he's throwing strikes. His plus curve has long been his biggest weapon. He loosens it up as a 72-74 mph get-me-over pitch early in counts, but then tightens it into a harder 75-77 tight-breaking curve that generates swings and misses later in counts. Fried's 92-93 mph fastball touches 97 at its hottest. It is an above-average pitch, but his current below-average control limits his effectiveness. His fringe-average changeup is a usable pitch Fried unveils against righthanders. He fields his position well and has a dangerous pickoff move. He toys with hitters' timing by varying his time over the rubber in his delivery.Fried lacks the polish and control of younger system-mates Mike Soroka or Kolby Allard, but he also has better pure stuff. He figures to see big league time in 2018.

JAIR JURRJENS, RHP

The Braves have had a number of pitchers who reached Atlanta with all the force of a hurricane, but quickly dissipated into a breezy April day. Much like Steve Avery and Tommy Hanson, Jurrjens was a pitcher who was excellent in his early 20s, but couldn't maintain that quality of stuff as injuries sapped his arm strength. Acquired in a trade in 2007, Jurrjens led Braves starters in ERA in 2009 and 2011. That 2011 season proved to be the last time he held onto a big league job all season. Rumored in many trade talks, the Braves found other teams as skeptical about Jurrjens' ability to maintain his success. He was bounced from the rotation in 2012 and made only four more MLB appearances over the next five seasons.

RANKED DETROIT TIGERS NO. 22 PROSPECT AFTER THE 2004 SEASON

Jurrjens has pleased the Tigers with his development since former scouting director Greg Smith signed him out of Curacao in May 2003. His best attribute is his ability to control three pitches as a teenager. Not only does he throw his fastball, breaking ball and changeup for strikes, but he also locates them well within the zone. Jurrjens moved from the bullpen to the rotation in 2004, and his fastball got stronger. It sat at 90-92 mph, up from 88-90 in his debut, and he projects to add more velocity as he fills out. His fastball is fairly straight, so it's his command that makes it effective. Jurrjens has so much feel and poise that he could move quickly. He may never have a dominant pitch, but he has enough savvy to project as a possible end-of-the-rotation starter in the major leagues. With a good spring, he could start this season in low Class A.

RANKED ATLANTA BRAVES NO. 3 PROSPECT AFTER THE 2007 SEASON

Jurrjens became the first Curacao native to pitch in the majors last August when he held the Indians to one hit in seven innings. In need of a shortstop, the Tigers swapped him and Gorkys Hernandez for Edgar Renteria after the season. Jurrjens goes after hitters with a two-seam fastball with plenty of sink or a four-seamer than ranges from 92-95 mph with late life and armside run. He has good arm speed and sinking action on his changeup. His curveball can be inconsistent but has good downer action. Both his changeup and curve are plus pitches when they're on. He's athletic and throws strikes with a fluid delivery. He's fearless on the mound. Jurrjens' command isn't as fine as his control, and at times he leaves pitches up in the strike zone. Durability is his primary concern. He missed the end of 2006 with shoulder spasms, and was sidelined for two weeks in June (groin) and again in September (shoulder inflammation). It's not easy to trade for a quality young starter these days, but Atlanta did that thanks to its depth at shortstop. Jurrjens profiles as a No. 3 starter with a ceiling as a No. 2.

BRANDON BEACHY, RHP

Beachy was a scouting success story. Signed by area scout Gene Kerns for $20,000 after Kerns saw him in the summer wood bat Valley League, Beachy went from being undrafted to the big leagues in just two years. The Braves initially expected Beachy to be a reliever, but he showed plus control and command that eventually made it clear he had potential as a starter. Beachy was a valuable member of the Braves' rotation in 2011 and he was even better in 2012 before he blew out his elbow. His first Tommy John surgery didn't work and he ended up needing two T.J. surgeries in a two year span. As of 2019, Beachy had never made it back to the majors after that second Tommy John surgery, but he was quite good before the elbow injuries struck.

RANKED ATLANTA BRAVES NO. 8 PROSPECT AFTER THE 2010 SEASON

Beachy was a third baseman who moonlighted as a closer when he went undrafted following his junior season at Indiana Wesleyan in 2008. After starring as a pitcher in the collegiate Valley League that summer, he signed with the Braves for $20,000 as a free agent. He had a breakthrough season in 2010, leading the minors with a 1.73 ERA and making three solid starts for Atlanta in September. Beachy has a live, fresh arm with good overall command of three pitches. He gets ahead of hitters by establishing his 90-94 mph fastball with plus life, throwing it on a nice downhill plane and to both sides of the plate. His hard, sharp-breaking curveball has quality depth. After beginning last season in Mississippi's bullpen, he began using his effective changeup more often as a starter. Hitters rarely barreled Beachy's pitches last season, even when he reached the big leagues. His confidence has improved considerably, though he's still honing the mental aspects of pitching at the game's highest levels. He may not have a long track record of success on the mound, but Beachy's repertoire and feel for pitching bode well for the long term. He succeeded as both a reliever and a starter in 2010, enhancing his chances of making the Atlanta pitching staff this spring. His ceiling is as a No. 3 starter.

Greg Maddux
won the Cy
Young Award in
each of his first
three seasons
with Atlanta.

BECAME BRAVES

Savvy additions pushed Braves to playoffs

I n the 1980s, the Braves found time and time again that free agency could burn them. The Braves would spend to acquire a closer, or a first baseman or an outfielder, only to find they were acquiring a player on the downside of his career.

But in the 1990s, the Braves found that signing free agents could be vital additions that could pay off in playoff appearances. Terry Pendleton immediately became one of the best players in Atlanta's lineup when he signed in 1991. Sid Bream filled a need at first base as well.

Two years later, the Braves made one of the best free agent signings of all time. Greg Maddux hit free agency after a Cy Young award-winning 20-11, 2.18 season with the Cubs. The Braves already had the best pitching staff in the National League—their 3.14 ERA led the NL in 1992. But adding Maddux gave the Braves one of the best rotations of all-time. From the time Maddux arrived in 1993 until Tom Glavine departed after the 2002 season, the Braves finished first in the National League eight times. They finished second in the league in ERA in the other two seasons.

As good as the Pendleton and Maddux's additions were, the Braves needed one more piece in the early 1990s. Bream looked to be on his last legs in 1993 (he retired after the 1994 season), and Ryan Klesko wasn't viewed as ready.

With a hole at first base, the Braves dipped into their significant prospect depth to acquire Fred McGriff. Outfielders Vince Moore and Melvin Nieves and righthander Donnie Elliott were shipped to San Diego, where none of them would ever make a significant impact for the Padres. In return, the Braves landed their cleanup hitter.

So while none of these three Braves stars were Braves prospects they were very significant parts of the Braves success and therefore a logical addition to a book looking at the rise of Braves stars. It's hard to imagine the Braves teams of the early 1990s without looking at the contributions of Pendleton. And when Maddux went into the Hall of Fame, Braves fans claimed him as one of their own just as much as Cubs fans did. Similarly, if McGriff ever does make the Hall of Fame, it will be a victory for Braves fans as well.

Greg Maddux topped 200 innings for 14 consecutive seasons.

GREG MADDUX, RHP

PROPER NAME: Gregory Alan Maddux. **BORN:** April 14, 1966 in San Angelo, Texas.
HT.: 6-0. **WT.:** 195. **BATS:** R. **THROWS:** R. **SCHOOL:** Valley HS, Las Vegas.
FIRST PRO CONTRACT: Selected by Cubs in second round of June 1984 draft; signed June 19, 1984.

First, let's clear up a common misconception. There was a time when Greg Maddux threw hard. It's evident in the Draft Preview report on Maddux from 1984. At the time, no one knew that Maddux would end up being one of the smartest pitchers to ever step onto the mound. No one knew that one day he'd intentionally make a mistake with a pitch in a blowout win in May just for the possibility that he could use that to his advantage in a tougher start in July. No one knew that his fastball would have so much movement that it could almost be described as three or four different pitches. But Maddux could bring it, topping 90 mph at a time when that wasn't the norm for a high school arm. By the time he came to the Braves, Maddux's velocity was average at best, but he had figured out how to stay three steps ahead of hitters. That craftiness and feel helped him dominate until he was in his late-30s, and it allowed him to still be a useful pitcher into his 40s.

CAREER STATISTICS

Year	Club (League)	Class	W	L	ERA	G	GS	CG	SV	IP	H	R	ER	HR	BB	SO	AVG
1984	Pikeville (APP)	R	6	2	2.63	14	12	2	0	86	63	35	25	2	41	62	.205
1985	Peoria (MWL)	A	13	9	3.19	27	27	6	0	186	176	86	66	9	52	125	.245
1986	Pittsfield (EL)	AA	4	3	2.69	8	8	4	0	64	49	22	19	1	15	35	.214
	Iowa (AA)	AAA	10	1	3.02	18	18	5	0	128	127	49	43	3	30	65	.259
	Chicago (NL)	MAJ	2	4	5.52	6	5	1	0	31	44	20	19	3	11	20	.336
1987	Iowa (AA)	AAA	3	0	0.98	4	4	2	0	28	17	3	3	1	12	22	.179
	Chicago (NL)	MAJ	6	14	5.61	30	27	1	0	156	181	111	97	17	74	101	.294
1988	Chicago (NL)	MAJ	18	8	3.18	34	34	9	0	249	230	97	88	13	81	140	.244
1989	Chicago (NL)	MAJ	19	12	2.95	35	35	7	0	238	222	90	78	13	82	135	.249
1990	Chicago (NL)	MAJ	15	15	3.46	35	35	8	0	237	242	116	91	11	71	144	.265
1991	Chicago (NL)	MAJ	15	11	3.35	37	37	7	0	263	232	113	98	18	66	198	.237
1992	Chicago (NL)	MAJ	20	11	2.18	35	35	9	0	268	201	68	65	7	70	199	.210
1993	Atlanta (NL)	MAJ	20	10	2.36	36	36	8	0	267	228	85	70	14	52	197	.232
1994	Atlanta (NL)	MAJ	16	6	1.56	25	25	10	0	202	150	44	35	4	31	156	.207
1995	Atlanta (NL)	MAJ	19	2	1.63	28	28	10	0	210	147	39	38	8	23	181	.197
1996	Atlanta (NL)	MAJ	15	11	2.72	35	35	5	0	245	225	85	74	11	28	172	.241
1997	Atlanta (NL)	MAJ	19	4	2.20	33	33	5	0	233	200	58	57	9	20	177	.236
1998	Atlanta (NL)	MAJ	18	9	2.22	34	34	9	0	251	201	75	62	13	45	204	.224
1999	Atlanta (NL)	MAJ	19	9	3.57	33	33	4	0	219	258	103	87	16	37	136	.294
2000	Atlanta (NL)	MAJ	19	9	3.00	35	35	6	0	249	225	91	83	19	42	190	.238
2001	Atlanta (NL)	MAJ	17	11	3.05	34	34	3	0	233	220	86	79	20	27	173	.253
2002	Atlanta (NL)	MAJ	16	6	2.62	34	34	0	0	199	194	67	58	14	45	118	.257
2003	Atlanta (NL)	MAJ	16	11	3.96	36	36	1	0	218	225	112	96	24	33	124	.268
2004	Chicago (NL)	MAJ	16	11	4.02	33	33	2	0	213	218	103	95	35	33	151	.269
2005	Chicago (NL)	MAJ	13	15	4.24	35	35	3	0	225	239	112	106	29	36	136	.275
2006	Chicago (NL)	MAJ	9	11	4.69	22	22	0	0	136	153	78	71	14	23	81	.284
	Los Angeles (NL)	MAJ	6	3	3.30	12	12	0	0	74	66	31	27	6	14	36	.244
2007	San Diego (NL)	MAJ	14	11	4.14	34	34	1	0	198	221	92	91	14	25	104	.285
2008	San Diego (NL)	MAJ	6	9	3.99	26	26	0	0	153	161	80	68	16	26	80	.271
	Los Angeles (NL)	MAJ	2	4	5.09	7	7	0	0	41	43	25	23	5	4	18	.276
Major League Totals			355	227	3.16	744	740	109	0	5008	4726	1981	1756	353	999	3371	.250
Minor League Totals			36	15	2.86	71	69	19	0	491	432	195	156	16	150	309	.235

The smartest man on the mound

JULY 1994

SIMPLY THE BEST

by BILL BALLEW

Pitch 23 years in the major leagues, win 324 games, then spend another half-dozen seasons broadcasting baseball's best starting rotation, and chances are you might pick up a thing or two about pitching.

"Pitching is an art, an art that few care to learn and less than that ever master," says Don Sutton, who has witnessed the efforts of such greats as Sandy Koufax, Don Drysdale, Bob Gibson, Tom Seaver . . . and Greg Maddux.

"Greg Maddux is the best pitcher I've ever watched work," Sutton says. "He knows how to go out there with that he is given and win ball games. You watch a lot of other guys, they seem to try to pitch to embarrass the hitter and have the hitter avoid making contact with the ball. Maddux pitches as though he knows every pitch that it's going to get hit, but knows it isn't going to get hit hard.

"Hands down, he's the best pitcher I've ever seen."

Though such lofty praise might be expected from the home-team announcer, Sutton is far from the lone member of the Maddux Admiration Society. Writers thought enough of Maddux's efforts to honor him with consecutive Cy Young Awards the past two seasons. Even Atlanta skipper Bobby Cox, who rarely is moved to make definitive comments about anyone, can't help but express his adulation for the righthander.

"Pure pitching-wise, he's the best I've ever seen," Cox said. "He goes out there with a report in his mind on every hitter. He's never confused. He's always prepared. When that game starts, he knows exactly what he's doing."

The average fan might have a hard time placing "Baseball's Best Pitcher" medal around Maddux' neck. His fastball fails to light up the radar gun, topping out around 88 mph. His curveball doesn't fall out of the sky. And while his slider and changeup are solid pitches, neither one strikes fear into hitters' hearts.

But if you tie the four into one package and combine them with a fine pitching mind, you have the best pitcher in the game.

Exactly what makes the 28-year-old Maddux the game's best isn't the easiest thing to determine.

His teammates joke that the 6-foot, 175-pound righthander has a body better suited for a college professor or a librarian than a professional athlete. A few Braves players go so far as to insist that there's a dark side to the quiet, scholarly-looking pitcher, yet they fail to be specific.

Adding to the Maddux mystique is his rather boring personality. For him, getting carried away is wearing his cap backwards in the clubhouse while playing cards with his teammates. Modest to no end, even Maddux says the success he has attained since reaching the major leagues with the Cubs late in the 1986 season surprises him.

"I'm pretty basic," says Maddux. "I just try to be fundamental. I try to stay out of the big inning early. I try to let our team score first if at all possible. Usually the team that scores first wins 65-70 percent of the time. I want to stay out of the big inning for five or six innings, then pitch accordingly from there."

The results speak for themselves. Maddux hadn't allowed a run in the first inning all year. Additionally, he had surrendered more than two earned runs in a game only once in his last 20 starts. That equates to a 22-4, 1.60 record since last year's All-Star Game.

"I have four pitches," says Maddux, who has averaged 18 wins in his six full seasons in the majors. "I'm not afraid to throw offspeed pitches when I'm behind in the count, and I'm not afraid to throw strikes when I'm ahead in the count. I work off my fastball, just cut it and sink it and throw the pitch on both sides of the plate. I try to take advantage by locating fastballs and changing speeds."

Maddux' textbook approach actually begins with the first pitch to the hitter. Nobody gets ahead in the count any better.

"He can go strike one with the best of them," Cox said. "That's a huge advantage if you can do that. You can talk about pitching and mechanics, but strike one is the first step to success."

Maddux' fastball moves anywhere from six to eight inches on its way to the plate. He throws a variety of cut fastballs, including one that appears to be down the middle before jamming righthanded batters. Another offering seems to be the same pitch until it suddenly tails away.

A craftsman at selecting the correct time to showcase his less-effective pitches, Maddux keeps hitters honest while going to great lengths to make sure those tosses don't hurt him.

"I try to stay away from that," Maddux says. "But if the situation calls for my curveball, which is my fourth pitch, if I feel like that's the best pitch to throw, I'll throw it. But I'm going

Draft Preview

May 1984

Another slightly built young pitcher who can throw extremely hard. His fastball has been clocked at 91, and is consistently in the high 80s. Also throws a split finger fastball, curve and slider. "He's a small kid who can really throw hard," confirmed one major league scouting director. In his first seven appearances this season, he was 6-1 with a 2.13 ERA and had struck out 61 while walking 12 and allowing 15 hits in his first 38 innings. In his first three outings, he did not allow and earned run, walked just two, gave up four hits and struck out 37 — in 21 innings. Younger brother of Mike Maddux, another hard throwing righthander the Philadelphia Phillies drafted on the fifth round out of Texas-El Paso in 1982. "Greg's better than Mike at the same age," says Valley High coach Roger Fairless. "He throws harder." Among the schools lining up for Maddux's services are Arizona State, Nevada-Las Vegas, Arizona, Miami (Fla.) and Texas.

to have a strong feeling that that's the right pitch to throw."

Maddux isn't necessarily religious in following the pitching textbook. In no area does he deviate more than in his refusal to waste a pitch.

"Everything he throws has a purpose," Atlantic pitching coach Leo Mazzone says. "Every single pitch."

While other pitchers will offer a weak breaking pitch once they get ahead in the count, especially 0-2. Maddux looks to finish the job. Should he surrender a hit with an 0-2 count, Maddux accepts it, even if the results have caused coronaries for pitching coaches throughout the minor leagues.

"I don't believe in wasting pitches," Maddux says. "Everyone says that 0-2 is the perfect time to waste a pitch. But if you look at the percentages of what hitters hit on certain counts, you'll find that 0-2 is the lowest average of any count. So why would you want to waste a pitch and go to 1-2? The average only goes up for the hitter.

"At 0-2, you're way ahead of the guy. So my thinking is to make the best pitch you can. Why put yourself in a hole?"

Maddux' approaches wouldn't be successful for just any pitcher. Three ingredients—flawless mechanics, unflappable confidence and constant preparation—must be included in the total package in order to get by without overpowering stuff.

The first ingredient was ingrained into Maddux during his prep days in Las Vegas. Valley High coach Rodger Fairless believes strongly in fundamentals, is a stickler on getting little things done and runs his team through countless hours of boring exercises that would make a drill sergeant proud.

"Rodger was a big influence," Maddux says. "I think I learned from him how important work habits are. We were always reminded where to be in certain situations. He taught me how to cover first, things like that.

"I took that for granted until I signed and went to Rookie ball. We had guys there who had no idea how to cover first. I just assumed everybody was getting that type of coaching. He taught me a lot of fundamentals that are used up here at this level."

Again, the results speak for themselves. Maddux is considered the best fielding pitcher in the game, having led the NL in putouts for five years running while winning four straight Gold Glove Awards.

His confidence, meanwhile, was formed at two specific times. Maddux' initial jolt came during early 1986, when he tossed eight games at Double-A Pittsfield.

His pitching coach, Dick Pole—now with San Francisco—persuaded Maddux to develop his own identity instead of trying to pitch like other people. Maddux responded by going 4-3, 2.69, followed by a 10-1 mark at Triple-A Iowa and a late promotion to the majors.

"He helped me learn myself as a pitcher," Maddux says. "He made me realize that not everybody can pitch the same way. You have to find a way that works for you, then try to improve off that and go from there. I think he gave me that starting point in terms of understanding myself as a pitcher."

Three seasons and 43 major league victories later, Maddux received a tuneup in confidence during sessions with a sports psychologist. Early in his career, the righthander would allow his defense's miscues to affect his approach to the next batter.

"That helped me with blocking out things I have no control over and focusing on things I can control," Maddux says. "For example, other than my at-bats, I have no control over the runs we're going to score. But I can control the pitches I make, how I handle my mechanics, how I control my frame of mind. That's what benefited me the most, and that's when I realized I can't control what happens outside of my pitching."

"He's never shaken, never," Cox says. "He's as tough as anybody I've ever seen. If there's a problem, he handles it."

Maddux also practices another mental side of his craft, studying opposing hitters. He doesn't keep records on a laptop computer or in a notebook, but spends countless hours examining how enemy batters perform against him. He also goes over with his teammates how he'll pitch everyone so they'll be as prepared as possible." I watch tapes if I have certain questions about hitters," says Maddux, who limited opponents to a .201 average in his first 13 starts this year. "I watch tapes to see how I'm pitching against a team. Are they hitting good pitches, or are they hitting bad pitches? Are they moving back or up on the plate? Those type of things. Then when the game starts, I can look for those things and pitch accordingly.

If all this sounds like Maddux had broken down the art of pitching to a science, it's because he has. In fact, Mazzone admits that Maddux has taught him a few things about the art. The pitching coach won't reveal the secrets, though, for understandable reasons.

His success and knowledge notwithstanding, no one even believes Maddux has reached his peak. He feels that adjustments still can be made, whether it's locating his fastball more accurately, making his slider break more or less, or taking a little speed off his changeup.

"There's always room for improvement," Maddux says. "The main thing I'm trying to stay away from is beating myself. You watch pitchers beat themselves all the time. I try to make the other team beat me. You can't give it away, but I know that's easier said than done."

"How do I think he can be a better pitcher?" Mazzone asks rhetorically. "Just keep doing what he's doing. If that ain't good enough, something's messed up." ■

OCTOBER 1985

MADDUX, SURPRISING DAVIDSON CATAPULT PEORIA TO TOP OF MIDWEST PACK

by JON SCHER

Peoria righthander Greg Maddux has been blowing away the rest of the Midwest League this season. The parent Chicago Cubs expected that.

But the Cubs didn't necessarily expect righthander Jackie Davidson to rebound from two disastrous seasons and show why he was the sixth player selected in the June, 1983 draft. They didn't really expect marginal righthanders Jeff Pico and Jeff Schwarz to become 100-strikeout men, either. And they didn't expect Dave Pavlas, a free agent from Rice University, to become a capable starter before an injury sidetracked his season.

"Pitching has been the name of the game," said Peoria manager Pete Mackanin, whose club has been in first place in the Southern Division most of the 1985 season. "As far as I'm concerned, it's been the key to our success. And a big reason for that is Jim Wright."

A former major league pitcher, Wright was a pitching coach for Chicago's Midwest League farmhands at Quad City last season. That team finished 50-88.

But it's been a different story for Wright this summer. Virtually every arm he's touched has turned to gold.

The staff has been led by Maddux, the Cubs second-round draft pick a year ago who owned a 12-7 record and 3.27 ERA despite gradually losing command of his curveball as the season wore on. He'd struck out 107 and walked 40 in 154 innings.

"He's been winning mainly on his fastball," said Mackanin. "When his curve and change were working early in the season, he was overpowering the hitters in this league. But he's got a good enough fastball to get by—he spots the ball so well."

Maddux throws his fastball consistently at 88 mph. "When he learns to control that curve he's going to move up as fast as anyone can move, in my opinion," Mackanin said. "He's going to be a major league pitcher."

Trouble is, at 6-foot and 150 pounds, Maddux looks more like an American Legion player than a National Leaguer. "A lot of people don't believe me when I tell them I play pro baseball," said Maddux, a 19-year-old from Las Vegas whose older brother Mike is a pitcher at Portland (Pacific Coast) in the Phillies' system. "They look at me like I probably play in a Pony League somewhere."

Although Maddux believes his lack of size might have scared off some scouts, it hasn't bothered Wright. "I couldn't believe how little (Ron) Guidry was either," Wright said of the New York Yankees' 5-11, 160-pound ace.

Maddux still has his detractors. "They say I'm too skinny to throw hard for a full season," he said. "I don't think I am." ■

Greg Maddux
scouting reports

APPALACHIAN LEAGUE
NO. 4 PROSPECT, 1984 SEASON

Drafted in the second round in June by the Chicago Cubs, Maddux impressed managers with an overpowering fastball, despite a slight build.

"He's got a live arm," said Biagini. "It's loose and limber, and he knows how to pitch for a high school pitcher. He throws hard for his size."

"He's the best pitcher in the league." said Fairey. "He throws 90, he's young (18), he has a good curve. And he has poise."

Maddux, whose older brother Mike is a pitcher in the Phillies system, was 6-2 in his first pro season, with a 2.63 ERA. He struck out 62 in 86 innings.

CHICAGO CUBS
NO. 7 PROSPECT AFTER 1985 SEASON

Despite his slight build, he throws an above-average fastball that moves well, and he has a power curve when he doesn't rush his delivery. He had a good season at Peoria (13-9, 3.19, 125 strikeouts and 52 walks in 186 innings), although physical fatigue took a toll in the final month.

The Cubs think he will get bigger and stronger. Mike Maddux, an older brother who pitches in the Phillies' system, was about the same size at the same age but has grown to 6-foot-2, 180 pounds.

CHICAGO CUBS
NO. 5 PROSPECT AFTER 1986 SEASON

He is the most advanced pitcher in the system and would be their best prospect if he was 20 pounds stronger. Maddux rushed through Pittsfield and Iowa last season (14-4, 2.91, with 45 walks and 100 strikeouts in 192 innings), but was hit hard in a September trial with the Cubs.

He has a good fastball that he can run inside or cut away, but it will be a five-inning pitch if he doesn't get stronger. His changeup is above average and his curve is strong when he pulls down properly. But in his immediate favor, he is not afraid to pitch inside and his control is superb, which could land him on the varsity this year as a spot starter and long reliever.

MIDWEST LEAGUE
NO. 3 PROSPECT, 1985 SEASON

He's only 19, but he's still got a major league arm—an 88 mph fastball and good control. Now Maddux needs to develop a consistent curve.

"For his age, he's got an excellent fastball," Appleton manager Sal Rende said. "He's got a decent breaking pitch, but (the Cubs) need to take their time with him so he can learn how to pitch."

Maddux, the Cubs' No. 2 pick in June 1984, was praised for his poise and was voted the league's best pitching prospect in a midseason poll. But some managers questioned whether the 6-foot, 150-pounder was strong enough to make it to the majors.

Peoria manager Pete Mackanin has little doubt. "When he learns to control that curve he's going to move up as fast as anyone can move," he said. "He's going to be a major league pitcher."

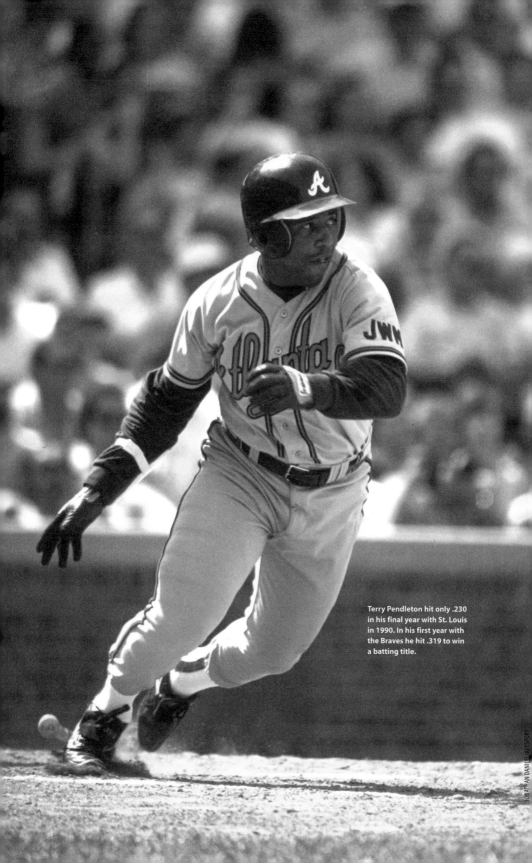

Terry Pendleton hit only .230 in his final year with St. Louis in 1990. In his first year with the Braves he hit .319 to win a batting title.

TERRY PENDLETON, 3B

BIOGRAPHY

PROPER NAME: Terry Lee Pendleton. **BORN:** July 16, 1960 in Los Angeles, Calif.
HT.: 5-9. **WT.:** 180. **BATS:** B. **THROWS:** R. **SCHOOL:** Fresno State.
CAREER TRANSACTIONS: Selected by Cardinals in seventh round of 1982 draft; signed .

Terry Pendleton was a good player for the Cardinals from 1984-1990, but no one expected that the Braves decision to sign him as a free agent would help reshape the direction of the franchise. Pendleton became the best player in the Braves lineup in 1991 and won the National League MVP. In 1992, he proved it wasn't a one year fluke. He did have to settle for second in NL MVP honors but he once again propelled the Braves to the World Series both with his glove at third and his middle-of-the-order bat. He also made his only all-star game appearance that season. Pendelton spent another two seasons with the Braves, but with Chipper Jones ready and waiting, Pendleton left in free agency after the 1994 season. He returned in a deadline-deal trade in 1996, but he wasn't able to recreate the magic of his first stint in Atlanta.

CAREER STATISTICS

Year	Club (League)	Class	AVG	G	AB	R	H	2B	3B	HR	RBI	BB	SO	SB	OBP	SLG
1982	St. Petersburg (FSL)	A	.261	20	69	4	18	2	1	1	7	2	18	1	.282	.362
1982	Johnson City (Appy)	Rk	.320	43	181	38	58	14	4	4	27	12	28	13	.359	.508
1983	Arkansas (TL)	AA	.276	48	185	29	51	10	3	4	20	9	26	7	.311	.427
1984	Louisville (A-A)	AAA	.297	91	330	52	98	23	5	4	44	24	51	6	.342	.433
1984	St. Louis (NL)	MAJ	.324	67	262	37	85	16	3	1	33	16	32	20	.357	.420
1985	St. Louis (NL)	MAJ	.240	149	559	56	134	16	3	5	69	37	75	17	.285	.306
1986	St. Louis (NL)	MAJ	.239	159	578	56	138	26	5	1	59	34	59	24	.279	.306
1987	St. Louis (NL)	MAJ	.286	159	583	82	167	29	4	12	96	70	74	19	.360	.412
1988	St. Louis (NL)	MAJ	.253	110	391	44	99	20	2	6	53	21	51	3	.293	.361
1989	St. Louis (NL)	MAJ	.264	162	613	83	162	28	5	13	74	44	81	9	.313	.390
1990	St. Louis (NL)	MAJ	.230	121	447	46	103	20	2	6	58	30	58	7	.277	.324
1991	Atlanta (NL)	MAJ	.319	153	586	94	187	34	8	22	86	43	70	10	.363	.517
1992	Atlanta (NL)	MAJ	.311	160	640	98	199	39	1	21	105	37	67	5	.345	.473
1993	Atlanta (NL)	MAJ	.272	161	633	81	172	33	1	17	84	36	97	5	.311	.408
1994	Atlanta (NL)	MAJ	.252	77	309	25	78	18	3	7	30	12	57	2	.280	.398
1995	Florida (NL)	MAJ	.290	133	513	70	149	32	1	14	78	38	84	1	.339	.439
1996	Florida (NL)	MAJ	.251	111	406	30	102	20	1	7	58	26	75	0	.298	.357
	Atlanta (NL)	MAJ	.204	42	162	21	33	6	0	4	17	15	36	2	.271	.315
1997	Cincinnati (NL)	MAJ	.248	50	113	11	28	9	0	1	17	12	14	2	.320	.354
1998	Kansas City (AL)	MAJ	.257	79	237	17	61	10	0	3	29	15	49	1	.299	.338
Minor League Totals			**.296**	**215**	**808**	**127**	**239**	**54**	**13**	**14**	**108**	**55**	**128**	**27**	**.339**	**.447**
Major League Totals			**.270**	**1893**	**7032**	**851**	**1897**	**356**	**39**	**140**	**946**	**486**	**979**	**127**	**.316**	**.391**

Terry Pendleton hit only .230 in his final year with St. Louis in 1990. In his first year with the Braves he hit .319 to win a batting title.

Terry Pendleton scouting reports

ST, LOUIS CARDINALS
NO. 7 PROSPECT AFTER 1982 SEASON

"He has the plusses," Cardinals field coordinator George Kissell said. "He's an intelligent kid and very aggressive. You tell him something once, and he's like Tommy Herr the way he remembers it.

"He had never switch hit before. He's going from righthanded to learning to hit lefthanded. He's got a little pop in his bat. He's a good bunter and an average runner. He's a big-legged guy like Jerry Bucheck used to be. That could be his only problem. He could play at Arkansas next year."

AMERICAN ASSOCIATION
NO. 6 PROSPECT AFTER 1984 SEASON

Pendleton, a 24-year-old third baseman came back from an injury-filled 1983 season with a solid performance that earned him a promotion to St. Louis in early August.

In 99 games, Pendleton, a former All-American outfielder at Fresno State, hit .297 with 23 doubles, four homers and 44 RBIs. He also played strong defense, committing just 10 errors.

"He's one of those guys you forget about until he beats you," one manager said of Pendleton.

Fred McGriff was an above-average hitter for 16 consecutive MLB seasons.

FRED McGRIFF, 1B

BIOGRAPHY

PROPER NAME: Frederick Stanley McGriff. **BORN:** Oct. **31, 1963 IN TAMPA, FLA.**
HT.: 6-3. **WT.:** 215. **BATS:** L. **THROWS:** L. **SCHOOL:** Jefferson HS, Tampa.
CAREER TRANSACTIONS: Selected by Yankees in ninth round of 1981 draft, signed June 11, 1981.

Franchise players are rarely traded. So it's hard to explain why McGriff was traded three times before his 30th birthday. What is clear is that two of the three teams that traded McGriff away came to regret their deals. Just a year and a half after drafting him the Yankees traded McGriff (along with Dave Collins and Mike Morgan) for Tom Dodd and Dale Murray. Dodd and Murray barely made an impact for the Yankees while McGriff soon became one of the Blue Jays top prospects. But facing a surplus of first basemen (McGriff never played another position), the Blue Jays then dealt McGriff to the Padres along with Tony Fernandez for Joe Carter and Roberto Alomar. That was a deal that helped both teams, but when the Padres decided to rebuild, they sent McGriff to the Braves—a deal they would soon regret.

CAREER STATISTICS

Year	Club (League)	Class	AVG	G	AB	R	H	2B	3B	HR	RBI	BB	SO	SB	OBP	SLG
1981	Yankees (GCL)	Rk	.148	29	81	6	12	2	0	0	9	11	20	0	.255	.173
1982	Yankees (GCL)	Rk	.272	62	217	38	59	11	1	9	41	48	63	6	.413	.456
1983	Florence (SAL)	A	.311	33	119	26	37	3	1	7	26	20	35	3	.414	.529
1983	Kinston (CAR)	A	.243	94	350	53	85	14	1	21	57	55	112	3	.354	.469
1984	Knoxville (SL)	AA	.249	56	189	29	47	13	2	9	25	29	55	0	.347	.481
1984	Syracuse (IL)	AAA	.235	70	238	28	56	10	1	13	28	26	89	0	.309	.450
1985	Syracuse (IL)	AAA	.227	51	176	19	40	8	2	5	20	23	53	0	.330	.381
1986	Syracuse (IL)	AAA	.259	133	468	69	121	23	4	19	74	83	119	0	.369	.447
1986	Toronto (AL)	MAJ	.200	3	5	1	1	0	0	0	0	0	2	0	.200	.200
1987	Toronto (AL)	MAJ	.247	107	295	58	73	16	0	20	43	60	104	3	.376	.505
1988	Toronto (AL)	MAJ	.282	154	536	100	151	35	4	34	82	79	149	6	.376	.552
1989	Toronto (AL)	MAJ	.269	161	551	98	148	27	3	36	92	119	132	7	.399	.525
1990	Toronto (AL)	MAJ	.300	153	557	91	167	21	1	35	88	94	108	5	.400	.530
1991	San Diego (NL)	MAJ	.278	153	528	84	147	19	1	31	106	105	135	4	.396	.494
1992	San Diego (NL)	MAJ	.286	152	531	79	152	30	4	35	104	96	108	8	.394	.556
1993	San Diego (NL)	MAJ	.275	83	302	52	83	11	1	18	46	42	55	4	.361	.497
	Atlanta (NL)	MAJ	.310	68	255	59	79	18	1	19	55	50	51	1	.392	.612
1994	Atlanta (NL)	MAJ	.318	113	424	81	135	25	1	34	94	50	76	7	.389	.623
1995	Atlanta (NL)	MAJ	.280	144	528	85	148	27	1	27	93	65	99	3	.361	.489
1996	Atlanta (NL)	MAJ	.295	159	617	81	182	37	1	28	107	68	116	7	.365	.494
1997	Atlanta (NL)	MAJ	.277	152	564	77	156	25	1	22	97	68	112	5	.356	.441
1998	Tampa Bay (AL)	MAJ	.284	151	564	73	160	33	0	19	81	79	118	7	.371	.443
1999	Tampa Bay (AL)	MAJ	.310	144	529	75	164	30	1	32	104	86	107	1	.405	.552
2000	Tampa Bay (AL)	MAJ	.277	158	566	82	157	18	0	27	106	91	120	2	.373	.452
2001	Tampa Bay (AL)	MAJ	.318	97	343	40	109	18	0	19	61	40	69	1	.387	.536
	Chicago (NL)	MAJ	.282	49	170	27	48	7	2	12	41	26	37	0	.383	.559
2002	Chicago (NL)	MAJ	.273	146	523	67	143	27	2	30	103	63	99	1	.353	.505
2003	Los Angeles (NL)	MAJ	.249	86	297	32	74	14	0	13	40	31	66	0	.322	.428
2004	Tampa Bay (AL)	MAJ	.181	27	72	7	13	3	0	2	7	9	19	0	.272	.306
Minor League Total			.249	538	1868	273	465	85	12	84	284	301	554	12	.357	.442
Major League Totals			.284	2460	8757	1349	2490	441	24	493	1550	1305	1882	72	.377	.509

On the day of Fred McGriff's Atlanta debut, he homered. The day is more remember for the Fulton County Stadium press box catching on fire.

Fred McGriff scouting reports

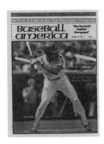

TORONTO BLUE JAYS
NO. 2 PROSPECT AFTER 1983 SEASON

What the Blue Jays scouting system hasn't uncovered at the amateur level, it has found waiting in the New York Yankees farm system. The Jays acquired McGriff a year ago as part of the package for Dale Murray. It will still be some time before he makes the Yankees regret that deal more than ever, but the time should come.

McGriff is the legitimate power hitter—the type, who with the inviting elements for a lefthanded hitter in Toronto, could be capable of 30 to 40 home runs. In his first full professional season last summer, he hit 28 home runs and drove in 93 runs, splitting the time between Kinston and Florence.

Like most young men with power, he creates some big breezes, too (147 strikeouts, 469 at-bats). That will decrease as his experience and knowledge of the strike zone increases, but it is foolish to think he will ever be a pure contact hitter.

He does not have a great deal of lateral movement, but then he is a first baseman. But he has soft hands and an excellent arm. He will field anything he gets, too, even if that's not as much as some would like.

He needs to increase his reaction time and get experience, but with his makeup and his natural power it won't be long before he makes the step to the big leagues.

TORONTO BLUE JAYS
NO. 1 PROSPECT AFTER 1984 SEASON

All right, he still has a ways to go. But once he arrives, he will give people plenty to talk about. Just like Willie Upshaw and Damaso Garcia, who like McGriff were raw talents the Blue Jays stole away from the Yankees system, McGriff has the ability. It just needs refining.

The only question on when he will make it to the big leagues is when he will make consistent contact. He has struck out 260 times in 894 at bats the last two minor league seasons, and he probably always will pile up strikeouts. But when he hits the ball, it goes a long way (50 home runs and 136 RBIs the last two years), a tempting sight for the Blue Jays, whose home park is a paradise for lefthanded hitters.

He has made a steady climb in the last two years since the Blue Jays got him as a throw-in in the trade for Dale Murray, having played at Kinston and Florence in 1983 and Knoxville and Syracuse last year.

Like other young power hitters, the curveball throws him for a curve. His defense is still in the marginal category, but he has good lateral movement, and an excellent arm. His reactions are slow, but his desire and work habits make him a good learner.

TORONTO BLUE JAYS
NO. 7 PROSPECT AFTER 1985 SEASON

McGriff has been a slow project, but one the Blue Jays are confident will be worth the wait once he harnesses the raw power he has shown. The 1985 season was pretty much a wash for McGriff. He suffered a stress fracture in his ankle and only had 176 at-bats for Triple-A Syracuse.

A big, free swinger, McGriff suffers a common ailment of power hitters—lack of enough contact. In the last three years, he has struck out 313 times in 1,070 at-bats. He does, however, show the power potential with 55 home runs, 48 doubles and seven triples. And when he makes contact, his home runs are the type that people talk about.

A throw-in in a deal that made Dale Murray a Yankee after the 1982 season, McGriff still needs to develop some patience with the curveball before he will make consistent enough contact to make a move to the big leagues.

Steve Avery was the No. 1 prospect for Baseball America's first-ever Top 100 Prospects list.

Top 100 Prospects

Baseball America began ranking the Top 100 Prospects in baseball in 1990. Over the next 30 seasons, 88 different Braves have made at least one Top 100 list. Steve Avery, Chipper Jones, Andruw Jones, Jason Heyward and Ronald Acuña Jr. are the five Braves players who have ranked No. 1 overall.

Rank	Player, Pos.	Year
1.	Steve Avery, LHP	1990
18.	Mike Stanton, LHP	1990
47.	Kent Mercker, LHP	1990
50.	Dennis Burlingame, RHP	1990
58.	Tom Redington, 3B	1990
80.	Tommy Greene, RHP	1990
92.	Tyler Houston, C	1990
3.	Ryan Klesko, 1B	1991
28.	Tyler Houston, C	1991
49.	Chipper Jones, SS	1991
4.	Chipper Jones, SS	1992
8.	Ryan Klesko, 1B	1992
13.	Mark Wohlers, RHP	1992
19.	Mike Kelly, OF	1992
56.	David Nied, RHP	1992
78.	Javy Lopez, C	1992
89.	Keith Mitchell, OF	1992
1.	Chipper Jones, SS	1993
20.	Javy Lopez, C	1993
26.	Ryan Klesko, 1B	1993
34.	Mike Kelly, OF	1993
39.	Melvin Nieves, OF	1993
2.	Chipper Jones, SS	1994
15.	Ryan Klesko, 1B/OF	1994
17.	Javy Lopez, C	1994
29.	Terrell Wade, LHP	1994
58.	Mike Kelly, OF	1994
64.	Glenn Williams, SS	1994
3.	Chipper Jones, SS	1995
21.	Andruw Jones, OF	1995
42.	Jason Schmidt, RHP	1995
54.	Terrell Wade, LHP	1995
76.	Glenn Williams, SS	1995
88.	Jermaine Dye, OF	1995
99.	Damon Hollins, OF	1995
1.	Andruw Jones, OF	1996
11.	Jason Schmidt, RHP	1996
30.	Jermaine Dye, OF	1996
64.	Terrell Wade, LHP	1996
75.	Bobby Smith, 3B	1996
95.	Damon Hollins, OF	1996
39.	Kevin McGlinchy, RHP	1997
83.	Bruce Chen, LHP	1997
86.	Wes Helms, 3B	1997
94.	George Lombard, OF	1997
27.	Bruce Chen, LHP	1998
44.	Luis Rivera, RHP	1998
68.	Rob Bell, RHP	1998
93.	George Lombard, OF	1998
4.	Bruce Chen, LHP	1999
26.	George Lombard, OF	1999
31.	Odalis Perez, LHP	1999
47.	Kevin McGlinchy, RHP	1999

Rank	Player, Pos.	Year
60.	Rafael Furcal, SS	1999
71.	Luis Rivera, RHP	1999
89.	Jason Marquis, RHP	1999
8.	Rafael Furcal, SS	2000
46.	George Lombard, OF	2000
51.	Luis Rivera, RHP	2000
74.	Marcus Giles, 2B	2000
99.	Wilson Betemit, SS	2000
28.	Matt Belisle, RHP	2001
29.	Wilson Betemit, SS	2001
51.	Matt McClendon, RHP	2001
54.	Marcus Giles, 2B	2001
92.	Jason Marquis, RHP	2001
97.	Adam Wainwright, RHP	2001
8.	Wilson Betemit, SS	2002
42.	Adam Wainwright, RHP	2002
47.	Kelly Johnson, SS	2002
66.	Brett Evert, RHP	2002
96.	Matt Belisle, RHP	2002
18.	Adam Wainwright, RHP	2003
40.	Andy Marte, 3B	2003
49.	Wilson Betemit, 3B	2003
58.	Bubba Nelson, RHP	2003
68.	Macay McBride, LHP	2003
95.	Jeff Francoeur, OF	2003
11.	Andy Marte, 3B	2004
27.	Jeff Francoeur, OF	2004
73.	Adam LaRoche, 1B	2004
75.	Bubba Nelson, RHP	2004
82.	Dan Meyer, LHP	2004
9.	Andy Marte, 3B	2005
14.	Jeff Francoeur, OF	2005
44.	Brian McCann, C	2005
53.	Kyle Davies, RHP	2005
92.	Jake Stevens, LHP	2005
99.	Anthony Lerew, RHP	2005
18.	Jarrod Saltalamacchia, C	2006
61.	Elvis Andrus, SS	2006
93.	Anthony Lerew, RHP	2006
98.	Chuck James, LHP	2006
36.	Jarrod Saltalamacchia, C	2007
65.	Elvis Andrus, SS	2007
90.	Matt Harrison, LHP	2007
93.	Brent Lillibridge, SS	2007
25.	Jordan Schafer, OF	2008
28.	Jason Heyward, OF	2008
49.	Jair Jurrjens, RHP	2008
70.	Brandon Jones, OF	2008
92.	Gorkys Hernandez, OF	2008
4.	Tommy Hanson, RHP	2009
5.	Jason Heyward, OF	2009
42.	Jordan Schafer, OF	2009
62.	Gorkys Hernandez, OF	2009

Rank	Player, Pos.	Year
87.	Freddie Freeman, 1B	2009
1.	Jason Heyward, OF	2010
32.	Freddie Freeman, 1B	2010
51.	Julio Teheran, RHP	2010
69.	Arodys Vizcaino, RHP	2010
5.	Julio Teheran, RHP	2011
17.	Freddie Freeman, 1B	2011
35.	Randall Delgado, RHP	2011
37.	Mike Minor, LHP	2011
86.	Craig Kimbrel, RHP	2011
93.	Arodys Vizcaino, RHP	2011
40.	Arodys Vizcaino, RHP	2012
46.	Randall Delgado, RHP	2012
92.	Andrelton Simmons, SS	2012
44.	Julio Teheran, RHP	2013
93.	J.R. Graham, RHP	2013
57.	Lucas Sims, RHP	2014
69.	Christian Bethancourt, C	2014
54.	Jose Peraza, 2B	2015
17.	Dansby Swanson, SS	2016
24.	Sean Newcomb, LHP	2016
55.	Hector Olivera, 3B	2016
60.	Aaron Blair, RHP	2016
63.	Ozzie Albies, SS	2016
84.	Kolby Allard, LHP	2016
90.	Touki Toussaint, RHP	2016
3.	Dansby Swanson, SS	2017
11.	Ozzie Albies, 2B/SS	2017
37.	Kolby Allard, LHP	2017
48.	Mike Soroka, RHP	2017
66.	Ian Anderson, RHP	2017
67.	Ronald Acuna Jr., OF	2017
77.	Kevin Maitan, SS	2017
78.	Sean Newcomb, LHP	2017
1.	Ronald Acuna Jr., OF	2018
23.	Luiz Gohara, LHP	2018
27.	Mike Soroka, RHP	2018
34.	Kyle Wright, RHP	2018
42.	Ian Anderson, RHP	2018
54.	Austin Riley, 3B	2018
65.	Kolby Allard, LHP	2018
72.	Max Fried, LHP	2018
22.	Austin Riley, 3B	2019
24.	Ian Anderson, RHP	2019
25.	Mike Soroka, RHP	2019
39.	Kyle Wright, RHP	2019
53.	Touki Toussaint, RHP	2019
80.	Bryse Wilson, RHP	2019
83.	Drew Waters, OF	2019
85.	Cristian Pache, OF	2019

Andy Marte was one of the rookies on the Braves' surprising 2005 playoff team.

The Braves' biggest busts

While the Braves have had plenty of success, like any other team they have also had some prospects that haven't panned out.

BRAD KOMMINSK, OF

After hitting 33 home runs for high Class A Durham in 1981, Komminsk hit .334/.433/.596 for Triple-A Richmond in 1983. It made him a Baseball America cover subject and seemed to put him on track to be an everyday outfielder for the Braves in 1984. That was the plan, but Komminsk's massive minor league production seemed to disappear somewhere on I-85 between Richmond and Atlanta. The Braves tried to give him a big league job in 1984 and again in 1985, but he failed both times. By 1986, he was back in Richmond full-time, hitting only .234/.333/.383. The Brewers and Indians gave him shots to try to regain his feel in the batter's box, but Komminsk never managed to regain his early-1980s form.

MIKE KELLY, OF

When Kelly was playing for Arizona State, he was viewed as potentially a better player than former Sun Devils outfielders Oddibe McDowell and Barry Bonds. Viewed as a well-rounded, toolsy outfielder, Kelly didn't hit enough. He did serve as a light-hitting backup outfielder on the Braves' 1995 World Series team, but he was a short-lived role player.

Wilson Betemit made four different Top 100 Prospects lists. He ranked eighth in 2002.

TYLER HOUSTON, 3B

The Braves picked in the top two in three consecutive years from 1989-1991. They drafted Houston second overall in 1989, then Chipper Jones No. 1 overall in 1990 followed by Mike Kelly No. 2 overall in 1991. One out of three isn't bad when one of them ends up as a Hall of Famer. Houston, the first of the trio of picks, was supposed to be a catcher who could hit and field. He never hit in the minors for the Braves, and he eventually traded in the catcher's mitt for a third baseman's glove. He spent parts of eight seasons in the majors as a backup corner infielder, but by then the Braves had traded him away in a low-impact deal.

ANDY MARTE, 3B

If Marte had continued to steadily improve off of his outstanding age-20 season (.269/.364/.525) with Double-A Greenville, he could have been a star. At that point, it seemed inconceivable that he wouldn't carve out a role as at least a solid MLB starter. But that proved to be the high point of his career, as his bat surprisingly backed up over the next few seasons. The Braves tried to sell high, trading Marte to the Red Sox for Edgar Renteria in the offseason after the 2005 season. The Red Sox then turned around and swapped him to the Indians later that same offseason. Cleveland gave Marte multiple chances, but he hit only .224/.281/.369 in five seasons with the Indians.

WILSON BETEMIT, SS/3B

Betemit played parts of 11 seasons in the majors and found a role as a utility infielder, so it may be unfair to include him on a list of prospect busts. But when the Braves signed him, he was expected to be so much more. After he signed, MLB discovered that Betemit was actually 14 at the time of his first contract. The Braves were fined and had to suspend signing players on the international market for a stretch as punishment, but they were allowed to keep Betemit. As he matured, Betemit's bat proved to be a grade lighter than expected and he moved down the defensive spectrum—instead of sticking at shortstop, he primarily ended up as a third baseman.

PHOTO CREDITS

Elvis Andrus by Tom Priddy. **PAGE 106:** Baby Braves by Scott Cunningham/Getty Images. **PAGE 107:** Adam Wainwright by Fernando Medina/Getty Images. **PAGE 110:** Jason Heyward by Setliff. **PAGE 116:** Jason Heyward by Chris Graythen/Getty Images. **PAGE 122:** Jason Heyward by Scott Cunningham/Getty Images. **PAGE 124:** Freddie Freeman by Chris Graythen/Getty Images. **PAGE 130:** Craig Kimbrel by Rodger Wood. **PAGE 134:** Brian McCann by Doug Pensinger/Getty Images. **PAGE 136:** Brian McCann by Scott Cunningham/Getty Images. **PAGE 138:** Rafael Furcal by Andy Lyons/Allsport. **PAGE 140:** Rafael Furcal by Sporting News via Getty Images. **PAGE 142:** Jeff Francouer by Scott Cunningham/Getty Images. **PAGE 143:** Kelly Johnson by Rick Stewart/Getty Images. **PAGE 144:** Kris Medlen by Chris Graythen/Getty Images. **PAGE 145:** Tommy Hanson by Bob Leverone/Sporting News via Getty Images. **PAGE 146:** Yunel Escobar by Elsa/Getty Images. **PAGE 147:** Yunel Escobar by Scott Cunningham/Getty Images. **PAGE 148:** Albies and Acuna by Scott Cunningham/Getty Images. **PAGE 150:** Sun Trust Park by Carmen Mandato/Getty Images. **PAGE 151:** Max Fried by Tony Farlow. **PAGE 154:** Andrelton Simmons by Matthew Stockman/Getty Images. **PAGE 160:** Julio Teheran by Tom Priddy. **PAGE 166:** Mike Soroka by DannyParker. **PAGE 172:** Ozzie Albies by Cliff Welch/Icon SMI/Corbis-Icon Sportswire via Getty Images. **PAGE 176:** Ozzie learned by Tony Farlow. **PAGE 178:** Ronald Acuna by Tom Priddy. **PAGE 182:** Ronald Acuna by Setliff. **PAGE 184:** Ronald Acuna by Icon Sportswire. **PAGE 186:** Mike Minor by Mike Ehrmann/Getty Images. **PAGE 187:** Max Fried by Joe Robbins/Getty Images. **PAGE 188:** Jair Jurrjens by Al Messerschmidt/Getty Image. **PAGE 189:** Brandon Beachy by Mitchell Layton/Getty Images. **PAGE 190:** Greg Maddux by Andy Cross/The Denver Post via Getty Images. **PAGE 192:** Greg Maddux by Steve Schaefer/AFP/Getty Images. **PAGE 200:** Terry Pendleton by Jonathan Danilel/Allsport. **PAGE 202:** Terry Pendleton by Focus on Sport/Getty Images. **PAGE 204:** Fred McGriff by Ron Vesely/MLB Photos via Getty Images. **PAGE 206:** Fred McGriff by Stephen Dunn/Allsport. **PAGE 208:** Steve Avery by Ronald C. Modra/Getty Images. **PAGE 210:** Andy Marte/Rick Stewart/Getty Images. **PAGE 212:** Wilson Betemit by Scott Cunningham/Getty Images.eps